HALLECK: *Lincoln's Chief of Staff*

Stephen E. Ambrose

HALLECK:

Lincoln's Chief of Staff

LOUISIANA STATE UNIVERSITY PRESS
BATON ROUGE

To My Parents

Copyright © 1962, 1990 by Louisiana State University Press
All rights reserved
Manufactured in the United States of America
Library of Congress Card Catalog Number: 62—11740
Louisiana Paperback Edition, 1996
ISBN 0-8071-2071-5 (pbk.)
05   5

The paper in this book meets the guidelines for permanence and
durability of the Committee on Production Guidelines for Book
Longevity of the Council on Library Resources. ∞

PREFACE

This study centers its attention on three movements basic to the development of the American military establishment: the application, and ultimate rejection, of the theories and principles of Baron Henri Jomini to the art of war as practiced in the United States; the growth of a national, professional army at the expense of the militia system; the beginnings of a modern command system. Henry Wager Halleck was intimately associated with all three movements. Before the Civil War he was one of America's few important theorists on the higher art of war, and it was in large part due to his efforts that the doctrines of Jomini were widely accepted by Civil War generals. Halleck himself, however, was one of the first of those generals to realize that Jomini's doctrines badly needed modification when applied to the American scene. As general-in-chief, Halleck was in the forefront of the movement to professionalize and nationalize the army; as chief of staff he was a central figure of primary importance in the embryonic command system President Abraham Lincoln created. An examination of the Civil War career of Halleck should make these and other facets of the Civil War clearer; it also could aid in making the modern command system more understandable by showing, at least in part, how it developed. Finally, the author hopes that this study will throw some light on the complex personality and the multifarious activities of Henry Wager Halleck.

I have been extremely fortunate in the help and encouragement I have received in the process of completing this study. Professor William B. Hesseltine of the University of Wisconsin first suggested an examination of Halleck and has patiently given of his time and his great knowledge; Professor T. Harry Williams of the Louisiana State University generously supplied me with ideas, criticisms, and direction. It is quite literally true that without Professors Hesseltine and Williams this study could never have been completed. I should also like to thank Professors John Duffy and John Loos of the Louisiana State University; Dr. Archer Jones of Virginia Polytechnic Institute, Blacksburg, Virginia; Lieutenant John Coussons of the Citadel, Charleston, South Carolina; Dr. Frank L. Byrne of the Creighton University, Omaha, Nebraska; Dr. Thomas Africa of the University of Southern California; Professor John L. Fluitt, Louisiana State University in New Orleans, for making the maps; and each of my fellow graduate students at the Louisiana State University and the University of Wisconsin who read and criticized the manuscript. Mr. E. B. Long of Chicago put me forever in his debt by graciously allowing me to examine his copious notes from the Francis Lieber Papers at the Henry Huntington Library. The staffs at the State Historical Society Library of Wisconsin, the Louisiana State University Library, the Illinois State Historical Library, and the Manuscript Division of the Library of Congress have been extremely helpful. Special thanks are due for the Carnegie Corporation grant, made available through the National Security Studies Group, University of Wisconsin, which made it possible for me to continue this study. Finally, I want to thank my wife for her encouragement and consideration.

CONTENTS

MAPS AND
ILLUSTRATIONS

HALLECK: *Lincoln's Chief of Staff*

CHAPTER ONE

THE FORMATIVE YEARS

His story is the story of the Civil War. His hand shaped strategy in every theater of the war. No man on either side took part in more campaigns, and in 1861 no one of the generals whose names later became household words was better prepared for the war than Henry Wager Halleck. Of him, General Ulysses S. Grant said: "He is a man of gigantic intellect and well studied in the profession of arms."

Yet he became one of the most vilified of all Civil War generals. "Heavy headed" Old Brains, they sneered, "Originates nothing, anticipates nothing, . . . takes no responsibility, plans nothing, suggests nothing, is good for nothing." During his tenure as general-in-chief of all the Union armies the North won two of her decisive victories—Vicksburg and Gettysburg. Halleck played a major role in shaping both triumphs; still, a member of Lincoln's cabinet maintained that "his being at Headquarters is a national misfortune."[1]

The nature of the role he assumed in the conflict provoked antagonism, hatred and contempt. He was the organizer, the coordinator, the planner, the manager, who advised and suggested and sometimes ordered where and when to make a move, but never made it himself. Consequently the romantic age in which he lived consid-

[1] U. S. Grant to E. B. Washburne, July 22, 1862, in the Ulysses S. Grant Papers (Illinois State Historical Library, Springfield, Illinois); Gideon Welles, *Diary of Gideon Welles, Secretary of the Navy Under Lincoln and Johnson* (Boston and New York, 1909), I, 383.

ered him a moral, if not a physical, coward. Halleck had a penchant for working indirectly and never deigned to justify his clandestine activities to a demanding public. He seldom performed openly. As departmental commander in the West, as general-in-chief, and ultimately as chief of staff, he always operated at the top, away from the heat of battle and the comradery of camp life. His decisions were the result of neither snap judgments nor friendly intercourse, but calculated thinking. Given to violent hating, and never cultivating close friendships, he inspired neither love, confidence, nor respect. A reporter, summarizing the opinion of his contemporaries, described him as a "cold, calculating owl," brooding "in the shadows," and "distilling evil upon every noble character." [2]

Only one high ranking officer recognized Halleck's abilities. Near the end of the war, General William Tecumseh Sherman told him: "You possess a knowledge . . . of the principles of war far beyond that of any other officer in our service. . . . Stand by us and encourage us by your counsels and advice." [3] It was small praise for the four years of silent, arduous managerial work; his background led him to expect much more.

Halleck's ancestry was German and English. His father, Joseph, owed his American heritage to Peter Hallock, an Englishman who landed on Long Island in 1640. In 1814 Joseph, who ran a farm in the Mohawk Valley of New York, married Catherine Wager, daughter of a respected German pioneer in Syracuse. Catherine named the first of her thirteen children, born January 16, 1815, after her father—Henry Wager. For sixteen years the boy lived and worked on his father's farm, until in 1831 he rebelled against the drudgery of plowing and escaped to his grandfather. Wager sent him to Fairfield Academy in Hudson, New York, and later to Union College in Schenectady. When his grandson was twenty, Wager se-

[2] New York *World*, May 31, 1864.
[3] Sherman to Halleck, in *War of the Rebellion, Official Records of the Union and Confederate Armies* (Washington, 1880–1901), Ser. I, XXXII, Part 3, p. 469, hereinafter cited as *O.R.*

cured a West Point appointment for him. In the fall of 1835 Halleck entered the military school. He was graduated third in the class of 1839 with an outstanding record.[4]

Dennis Hart Mahan was the only instructor at West Point who decisively shaped Halleck's thinking. Recently returned from Europe where he studied war with experts, Mahan taught Halleck military and civil engineering, which included instruction in the "art of war." In Europe Mahan became convinced that the soldier could learn this "art" from the study of military history.

Mahan used the Napoleonic campaigns as his examples; he saw the Corsican through the eyes of Baron Henri Jomini, Swiss military historian and interpreter. Unlike his contemporary, Karl von Clausewitz, Jomini taught that Napoleon's success stemmed from the use of principles established by Frederick the Great rather than from the radical innovations which Clausewitz emphasized. Jomini wanted to introduce a rationality and system to the study of war; to make war less barbarous he created rules that emphasized movement rather than annihilation. Disliking the destructive warfare of his own time, Jomini wrote: "I acknowledge that my prejudices are in favor of the good old times when the French and English guards courteously invited each other to fire first. . . ."

Mahan accepted Jomini's ideas. Referring to the horrors of the French Revolution, the West Point instructor told his students that, when Napoleon took command, "reason and discipline again claimed their rights. . . ." Halleck accepted Mahan's assertion that the Corsican's only mistake was in neglecting fortifications and entrenchments, which led the First Counsel to make audacious and foolish attacks. As Mahan told the impressionable Halleck, "to do the greatest damage to our enemy with the least exposure to our-

---

[4] James Grant Wilson, "General Halleck, a Memoir," in *Journal of the Military Service Institution of the United States* (Governor's Island, 1905), XXXVI, 537; Daniel E. Wager, *Our County and its People, A Descriptive Work on Oneida County, New York* (Boston, 1896), 598; Samuel W. Durant, *History of Oneida County, New York* (Philadelphia, 1878), 597; Charles Hallock, *The Hallock-Holyoke Pedigree* (Amherst, 1906), 16.

selves is a military axiom lost sight of only by ignorance of the true ends of victory."

Daily Halleck heard Jomini's interpretations and adopted them for his own. He learned that success in the art of war began with the choice of a base of operations. The ideal was an interior line of communications which emanated from a strong base and lay between the two wings of the enemy. From an interior line a soldier could, after the fashion of Frederick the Great, strike first one wing and then another before the enemy could join forces. Interior lines simplified supply and mobilization problems while facilitating concentration on the battlefield. And concentration, both strategically and tactically, was of primary importance to the Jominian system. The Swiss theorist stressed three basic principles, all of which revolved around the idea of concentration: The commander should bring his forces to bear on the decisive areas of the theater of war; strategically, he should manoeuvre to engage his masses against fractions of the enemy; tactically, he should attack with his masses against the decisive point on the battlefield. Jomini emphasized the offensive only insofar as it resulted in the capture of places—he believed the occupation of territory or strategic points more decisive than the destruction of enemy armies. Never did Jomini emphasize attack or the concept of a *levee en masse;* instead, his geometrical diagrams impressed upon Halleck the scientific and rational aspect of war. When he made his own contribution to the "art of war," Halleck changed none of Mahan's and Jomini's dogmas.[5]

After serving one year as an instructor in French, Halleck left

[5] For a summary of Jomini's views, see Lt. Col. J. D. Hittle, *Jomini and His Summary of the Art of War* (Harrisburg, 1947); an excellent interpretation is offered by T. Harry Williams, "The Military Leadership of the North and the South," in *The Harmon Memorial Lectures in Military History, Number Two* (United States Air Force Academy, Colorado, 1960); D. H. Mahan, *An Elementary Treatise on Advanced Guard, Out Post, and Detachment Service of Troops* (New York, 1847), contains his views; for Mahan's teaching technique see R. Ernest Dupuy, *Where They Have Trod, The West Point Tradition in American Life* (New York, 1940), 228–38. D. H. Mahan was, of course, the father of naval captain Alfred T. Mahan.

West Point in 1840 to work on fortifications in New York City. There he wrote a paper for the United States Senate on sea coast defenses.[6] General Winfield Scott had asked the young lieutenant to submit his views on defenses, and was so pleased with the results that he rewarded Halleck with a trip to France. After six months of study in Europe, Halleck returned to New York and wrote *Elements of Military Art and Science.*

The work was in large measure a translation of Jomini's writings. "The first and most important rule in offensive war," Halleck copied from the master, "is to keep your forces as much concentrated as possible. . . . *Interior* lines of operations," he carefully noted, "have almost invariably led to success." The book had a major influence on American military thought. West Point accepted the study as a text, President Lincoln read it in the midst of the Civil War, and it was widely distributed to amateur soldiers during that conflict. Partly because of *Elements of Military Art and Science,* the practice of using interior lines of operations, a strong base of supply, fortifications, concentration on decisive points, a campaign of positions—all derived from the ideal of limited war—recurred time and again during the four year struggle.[7]

When the Mexican War came in 1846, Halleck found himself assigned to California, relatively removed from the scene of combat. There, with only one brief excursion against a semihostile hacienda, he found life dull. But his talents as a student, writer, and casual student of law soon led to his assignment as secretary of state to the military governor. The position carried with it a minimum of responsibility, but in it he learned the elements of administration. Hal-

[6] Henry Wager Halleck, "Report on the Means of National Defense," 28th Congress, 2nd session, Senate Document 85, p. 2–76, series no. 451; G. W. Richards, *Lives of Generals Halleck and Pope* (Philadelphia, 1862), 4.

[7] Henry Wager Halleck, *Elements of Military Art and Science* (2nd ed., New York, 1861), 5, 398, 383; chapter two, "Strategy," encompasses most of Halleck's views on the art of war; on Civil War military thinking, see Francis A. Lord, "Army and Navy Textbooks and Manuals Used by the North During the Civil War," in two parts, in *Military Collector and Historian* (Washington, D. C., 1957).

leck found that it had other advantages. He had access to records of
land titles, and in the confused state of transferring sovereignty from
Mexico to the United States, the young officer succeeded in acquir-
ing considerable land and valuable mineral rights.

Halleck's duties involved assisting in the establishment of a civil
government for conquered California. Partly moved by a desire to
divest himself of his duties as secretary of state, and partly to insure
a stable government to protect his speculative investments, he took
an active part in organizing a constitutional convention to adopt a
constitution for the state of California. In September, 1849, the
convention assembled in Monterey, and Halleck acted as the liaison
officer between the military government and the convention. He did
more. He exercised his personal influence to conciliate and persuade
delegates, while he made his knowledge of law available to the
assembled state-makers. Most of the constitution which emerged
from the deliberations was his personal handiwork.[8]

In the winter of 1849–50, he helped form the law firm of Halleck, Peachy and Billings, which quickly became one of the most
respected and wealthy in California.[9] In 1855 he married Elizabeth
Hamilton, the granddaughter of Alexander Hamilton. Halleck had
retired from the army in 1854. He was on the board of directors of
a bank and two railroads, and owned part of the second richest
quicksilver, or mercury, mine in the world.[10] By the time Beauregard
fired on Fort Sumter, Halleck's estate was worth $500,000.[11]

[8] William T. Sherman, *Memoirs* (New York, 1875), I, 40; Wilson,
"General Halleck," *loc. cit.,* XXXVI, 538; Theodore H. Hittell, *History of
California* (San Francisco, 1885), II, 630; Rev. S. H. Willey, "Recollections of General Halleck as Secretary of State in Monterey, 1847–
1849," in *The Overland Monthly* (San Francisco, 1872), I, 1–7, and
10–11; Joseph Ellison, "The Struggle for Civil Government in California,
1846–1850," *California Historical Society Quarterly* (San Francisco,
1929), X, 9–22; Milton H. Shutes, "Henry Wager Halleck, Lincoln's
Chief-of-Staff," *Ibid.,* XVI, 196; J. Ross Browne, *Report on the Debates in
the Convention of California* (Washington, 1850), *passim,* for Halleck's
activities in the Convention.

[9] Shutes, "Henry Wager Halleck," *loc. cit.,* XVI, 200.

[10] *Ibid.*   [11] *Ibid.*

The Civil War uprooted him. The shouts of joy with which the people of Charleston greeted the secession of South Carolina were heard as far away as the West Coast. Halleck viewed the situation with a "deep feeling of regret," for it would have a "very depressing effect upon property and business." He was skeptical about the future. The North, he predicted, "will become ultra anti-slavery, and I fear, in the course of the war will declare for emancipation and thus add the horrors of a servile to that of a civil war." The only solution, he thought, was to keep Maryland in the Union. If she could be retained, "slavery will still be recognized and protected under the Constitution, and the door kept open for a compromise or reconstruction, if either should become possible." He had hoped to see the party of Jackson returned to the White House and when that failed could only say: "In all probability a militia force will be ordered out, and it is possible that I may have to put on the old uniform." [12]

He would indeed. In August of 1861, Halleck returned to the army. General Scott remembered the young theorist on war and recommended Halleck for appointment as a major general in the regular army. Scott reportedly wanted Halleck to replace him as general-in-chief. [13]

The new major general hardly looked the part of a dashing leader of men. Standing about five feet, nine inches tall, weighing 190 pounds, he had a double chin and a large bald spot just above his forehead. One observer commented disparagingly on his "flabby cheeks . . . slack-twisted figure and . . . slow and deliberate movements." [14] Others noticed that when he spoke, his words were "few, pithy, and to the point." [15]

Halleck's eyes, like the man himself, impressed people in various

---

[12] Halleck to Reverdy Johnson, in Wilson, "General Halleck," *loc. cit.,* XXXVI, 553.

[13] *Ibid.,* 544; T. Harry Williams, *Lincoln and His Generals* (New York, 1952), 43.

[14] James Harrison Wilson, *Under the Old Flag* (New York, 1912), I, 98.

[15] William E. Doster, *Lincoln and Episodes of the Civil War* (New York, 1915), 178.

ways. A friendly newspaper reporter thought his eyes were "of a hazel color, clear as a morning star, and of intense brilliancy," while a critic commented on his "sideways carriage of the head," and thought his "habit of looking at people with eyes wide open, staring, dull, fishy even," made him look "more than owlish." [16] All agreed that "when he looks at a man" it seemed "as though he were going literally to read him through and through. . . . It is an eye to make all rogues tremble, and even honest men look about them to be sure they have not been up to some mischief." [17]

On October 10, accompanied by his wife and child, Halleck sailed for the East. His sense of duty compelled him to leave California, his home, his friends, his practice. Behind him were the happiest days of his life. On the day he left, the Pioneer California Guards gave him a salute of thirteen guns on the Folsom Street Wharf. A local newspaper expressed the sentiments of many: "California will lose one of her most patriotic and useful citizens." [18]

Just as he had used his talents to help build California and to protect his interests, now he moved to a larger scene with the same intent. But the years of quiet, orderly, successful living in California had left their mark. He was no longer a promising young army officer; he was an established, respected and powerful lawyer-businessman. His social, political, and military thinking was conservative; he entertained no thought of becoming an innovator. He was certain that he understood war and could control the course of the conflict; he knew that he would command respect in Washington. Businessman, lawyer, politician, statesman, soldier—he spoke the language of all. The army officers and Washington leaders considered him the foremost exponent of the art of war in America. Halleck never doubted that the war would be a limited one, fought along the lines that he had so carefully absorbed from Jomini.

---

[16] The New York *Herald*, July 21, 1862; Lew Wallace, *Autobiography* (New York, 1900), II, 570.

[17] The New York *Herald*, July 21, 1862.

[18] Shutes, "Henry Wager Halleck," *loc. cit.*, XVI, 200.

CHAPTER TWO

FROM CHAOS TO ORDER

"General," General-in-chief George B. McClellan was saying, "you have . . . the . . . difficult task of reducing chaos to order."[1]

It was a brisk November afternoon in the nation's capital. Major General Henry Wager Halleck was talking with McClellan about his new post, the Department of the Missouri, a command that included the key state of Missouri and the important area of Western Kentucky. President Abraham Lincoln had dismissed the former commander, General John C. Fremont, largely because the "Pathfinder" was a rabid abolitionist, and had hastily replaced the political troublemaker with an old friend, General David Hunter. After arriving in Washington, Halleck learned that he had originally been slated for the post of general-in-chief, but since Fremont had created so much confusion in Missouri, Lincoln required Halleck's services there. Besides, McClellan already had been made general-in-chief. Hunter would hold the command in Missouri until Halleck arrived.

General McClellan, Halleck's superior officer, appeared to be a soldier in the Napoleonic tradition; like the Corsican, he was short, swarthy, dramatic. His thinking, however, was more akin to Halleck's. McClellan agreed with the author of *Elements of Military Art* that concentration and fortification were the keys to victory; that in war civilians and their property should be held sacred; that civil-

[1] *O.R.,* Ser. I, V, 37.

ian leaders should abstain from military affairs; and that any excess blood-letting was criminal. McClellan delighted in the nickname, "Young Napoleon," but was a better organizer and administrator than fighter. Vain and egotistical beyond a point which Halleck, even in moments of supreme victory, could ever reach, McClellan was simultaneously beset with fears. The whole world seemed to be jealous of his superiority and plotting against him. He worried more about vague enemies to his rear than the real ones at his front, and never trusted anyone who did not absolutely worship him. After two years of fighting against him, one Confederate staff officer said of McClellan: "There was no lack of physical courage; it was a mental doubt with him." [2]

On November 11, 1861, the two generals, so different in appearance and yet so alike in mind, were discussing the problems Halleck would face in St. Louis. Fremont, who had been more interested in freeing slaves and enlarging his reputation than in organizing and running a military department, had signed fraudulent contracts and issued many illegal commissions to general and staff officers. The troops lacked food, clothing and pay. McClellan described the situation to Halleck in exaggerated terms: "You are facing a system of reckless expenditure and fraud, perhaps unheard of before in the history of the world." [3]

Halleck had problems other than administrative chaos. Briefly reviewing the military situation, McClellan suggested that Halleck hold the cities of Rolla and Sedalia, southwest of St. Louis. These places were railheads connecting with St. Louis and, since Hunter had placed his men there soon after taking command, were already centers of troop concentration. The enemy's main army, under the command of General Sterling Price, was located about one hundred miles southwest of Rolla, at Springfield, Missouri. It reportedly consisted of 33,000 to 50,000 men. Price was a former congressman and governor of Missouri who had been opposed to secession, but joined the South when fighting began in his state. On August 10,

[2] G. Moxey Sorrel, *Recollections of a Confederate Staff Officer* (new ed., New York, 1958), 127.   [3] *O.R.,* Ser. I, V, 37.

1861, he had won the battle of Wilson's Creek and after some jockeying for position had settled in Springfield.[4] In addition to this force led by a proven fighter, Halleck faced other opposition. Over the entire state, but especially north of the Missouri River, guerilla bands were anxious to join their former governor. Until they could do so, they busied themselves in hindering the Federal "occupation" of Missouri.

Properly briefed, Halleck boarded the train for St. Louis, confident he would be a success. On November 20, one day after he arrived, he began his administration by attacking the issue that cost Fremont his job—runaway slaves. The new commander wanted a well-ordered department and also to show McClellan that his own views on the peculiar institution were sound. Halleck knew the difficulties other commands had in dealing with fugitive slaves who fled into the army camps, and he knew that McClellan wanted them returned to their owners. Therefore, in General Orders, No. 3, he declared that no "contrabands" would be allowed within his lines. His reason, officially, was that the slaves conveyed military information to the enemy.[5]

This settled, Halleck turned his attention to corruption in the department. His task was Herculean. Most of the firms with which Fremont had done business were dishonest; even the supplies they did send were either stolen en route or "lost" by the quartermasters. The whole enterprise, Halleck said, had been conducted "in such a manner as to leave the least possible trace behind."[6] He sent out a systematic order for tightening the purchase of substance stores, one that resembled his law briefs in California, increased the number and quality of inspection officers, and soon reduced the losses.

His conduct at interviews underscored his determination. Invariably he began an interview with the curt question: "Have you any business with me?" When one officer replied "I have a moment's,"

---

[4] Thomas L. Snead, "The First Year of the War in Missouri," in Robert Underwood Johnson and Clarence Clough Buel (eds.), *Battles and Leaders of the Civil War* (new ed., New York, 1956), I, 266.

[5] John G. Nicolay and John Hay, *Abraham Lincoln, a History* (New York, 1886), V, 94–95.　　　[6] *O.R.*, Ser. I, VIII, 389.

Halleck ejected, "Very well, Sir, a moment let it be."[7] During his
conferences Halleck paced the floor, stooped over, hands in his
pockets or behind his back, or occasionally scratching his elbow, but
always with "the incessant activity of his eyes showing much wari-
ness and circumspection."[8]

Halleck's efforts, which extended into finance, clothing, regimental organization and pay for his troops,[9] brought praise even from
the enemy. Confederate President Jefferson Davis felt that "the Federal forces are not hereafter, as heretofore, to be commanded by
Pathfinders and holiday soldiers, but by men of military education
and experience in war." Measuring Halleck's activities in relation to
those of Fremont and Hunter, Davis predicted, "the contest is therefore to be on a scale of very different proportions than that of the
partisan warfare witnessed during the past summer and fall."[10]

Halleck agreed. He was becoming supremely confident and prone
to ignore the suggestions or criticisms of others, especially bother-
some and misinformed civilians. A visitor noted that he "abhorred
circumlocutions, introductions, and prefaces. He would anticipate
what you had to say, and decide before you were half way
through."[11] Nor was this dogmatism reserved for civilians. General
Lew Wallace, remarking on the first time he met Halleck, remembered that "he asked no questions, but indulged in very positive
speach. . . ."[12]

Though gruff, the general did not lack a sense of humor. Unionist
citizens of St. Louis later remembered, with a laugh, how Halleck
handled the Southern sympathizers among the women of the city.
The ladies showed their contempt for the North by wearing red
rosettes, so Halleck, as "Beast" Ben Butler did later in New Orleans,

[7] New York *Tribune*, January 3, 1862.
[8] Doster, *Lincoln and Episodes of the Civil War*, 178.
[9] See a series of General Orders in *General Orders, Department of the
Missouri and Mississippi, 1861–1862* (n.p., n.d.). The Orders are
chronological; see also Halleck to M. Meigs, January 18, 22, and May 23,
1862, in the Henry Wager Halleck Collection (Library of Congress,
Washington, D. C.).   [10] *O.R.*, Ser. I, VIII, 701.
[11] Doster, *Lincoln and Episodes of the Civil War*, 178.
[12] Wallace, *Autobiography*, II, 570.

purchased a large quantity of the rosettes and distributed them among the streetwalkers in St. Louis. Ladies who saw prostitutes wearing badges quickly shed their own.[13]

On the day that Halleck began his administrative campaign he also reviewed the military situation. The forces he inherited in Missouri were situated on a general northwest to southeast line, cutting across the Osage and protecting the Missouri River. On the eastern side of the Mississippi River, Halleck had a small force stationed at Cairo, Illinois, under the command of Brigadier General Ulysses S. Grant. Cairo lay next to the Ohio River near the mouth of the Tennessee. Opposite Grant's force was the center of Confederate Albert Sidney Johnston's line, bolstered by Forts Henry and Donelson. The Confederates had been content to watch Grant after repulsing him at Belmont, Missouri on November 7, 1861, but Halleck knew his position was one of potential danger. Fortunately, the Southern government had dictated a defensive policy and Johnston, like Halleck, had organizational problems.[14] Rebel troops west of the Mississippi, who were concentrated with Price at Springfield, were not under Johnston's direct command.[15]

On November 23, Halleck heard a rumor that Price was on the move. Colonel Frederick Steele reported from Sedalia that the Rebel general was traveling north at the fantastic rate of thirty miles a day. He was expected to cross the Osage that day and attack Sedalia.[16] Halleck handled the threat with a firm, calm hand. Refusing to take the field dramatically to repress the "onrushing" enemy, he merely ordered all his subordinates to prepare to resist attack.[17] The rest was up to them.

One lieutenant was not able to accept the delegated responsibility. William T. Sherman, West Point graduate and Halleck's friend of long standing, was one of the officers helping to organize the department. He was still recuperating from the mental strain caused

---

[13] Clarence Macartney, *Grant and His Generals* (New York, 1953), 153.
[14] Snead, "The First Year of the War in Missouri," *Battles and Leaders,* I, 268–70.   [15] *Ibid.*
[16] *O.R.*, Ser. I, VIII, 374.   [17] *Ibid.,* 375.

by a command in Kentucky. Nervous, muscular Sherman had a sharp, well-cut mouth, bluish-grey eyes, fair complexion and sandy-red hair and beard. He was known to his friends as "Cump." Unlike Halleck, who lived continually on an even emotional plane, Sherman alternated between fits of despair, when he often thought of suicide, and moments of extreme exhilaration. In conversation he was excitable and inclined to heavy profanity; he was highly sensitive and had a hidden desire to be a painter. Though temperamentally his opposite, Sherman liked the stolid Halleck, with whom he did have something in common—both men were theorists on war. Sherman had admired Halleck since their days at West Point, when Halleck, the honor student, condescended to take notice of him. His veneration grew during their voyage to California together in the 1840's. It matured during the Civil War. In 1864 he told Halleck: "You are frank, honest and learned in the great principles of history," while "both Grant and I are deficient in these and are mere actors in a grand drama, the end of which we do not see." [18] Halleck in turn always treated Sherman as if he were a promising student. When Sherman's nervousness required attention, Halleck, moved by a genuine concern and a desire to maintain his one deep friendship, acted like an indulgent teacher.

Sherman had come to Missouri to rest, but when Price moved north, Sherman, who was near the front, became involved in the campaign. On November 28, he excitedly warned Halleck to "look well to Jefferson City," for Price was moving on the camp there with "large numbers." Another Confederate force was aiming at Rolla, Sherman prophesied, and after capturing the town it would join Price. The consequences of such a junction would be disastrous; the combined forces might well threaten St. Louis.[19]

The cautious, methodical Halleck checked with General John Pope, at Syracuse. Pope found no signs of the enemy and no possibility that Price would storm northward. Nevertheless, Sherman

[18] Lloyd Lewis, *Sherman, Fighting Prophet* (New York, 1932), 71, 106, 203; *O.R.*, Ser. I, XXXIX, Part 3, p. 203.
[19] *O.R.*, Ser. I, VIII, 379.

feared an attack and ordered all commanders to fall back.[20] To stop
the panic-stricken general, Halleck countermanded Sherman's order
and directed him to St. Louis to report his "observations on the condition of the troops you have examined." When Sherman returned,
Halleck gave the over-wrought general a twenty-day rest.[21]

Sherman decided to go home, and shortly after he arrived in Ohio,
his wife sent an irate demand to Halleck. Newspapers throughout
the North accused her husband of being crazy and Ellen Sherman
demanded an explanation. Halleck, who honestly felt that "General
Sherman was completely stampeded, and was stampeding the army,"
told Mrs. Sherman he would make a "Yankee trade" with her husband; he was willing to "take all that is said against him if he will
take all that is said against me. I am certain to make 50 per cent
profit by the exchange." [22] Halleck told his wife "I treated the whole
matter as a joke," but candidly added: "He certainly has acted insane." However, he told one of Cump's politically powerful in-laws
that anyone who knew the general as well as he did, "thought that
nothing was the matter with . . . [Sherman] except a want of
rest." [23] The diagnosis proved correct, and Sherman was soon back at
his post, refreshed and in a better frame of mind. Halleck's careful
handling of the situation brought personal rewards. Sherman regarded him as a benefactor, and Halleck saved Cump for the Union
when he might otherwise have sunk to obscurity.

Meanwhile, Halleck had taken steps to rid Missouri of Price. To
head the coming offensive he chose General Sam Curtis, a fifty-four
year old West Point graduate, who had practiced law in Iowa after
seeing action in the Mexican War. A tall, thin, stern soldier, he
proved an able campaigner. Halleck had already—on Christmas
Day, 1861—ordered all his commanders to wipe out the guerillas in
their areas, get the troops ready for the field, and prepare for a
southward movement under Curtis against Price.[24] Even before Cur-

---

[20] *Ibid.*, 393.   [21] *Ibid.*, 391, 393.

[22] Lewis, *Sherman, Fighting Prophet*, 203.

[23] Wilson, "General Halleck," *loc. cit.*, XXXVI, 554; Lewis, *Sherman, Fighting Prophet*, 203.   [24] *O.R.*, Ser. I, VIII, 461.

tis could get his force effectively organized, Price was in retreat. Halleck ordered a cavalry pursuit and left the rest to Curtis. He felt it impossible to direct a campaign in southwestern Missouri from a map in St. Louis. Moreover, Washington demanded his attention east of the Mississippi.

The command situation in Kentucky and Tennessee was confused. Neither Halleck in St. Louis nor General Don Carlos Buell in Louisville, commander of the Department of the Ohio, knew where his departmental authority ended. Halleck's command reached to the banks of the Cumberland River, but applied only to the state of Kentucky. Tennessee, in Confederate hands, had not been divided.[25] Lincoln wanted Buell to advance into East Tennessee, a stronghold of Unionist sentiment in the South, but Buell could not "determine on it absolutely." [26] With his offensive in Missouri just getting underway, Halleck had neither time nor troops for an immediate advance in Kentucky. The absence of a single command for the entire West did not encourage offensive action.

The Confederates east of the Mississippi also had their problems. General Albert Sidney Johnston was making an effort to protect Bowling Green and Columbus, Kentucky, while guarding the state of Tennessee with the flanks of his line. The middle of the geographical line was at Dover, just inside the state of Tennessee, where the Cumberland and Tennessee Rivers flowed within ten miles of each other. Although these rivers were natural highways leading into the states, Johnston had failed to protect them adequately. Fort Henry, on the Tennessee River and Fort Donelson, at Dover on the Cumberland, were not good natural defenses, nor were they strongly garrisoned. One officer in the Confederate navy stationed at Henry thought that "extraordinarily bad judgment, or worse, had selected the site for its erection." [27]

Halleck had Union troops stationed at Cairo, less than one hun-

---

[25] *Ibid.,* 369.   [26] *Ibid.,* VII, 450.
[27] Captain Jesse Taylor, "The Defense of Fort Henry," in *Battles and Leaders,* I, 368.

dred miles from Fort Henry, and knew that he should take advantage of the Southerners' "bad judgment." One night in December, after dinner at his headquarters in the Planter's House with General George Cullum, his chief of staff, and the recently-returned Sherman, Halleck lit a cigar and turned the conversation to the "much-talked-of-advance." Newspapers were speculating that it would take place on the Mississippi River, but Generals Gideon J. Pillow and Leonidas Polk had a large Confederate force at Columbus, Kentucky, eighteen miles below Cairo, which forced Halleck to consider other places.

Pointing to a map on his table and taking a pencil in his hand, he asked: "Where is the rebel line?" Cullum took the pencil and drew a line through Bowling Green, Forts Henry and Donelson, and Columbus, Kentucky. "Now, where is the proper place to break it?" Both Cullum and Sherman replied, *"naturally* the center." It was basic Jominian strategy. The enemy had the immense advantage of interior lines, and only concentration by the Federals would counterbalance their ease of movement. If Halleck could set up a base in the heart of Johnston's territory he could fan troops out from it. They could be supplied by the Cumberland and Tennessee Rivers and would have a central point to which they could retreat or from which they could draw reinforcements. Drawing a mark perpendicular to the Confederate line, a mark that coincided with Fort Henry on the Tennessee River, Halleck pronounced: "That's the true line of operations." [28]

But for the moment his plan for advance was pure speculation. Halleck refused to move in Tennessee until he had complete control of Missouri. He did not have enough troops and did not feel competent to start two separate movements. The widely split offensives would be on exterior lines, anathema to Jominian theory. The day after the Missouri offensive began Halleck told McClellan that

[28] Sherman, *Memoirs*, I, 219–20. Sherman recorded: "This occurred more than a month before General Grant began the movement and I have always given Halleck the full credit of it."

when his "present plans" were executed he would turn on Tennessee.[29]

Buell, however, thought Halleck should advance. The suggestion sounded doubly sweet to Lincoln, for Buell sang it on a key that other generals would repeat with liturgical regularity throughout the war—East Tennessee. Buell said that if Halleck cut the Memphis and Nashville Railroad he would take Bowling Green. Lincoln, whose judgment was often thrown out of balance by the political pressure of the Unionists of East Tennessee, eagerly asked Halleck his opinion.[30] Halleck tartly replied: "It would be madness." Men could not be withdrawn from Missouri "without risking the loss" of the state; there were not enough troops available at Cairo; and the Confederates had no intention of withdrawing troops from Columbus, advance by Buell or not.[31]

On New Year's Day, tired of what he deemed were excuses, Lincoln told Halleck to contact Buell.[32] Halleck refused: "I am not ready to co-operate with him. Too much haste will ruin everything." Just to leave the President in no doubt about the protocol of army communications—according to the West Point texts—Halleck added: "I have written fully on the subject to Major-General Mc-Clellan." [33]

Halleck was clearly determined to run his department without interference from political bosses or rival commanders. When McClellan suggested that he should send some of his troops to Buell, Halleck complained: "The authorities at Washington do not understand the present condition of affairs." The result of shipping the troops to Kentucky would be the Union's loss of Missouri.[34] McClellan did not press the issue, and Halleck kept his men.

But if Halleck would not let go of the troops he must use them

[29] *O.R.*, Ser. I, VIII, 463. Halleck said: "If I receive arms in time to carry out my present plans . . . I shall be able to strongly re-enforce Cairo and Paducah for ulterior operations by the early part of February," which was a very accurate prediction of when the move would come.

[30] *O.R.*, Ser. I, VII, 450, 524.   [31] *Ibid.*, 532.
[32] *Ibid.*, 526.   [33] *Ibid.*, 526.
[34] *Ibid.*, 543.

himself. The General-in-chief ordered him to send an expedition up
the Cumberland River, acting in concert with Buell, who was finally
advancing into East Tennessee, and demonstrate toward Columbus.
McClellan also suggested a feint up the Tennessee River.[35]

The disgruntled Halleck felt it was impossible to do all three, and
informed the President on January 6 that he had only 10,000 effectives east of the Mississippi, while the Confederates had 22,000.
"We are virtually in an enemy's camp," and he added a simile to reinforce his point: "I am in the condition of a carpenter who is required to build a bridge with a dull ax, a broken saw, and rotten
timber." Then the author of a work on military tactics proceeded to
lecture the Western politician on war. "To operate on exterior lines
against an enemy occupying a central position will fail, as it has always failed, in 99 cases out of 100." Receiving this information
Lincoln sighed, "It is exceedingly discouraging. As everywhere else,
nothing can be done." [36]

Another factor accounting for Halleck's hesitancy was the lack of
a thoroughly reliable general in the Kentucky area. The top-ranking
officer was Ulysses S. Grant, a West Point graduate who had followed a career diametrically opposed to Halleck's. Grant left the
army after the Mexican War because of his drinking and had been
a complete failure ever since. With his shaggy beard and ill-kempt
clothes he looked more like the town joke than a great soldier.
When the Civil War started, Grant became a colonel on the
strength of his professional background. Halleck was in Washington when Grant became a general and knew that the promotion
came through political aid. For his one battle, Belmont, Grant
claimed a victory. Actually he had been fortunate to escape without
having to surrender his entire force.[37] Halleck and Grant had a poor
personal relationship—Halleck thought Grant a brave but reckless
fighter, and Grant felt eclipsed by Halleck. However, Grant had
done a good job of organizing his troops and was anxious to move

[35] *Ibid.*, 527.   [36] *Ibid.*, 532.
[37] See Chapter One, "Forty Years of Failure," in William B. Hesseltine,
Ulysses S. Grant, Politician (New York, 1935).

south. A desperate Halleck gave him permission to make a demonstration on January 6, telling him to begin the move whenever he
was ready.[38] The general embarked almost immediately on an un-
eventful expedition.

In the middle of January, Halleck, in bed with camp measles, mo-
mentarily forgot about Washington, Grant, and Kentucky as he
turned his full force on Price. The Rebel general had counter-
attacked Curtis' army, but had run into a flexible cavalry force that
retreated before him. Halleck ordered Curtis to move his artillery
and infantry forward from behind the cavalry screen and prepare
for a general advance, a movement that was soon underway. It was
elementary tactics, but it worked.[39] Curtis was soon driving Price
south and Halleck could finally see his objective of two months in
sight: Missouri was fast being cleared of Confederates and, thanks
to Halleck's strenuous efforts and ability, the department was in
smooth running order. Now he could devote his attention to planning military moves on a larger scale.

[38] *O.R.,* Ser. I, VII, 533.   [39] *Ibid.,* VIII, 498.

CHAPTER THREE

"GIVE ME COMMAND IN THE WEST"

A much more feasible plan" than an advance by both Buell and Grant, Halleck instructed McClellan on January 20, 1862, "is to move up the Cumberland and Tennessee, making Nashville the first objective point." His strategy was based on a principle put forth in his *Elements of Military Art:* "The configuration of the ground and the position of the hostile forces may *sometimes* render it advisable to direct our line of operations against the extremity of the enemy's line of defence; but, *as a general rule,* a central direction will lead to more important results." Halleck also rejected the "bad strategy" of a twin advance by his forces and those of Buell, because it would require a "double force to accomplish a single plan;" in other words, it violated the principle of concentration. Instead, Halleck would take Fort Henry, which flanked Columbus and Bowling Green, and force the Confederates to evacuate those cities. He implied that Buell should help in the campaign. In Missouri, which he considered a separate theater, Halleck would move part of his army on Pocahontas, in the northeastern corner of Arkansas, cut Price's supply line, and have Curtis follow the Southerner into Arkansas. At the same time, General John Pope would take New Madrid, a Mississippi River town. Halleck maintained that the plan was sound because it followed the "great central line of the Western theater of war."[1] Actually, Halleck already was

[1] Halleck, *Elements of Military Art and Science,* 52; O.R., Ser. I, VIII, 508–11.

modifying Jomini. The Swiss master insisted on concentration at the
decisive *point*, but distance and nature of the terrain made it impossible for Halleck to concentrate his Missouri, Kentucky, and Illinois
troops for one big push at any one point. Instead he would advance
on a broad front, attacking with Curtis, Pope and Grant, and clear
the Mississippi River—the great central *line* in the West. In each of
the three separate theaters of action—southwestern Missouri, southeastern Missouri, and northern Tennessee—he would keep the attacking forces well concentrated. One huge force marching down
either bank of the Mississippi would have been more in line with
Jomini's teachings, but less likely to succeed, if indeed such a force
could have been supplied or even brought together.

While he waited for McClellan's approval of his plans, Halleck
moved into the planning stage for his offensive against Fort Henry.
On January 22, 1862, in response to repeated requests and in order
to discuss his ideas with the general closest to the "central line,"
Halleck allowed Grant to come to St. Louis.[2]

Grant arrived for the appointment eager to attack Fort Henry, but
Halleck's usual blunt reception made the general nervous and in-
articulate. Halleck had no time for the advice of subordinates; what
he wanted was information and when Grant did not give it, Halleck
summarily dismissed him. Grant later complained that Halleck
treated him with "so little cordiality that . . . I returned to Cairo
very much crestfallen," but did admit: "I perhaps stated the object
of my visit with less clearness than I might have done."[3] Still their
conversation had been somewhat fruitful. After his demonstration
on the Tennessee, Grant had received a report on Fort Henry from
General Charles Smith, a West Pointer in whom Halleck placed

[2] *O.R.*, Ser. I, VII, 561.
[3] E. B. Long (ed.), Ulysses S. Grant, *Memoirs* (new ed., Cleveland and
New York, 1952), 147; George Bruce, "The Donelson Campaign," in
*Campaigns in Kentucky and Tennessee, The Papers of the Military His-
torical Society of Massachusetts* (Boston, 1908), VII, 9; J. F. C. Fuller,
The Generalship of Ulysses S. Grant (London, 1929), 82.

great trust. Smith believed that two gunboats could take Henry, and Grant managed to tell Halleck of the report.[4]

But Halleck was still dubious and for the next five days ignored Grant's numerous requests for permission to attack Fort Henry. On January 28, Grant added the voice of Flag Officer Andrew Foote to his own. As commander of the river gunboats, Foote's opinion added weight to Grant's side, but Halleck continued to procrastinate.[5] He wanted everything absolutely ready before he made the move, for although Curtis was making headway against Price, Halleck had minor problems, such as pay for his troops, that caused him to hesitate.

Continuing to press, Grant pointed out the advantages of holding Fort Henry. The Union troops could use it as a base and from it they would be in striking distance of Columbus, Memphis, or the Cumberland River. Grant ingratiatingly concluded: "The advantages of this move are as perceptible to the general commanding as to myself." [6]

On January 29, news arrived that forced Halleck to push the operation forward. McClellan reported that the Confederate General P. G. T. Beauregard and fifteen regiments were en route to Kentucky or Tennessee. Halleck immediately decided to establish his forces in Tennessee before the Creole and his men occupied the state. He promptly ordered Grant to take Fort Henry and hold it at all hazards.[7]

Grant received detailed instructions. He should take Fort Henry as soon as possible, send a cavalry force up the Tennessee River to break up the railroad track that connected the Confederate lines, leave a garrison in Cairo to hold the city in case of an attack from Columbus, and extend a telegraph cable from Paducah, Kentucky, to Fort Henry.[8] Halleck was determined to be master of the situation; he had given Grant a limited objective and almost no freedom

---

[4] Fuller, *The Generalship of Ulysses S. Grant*, 82.
[5] *O.R.*, Ser. I, VII, 120, 121.   [6] *Ibid.*, 120.
[7] *Ibid.*, 121, 571–72.   [8] *Ibid.*, 572.

of movement. To solidify his position and simplify the confused command system, Halleck explained to McClellan what was happening and asked to have Tennessee put in his department.[9] McClellan ignored the request.

As the preparations for the movement were getting underway, Halleck heard from General Buell. The Louisville commander had just found out about the advance. He asked what Halleck's plans were and if he could be of any service.[10] Halleck replied that his plans were to take and hold Fort Henry and he could do it without Buell's assistance.[11]

But on February 3, when he heard that Grant was actually on his way, Halleck began to worry. This was the first major offensive in which he had participated, and although he could draw strategy on paper calmly and assuredly, forces beyond his control unnerved his quiet office manner. He now anxiously asked Buell to make a diversion toward Bowling Green.[12] Buell, still fuming over Halleck's initial rebuff, refused and retorted that Halleck's "moves must be in earnest." The Missouri commander turned to McClellan for reinforcements, telling him that 10,000 men were moving on Fort Henry from Bowling Green.[13] McClellan had no troops, but he did order Buell to reinforce Grant. The Ohio general sent one green brigade.[14]

Halleck nearly panicked. The Creole with his 15,000 men never left his mind—he was certain they would prove far too strong for the inexperienced Grant and his little force. Feverishly he did what he could to build up Grant's force, but three regiments were all he could scrape together.[15] Again he turned to Buell, pleading for more men and material. But Buell refused. "This whole move," Buell thought, was started by Halleck "without appreciation— preparation or concert."[16] Halleck struggled to show the general that he was not a reckless soldier, claiming: "I had no idea of com-

[9] *Ibid.*, 571–72.   [10] *Ibid.*, 574.
[11] *Ibid.*, 576.   [12] *Ibid.*, 583.
[13] *Ibid.*, 583.   [14] *Ibid.*, 584.
[15] *O.R.*, Ser. I, LII, Part 1, p. 206.   [16] *O.R.*, Ser. I, VII, 587–88.

mencing the movement before the 15th or 20th instant till I received General McClellan's telegram about the reinforcements sent to Tennessee or Kentucky with Beauregard." Although he hedged a little on his dates, Halleck showed Buell he had not abandoned caution for an idle cause. "Although not ready," he added, "I deemed it important to move instantly." If Buell still did not have a proper fear of Beauregard, Halleck reminded him that "the holding of Fort Henry is of vital importance to both of us." He argued in vain; Buell did nothing.[17] Halleck gave the same evidence to McClellan and then went into a rhapsody about what he could accomplish if only he had more troops—if McClellan would give him 10,000 additional men he would take Fort Henry, cut the enemy's railroad line and "paralyze Columbus"; with 25,000 he would threaten Nashville and force the Southerners to abandon Bowling Green without a battle.[18] McClellan did nothing.

Halleck's frustrations illustrated the inherent defects of the command system. The General-in-chief refused to take an active role in the campaign; he let his two subordinates argue and fight. Already jealous of each other, and never close friends, Halleck and Buell did just that. Buell actually demanded proof of the necessity of Halleck's drive south and even after Halleck furnished it refused to help. Obviously one of the two independent commanders would have to be made subordinate to the other if the Union ever hoped to get maximum efficiency from either. Their bickering produced only minor results. In the space of two days, Halleck, Buell, and McClellan exchanged twenty-two telegrams in regard to the operation. The result was the transfer of one brigade from Buell to Grant.

While Halleck, Buell, and McClellan debated, Grant took Fort Henry. The few Confederates there hardly put up a fight. In fact, Grant did not have time to get his troops in position before the enemy surrendered. Buoyed up by the ease of victory, Grant casually informed Halleck he would destroy Fort Donelson in two days, then return to Fort Henry unless he found it advisable to occupy Donelson with a small force. If he did, Halleck need not

[17] *Ibid.,* 593.   [18] *Ibid.,* 587.

worry, for in case of danger they could easily retreat to the main body at Henry. "I shall regard it more in the light of an advance guard than as a permanent post," Grant remarked. The task looked so unexacting that Grant decided to take no transportation and little artillery with him.[19]

Grant's plan corresponded with Halleck's. Fort Henry would be a base of operation in the heart of enemy territory; from it troops could fan out in all directions and still, like spokes on a wheel, have a central hub to which they could return. It was an advantageous outpost from the standpoint of communications, for the Tennessee River was navigable and in the hands of the superior Union fleet. To strengthen the position further, Halleck ordered the railroad bridges up river, or south of Henry, destroyed. To make Fort Henry itself impregnable, he sent shovels and picks to Grant, gave him permission to use slaves of secessionists on the fortifications, and ordered all artillery placed to resist an enemy attack by land.

Immediately after giving the order Halleck informed McClellan of his fears and objectives. He thought the enemy would concentrate at Paris, Tennessee in order to operate on Grant's right flank. Halleck wanted Grant to take Paris as soon as Donelson fell. He rejected the prospect of a dash on Columbus, since he lacked the necessary troops, but would endeavor to occupy New Madrid and thereby cut off the communications of Columbus. The key to the whole process was to "hold Fort Henry at all hazards," a phrase that continually ran through Halleck's mind.[20]

The general was thinking negatively. If Fort Henry fell, what Grant's troops should do did not bother Halleck as much as what he imagined the Confederate forces would do. He thought of entrenching, solidifying, strengthening the new base, without taking into account the lowered Confederate morale and the inherent possibilities of Grant's force. Other high officials in the West were similarly worried about Grant. Buell thought he would soon be at least forced out of Fort Henry, if not captured. Assistant Secretary of War

[19] *Ibid.*, 124.   [20] *Ibid.*, 590.

Thomas A. Scott believed that Grant was in "extreme danger of being cut off by Beauregard." [21]

Halleck's trepidation, however, did not prevent him from devoting much of his time and energy to obtaining a larger personal command. He believed the command system in the West archaic, that a general needed autonomy to make his plans effective, and that he was the only general qualified to command the entire area. On February 8, he asked McClellan to create a "Western Division." The wing commanders could be Generals Buell and Hunter, while General E. A. Hitchcock, an old regular army man, could take charge of the center. Two advantages would result if McClellan initiated the plan: orders would go through a single officer, simplifying the command system, and the new division would eliminate departmental lines. Halleck summarized his proposal in a powerful argument that took into account all of the disagreements of the preceding five days: "This would avoid any clashing of interests or difference of plans or policy." Then, although he claimed to have "no desire for any larger command," Halleck offered to take charge of the whole. [22] But his proposal availed nothing and after McClellan refused Halleck returned to running his own department.

While Halleck was petitioning McClellan, Grant told him that he would destroy Fort Donelson on February 8. On the eleventh, delayed by rain, he was still in Fort Henry. Almost hourly during this "crisis of the war in the West," Halleck saw opportunities for the Southerners. At one time he believed they were concentrating at Dover, preparing to knock Grant out of Tennessee. Later he imagined they possessed an "immense number" of boats, which would carry the Bowling Green force to Donelson, attack the rear of Grant's lines, and return to Nashville before Buell even started after them. [23] Anxiously he turned to Foote, whose gunboats were not hampered by the weather, telling the naval commander that the destruction of Fort Donelson "is of vital importance," and should

---

[21] Richey Kamm, *The Civil War Career of Thomas A. Scott* (Philadelphia, 1940), 105.

[22] *O.R.*, Ser. I, VII, 595.   [23] *Ibid.*, 588, 599.

be carried out "immediately. . . . The taking of these places [Donelson and Paris] is a military necessity." [24]

But when he decided that the Confederates had reinforced Fort Donelson by at least 40,000 men from Bowling Green, Halleck became less convinced of the auspiciousness of attacking it. Perhaps it would be better to strengthen Fort Henry further before doing anything else. At any rate, Grant must have more men and Halleck endeavored to secure reinforcements by ordering Sherman, Hunter, and General George W. Cullum to send troops from Illinois, Kansas and Missouri to Tennessee. [25] Then he pleaded with Assistant Secretary of War Scott, asking him to urge McClellan to send men, and emphasizing that he had not "the slightest doubt" that the expedition would succeed, *"if they will give me the forces which are now useless elsewhere."* [26]

Halleck left nothing to chance. He approached McClellan through Scott while trying to bribe Buell by offering him command of the Cumberland expedition. Halleck even proposed to transfer Grant out of the department, hoping Buell would bring some troops with him, but Buell scorned the bait. [27]

That night Grant finally started for Donelson; when he did, anxiety gripped Halleck's methodical mind. Grant had violated almost every one of Halleck's orders and his own promises. He failed to entrench at Henry, leaving himself with no central fortified spot to which he could return if difficulties appeared. He took almost all of his force and equipment from Henry on his move to Donelson. The reckless subordinate was in the heart of the enemy's territory with nothing to hold to in case of disaster. In effect, he was in a bag, with the enemy to the northeast and northwest. If Johnston saw his opportunity and pulled the strings, Grant would be trapped. Foote's gunboats had been driven off by the batteries of Donelson and the transports that carried Grant's men up to Henry had gone back down the river. Well might Halleck worry. He was desperate over the fate

---

[24] *Ibid.,* 604.   [25] *Ibid.,* 580–610, *passim.*
[26] Halleck to Scott, February 12, 1862, in the Edwin M. Stanton Papers (Library of Congress).   [27] *O.R.,* Ser. I, VII, 607, 617.

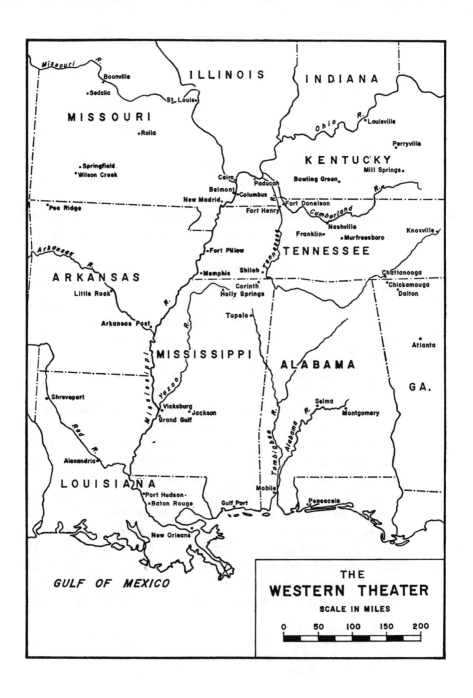

THE
WESTERN THEATER

SCALE IN MILES

0   50   100   150   200

of his troops and displeased with his general. His men were almost surrounded by a superior enemy.

But Halleck believed that he was neither authorized nor qualified to send Grant suggestions, orders or plans. He convinced himself that since he was not on the scene he should not make decisions; all he could do was send men and more men to Grant. Besides, he could see no way to withdraw his general safely. Afraid of aggravating the situation, he decided to let his subordinate fight it out.

To help Grant, Halleck appealed to Buell, asking for a cavalry demonstration on Bowling Green or, failing that, a "mere feint." Again he tried to bribe Buell by offering him command of the Cumberland column and again offered to transfer Grant.[28] When Buell refused to bring reinforcements, Halleck's anxiety and exasperation mounted. There were 30,000 troops in the garrison of Fort Donelson and even more were coming from Bowling Green, just evacuated by the Confederates. "I must have more troops," he told McClellan.[29]

Among a host of nervous strategists, President Lincoln alone kept himself under control. He saw nothing particularly alarming about the situation, although he did warn Halleck to be cautious. When a friend asked Lincoln if he thought *that* warning was necessary, the President replied he "didn't know that he did, but there was too much at stake on the battle," and "no hazard must be run which could be avoided."[30] McClellan, meanwhile, continued to argue strategy with Halleck.[31] The only piece of welcome information the general received was Price's continuing retreat before Curtis.[32]

The sky finally began to clear for Halleck as it became increasingly evident that the Confederates were not going to take advantage of Grant's exposed position. Instead of planning an offensive against the isolated enemy general, the Rebels spent their time trying to find a way out of the besieged Fort Donelson. By

[28] *Ibid.,* 609.   [29] *Ibid.,* 617.
[30] Francis Fessenden, *Life and Public Services of William Pitt Fessenden* (Boston and New York, 1907), I, 261.
[31] *O.R.,* Ser. I, VII, 625.   [32] *Ibid.,* 617.

11 P.M. of February 15, Halleck was satisfied with the progress of the siege; the next day he received word that Grant had captured the fort.[33]

St. Louis went wild with joy, Halleck right along with it. He posted the news on the bulletin board outside the Planter's House; then sat vigorously puffing his cigar. "Palmer," he called out to the clerk, "send up two dozen baskets of champagne, and open them here for the benefit of the crowd. . . . And I want you to give public notice that I shall suspect the loyalty of any male resident of St. Louis who can be found sober enough to walk or speak within the next half hour." [34]

In the muddy streets the news rang forth. "The Star Spangled Banner" and "Red, White and Blue" resounded. Banding together 1,500 strong, the mob tottered two-abreast through the ankle-deep mud to Halleck's recently quiet headquarters. They raised three cheers for Halleck, then Foote. To their cry, "Speech! Speech!" Halleck, limp from the sudden release of tension, gladly responded.

"When I came here," he shouted, "I said . . . the flag of the enemy should be driven from Missouri." He paused as if to imbibe his own words. "It is now out of Kentucky." The crowd below cheered wildly. As a hush finally settled, he cried triumphantly: "And will in a short time be out of Tennessee." Raising its voice to acclaim Halleck again, the mob sloshed off to decorate the city in carnival attire.[35]

With his faith in himself never higher, Halleck moved inside his office to telegram McClellan. "Give me command in the West," he demanded; "I ask this in return for Forts Henry and Donelson." [36] The general had seen, and seized, the chance for the power he desired. When Grant's campaign proved a success, Halleck pro-

[33] *Ibid.,* 159, 616.

[34] Miles O'Reilly (pseudo. for Charles G. Halpine), *Baked Meats of the Funeral* (New York, 1866), 166.

[35] Chicago *Tribune,* February 18, 1862.

[36] *O.R.,* Ser. I, VII, 628.

claimed himself the architect of victory, convincing himself that he had ordered Grant to take Fort Donelson.

After waiting a day for McClellan's reply, Halleck repeated his request. This time he promised to "split secession in twain in one month" if he were given the command.[37] Again he waited in vain, before telegraphing hopefully, almost prayerfully: "May I assume the command? Answer quickly."[38] The General-in-chief's quick answer was a flat refusal.[39] Desperately, Halleck went over his commander's head and told the new Secretary of War, Edwin M. Stanton, that nothing could be done in the West until he had the overall command. "Give me the authority," he boasted, "and I will be responsible for the results." Earlier he had told Scott to have Stanton send him 50,000 troops from the Army of the Potomac. Scott had been impressed with Halleck's abilities and told Stanton that if he sent the troops and gave Halleck command "there can be no such thing as fail."[40] But Stanton also refused and Halleck shifted from his bold offensive tactics to guerilla warfare.

Halleck had not relinquished his attempts to induce Buell to come into his department and thereby be under his orders. For the third time he tempted Buell with command of the Cumberland force and tried to persuade him to come into the area by pointing out what might have happened in the recent campaign. "We came within an ace of being defeated," he told the hesitant Buell, because: "You and McClellan did not appreciate the strait I have been in. . . . Help me, I beg of you," Halleck pleaded. "You will not regret it."[41] Buell probably agreed that the command system needed complete revision; he undoubtedly did not concur with the proposal that placing Halleck in charge would solve all the problems.

Later the same day Halleck repeated the theme in another telegram to Buell, saying: "Had the enemy thrown his force rapidly down the river he could have crushed me at Fort Donelson, and

[37] *Ibid.*, 636.   [38] *Ibid.*, 641.
[39] *Ibid.*, 645.
[40] *Ibid.*, 655; Kamm, *The Civil War Career of Thomas A. Scott*, 109–10.
[41] *O.R.*, Ser. I, VII, 632.

have returned to Nashville before you could have reached that place." Halleck believed the Confederates made a "terrible mistake" in the opening movements of the campaign by "not falling back from Bowling Green or Clarksville, driving me out of Fort Henry, reinforcing Fort Donelson, and connecting again with Columbus." Quite correctly he saw that their failure to do so cost them a "golden opportunity." [42] If Halleck had supreme command he could take advantage of their loss. But Buell, like his friend Mc-Clellan, turned Halleck down. He went straight south and took Nashville on his own.

Again Halleck turned on McClellan, sending the General-in-chief a masterfully composed letter which appealed to McClellan's vanity, his fear and hatred of the abolitionists, and his desire for new honors. Radical Republicans, Halleck said, had been trying to promote antislavery officers to the rank of lieutenant general. Halleck temporarily blocked them by informing a congressman that if McClellan "were superceded by *any one*, [the army] would be utterly demoralised," and he conjured a plan that would silence them permanently. Halleck would have Congress create the rank of "general," which would be between the positions of major general and lieutenant general, leaving the latter for brevet only. McClellan should see to it that the number of "generals" were limited to two—Halleck and himself. McClellan would be made a brevet lieutenant general when he took Richmond, and Halleck would "come in for it" at the close of the war. "This," Halleck pronounced, "will suit me perfectly." In sychophant fashion, Halleck concluded, "Be assured, General, that my name shall never be used in opposition to yours. I have too high a regard for your character and military skill to permit anything of that kind." [43] Halleck had spun his web too fine; McClellan could not be caught in it. Frustrated at every turn, Halleck temporarily shelved these plans and devoted all his talents to the Union's war.

[42] *Ibid.,* 632.
[43] Halleck to McClellan, February 24, 1862, in the George B. McClellan Papers (Library of Congress).

After the excitement of the Donelson campaign abated, Halleck started outlining new thrusts southward. In Missouri his main objective was clearing the Mississippi River. He had cleared the northern "flanks" of the river, Missouri and Kentucky, and had his forces driving into Tennessee and Arkansas. His broad front strategy forced the Confederates to evacuate their northernmost stronghold on the river, Columbus, and now he was prepared to push them farther back.

On February 18, Halleck pointed out to General Pope the possibilities and advantages of capturing New Madrid, Missouri, and Island No. 10, in the Mississippi River. Pope agreed with his chief and by February 21 had an offensive underway.[44] Halleck did everything he could to aid his subordinate. On February 25 he told Pope he was sending enough reinforcements to raise his command to 10,000 men, and by March 1 Pope was investing New Madrid. On March 3, shifting troops rapidly, Halleck ordered Sherman and Cullum, at Cairo, to send any available troops to Pope.[45] The next day he told the two subordinates to send the men to Grant's force in Tennessee if Pope took New Madrid before the troops were on the transports.

The troops in Tennessee no longer served under Grant. On February 26, "Unconditional Surrender," the nickname the stodgy Grant had recently acquired because of his demand for unconditional and immediate surrender at Donelson, had gone down to Nashville to talk with Buell. Halleck flooded Grant with requests for troop strength, but received no answer. Halleck began to complain to McClellan. "It is hard to censure a successful general," he admitted, "but I think Grant richly deserves it. . . . I am worn-out and tired with this neglect and inefficiency." Halleck was especially angry because McClellan hinted he was not capable of a larger command since he did not know the numbers he had in his present one. Halleck stated that he could not understand why Grant did not answer his requests, or why he had gone to Nashville, and said that he believed Charles F. Smith the only capable officer in the depart-

[44] *O.R.*, Ser. I, VII, 74.   [45] *Ibid.*, 573, 583.

ment.[46] McClellan sped back an order: "Do not hesitate to arrest him [Grant] at once if the good of the service requires it." [47] The next day Halleck removed Grant and placed Smith in his command. "Why do you not obey my orders to report strength of your command?" Halleck angrily demanded.[48]

By March 4, Halleck thought he found the answer. "A rumor has just reached me," he telegraphed McClellan, "that since the taking of Fort Donelson General Grant has resumed his former bad habits." To a seasoned regular army man like McClellan that meant just one thing—Grant was drinking. Halleck left no doubt in his chief's mind as to the validity he gave the rumor. "If so," he said, "it will account for his neglect of my often-repeated orders." However, "for the good of the service," Halleck did not "deem it advisable to arrest" the North's new-found hero "at present." [49]

Halleck finally learned the reason for Grant's neglect; the general had not received the requests. The local telegraph operator was a Rebel who ran off with the dispatches, leaving Halleck and Grant completely out of touch. Halleck retreated as gracefully as possible. "I am satisfied," he told Adjutant General Lorenzo Thomas, admitting that Grant had acted "from a praise-worthy although mistaken zeal for the public service" in going to Nashville. Halleck recommended that no further notice be taken of his charges.[50]

But with the misunderstanding glossed over, at least to Halleck's satisfaction (Grant still did not have a command), dissension began to develop along the muddy banks of the Mississippi among Halleck's subordinates. Pope and Foote were feuding. Pope wanted the naval officer to make a demonstration against Island No. 10, just up the river from New Madrid. When Foote refused, Halleck intervened on the side of his fellow West Pointer, telling Foote not to wait for repairs on his boats but to go ahead with the demonstra-

---

[46] *Ibid.*, VII, 679.   [47] *Ibid.*, 680.
[48] Grant, *Memoirs*, 166.
[49] *O.R.*, Ser. I, VII, 682, 683; Grant, *Memoirs*, 166–68.
[50] *O.R.*, Ser. I, VII, 683.

tion. He added that his instructions must be obeyed, "if possible." [51]
Foote responded with a refusal to attack Island No. 10, and Pope
declared that he would not move against New Madrid until he had
Foote's support. [52] Halleck stepped forward and displayed a latent
ability to ply stubborn officers like Pope, saying that he was giving
up and that he was pulling Pope's entire command out and sending
it off to Smith. [53] The next day a thoroughly frightened Pope
flanked New Madrid, took Point Pleasant and erected batteries. Now
that the Union troops had a strong position down river from New
Madrid, Halleck called off Pope's retreat. [54]

Pope responded with another victory. The Confederates evacuated New Madrid on March 13, sending troops to Island No. 10. [55]
Happily, Halleck told Pope and his men: "You have given the
final blow to the rebellion in Missouri and proved yourself worthy
members of the brave Army of the West." [56] The campaign worked
just as Halleck desired; he had planned it, and let his subordinate
act. After the fall of New Madrid, Pope turned on Island No. 10,
and Halleck promised: "I will not embarrass you with instructions." [57]

The sentence was a summary of Halleck's theory of command.
Control of a situation passed from his hands as he sent a subordinate out on a mission. Halleck held that "a General in command of
an army in the field is the best judge of existing conditions," and
that for the departmental commander to dictate to the field general
on the basis of incomplete information would be disastrous. The departmental commander's duties, as Halleck visualized them, involved outlining the operation before it began and supporting the
field commander with reinforcements and supplies while he
executed it. Halleck's practice had been successful at Forts Henry

---

[51] Halleck to McClellan, February 27, 1862, in the Robert Todd Lincoln
Papers (Library of Congress); *O.R.*, Ser. I, VIII, 588.
[52] *O.R.*, Ser. I, VIII, 582.   [53] *Ibid.*, 588.
[54] *Ibid.*, 597.
[55] *Ibid.*, 613. Pope telegraphed: "To my utter amazement the enemy
hurriedly evacuated the place last night, leaving everything."
[56] *Ibid.*, 641.   [57] *Ibid.*, 646.

and Donelson, at New Madrid, and would be again in the future.

While the New Madrid campaign was reaching a climax, Halleck finally saw the reorganization he deemed necessary to success become a reality. Lincoln, disgusted with McClellan's inactivity and impressed with Halleck's success, had Secretary Stanton ask Halleck on March 7 what areas he would desire in a new Western Department. Halleck replied, then addressed McClellan with the freedom that came from having an assured position. Both Buell and Hunter had been too late in recent campaigns to do any good and under such a system "there never will and never can be any cooperation at the critical moment; all military history proves it." As he thought of McClellan's obstinate refusal to help him solder the chain of command, he could not contain his anger. "You will regret your decision against me on this point," Halleck declared, and accused McClellan of letting friendship obstruct military necessity. "So be it," he ended ominously.[58]

The next day Halleck became commander of the new Department of the Mississippi, which included most of the area west of the Alleghenies, and Lincoln reduced McClellan to the head of the Army of the Potomac.[59] Thereafter Halleck could deal with Lincoln directly.

February and March, 1862, had been good months for Halleck. He had survived the strain of Grant's boldness and proclaimed he had fathered the entire campaign, bragging to his wife that Columbus, Bowling Green, and Nashville were evacuated as a consequence of his strategical moves. Actually he had managed, as much as he directed or planned, the offensive. Halleck had acted as a businessman-soldier, mobilizing both the civilian and military resources of an area for an operation. His field commanders did not suffer from a lack of men or supplies, nor were they overburdened with minute, impossible orders. Instead they could enter an operation confident that Halleck would keep them well supplied, just as he could depend on their fighting ability to make his simple strategical plans successful.

[58] *Ibid.*, 596, 602.   [59] *Ibid.*, 605.

The role Halleck played was important and Lincoln recognized it as such, by making Halleck supreme commander in a reorganized department of the West. From coast to coast his abilities were acclaimed. "I need not tell you how your brilliant exploits are in the mouths of all New Yorkers," his sister-in-law, Mrs. Schuyler Hamilton, remarked. A Californian informed him: "All California is now swearing by you; and, should you return to civil life among us, the U. S. Senate is your next sphere for action, unless the Democracy . . . make you President, which is not at all improbable." [60] It was not improbable. One more major victory in the West and he might be able to choose his position.

The icy weight of recent weeks melted, and Halleck overflowed with confidence. His men were "in excellent spirits," and basked in bright prospects for the future. "Of course I have been very, very busy," he confessed to his wife, "not only in carrying out these plans, but in forming new ones." [61]

[60] Mrs. Schuyler Hamilton to Halleck, March 16, 1862, and George F. Ihrie to Halleck, March 29, 1862, both in the Henry Wager Halleck Letter Book (Library of Congress).

[61] Wilson, "General Halleck," *loc. cit.,* XXXVI, 555.

CHAPTER FOUR

THE SIEGE OF CORINTH

The Confederates enjoyed no rest after evacuating Fort Donelson. The Yankees drove them south from Columbus, Bowling Green, Nashville, all of Kentucky and the western half of Tennessee. On the left flank Grant's army, now under Smith, pushed forward relentlessly; in the center Pope was on the point of eliminating the last shreds of resistance on the upper Mississippi River; on the right Curtis was preparing for a victorious battle with Price. If the Army of the West could continue to advance at that rate, it would be in New Orleans before winter.

Since his days at West Point, Halleck had visualized war as a chess game; now he was a player rather than a kibitzer. The enemy's main line of defense was the Mississippi, but the Confederate queen, Beauregard's and Johnston's army, was a free agent. It was operating in the northeastern corner of Mississippi—take it, and the king, Vicksburg, would be checkmated. Watching the board, Halleck decided that the battle to culminate the war in the West must soon take place. Johnston's new defensive line had its wings on the Mississippi and Tennessee Rivers, with the center at Corinth, in the northeastern corner of Mississippi. The Mobile and Ohio and the Memphis and Charleston railroads crossed there and made Corinth important. Halleck determined to move his queen to the square, eliminate the enemy's, again break Johnston's line in the center, and

all without incurring the risks of the Donelson campaign. By waiting for all his forces to concentrate around Smith's army on the
Tennessee River, Halleck could build up an overwhelming force
and assure himself of victory. Once committed to the policy, Halleck saw advantages in allowing the Confederates to bring all their
men into Corinth, for even when both sides built up to their maximum the Union would have superiority in numbers and could
demolish all enemy resistance with one blow.

The immediate objective was to clear the Confederates from the
river north of Memphis. They still held a strong position up river
from the city on the nondescript island called "No. 10." Pope tried
various methods of getting at the island, including digging an extensive channel, without success. An impetuous junior naval officer
saved him by taking a gunboat and running the batteries of Island
No. 10. The next night another sailor repeated the move. When
daylight came on April 7, Pope crossed the river. With nowhere to
turn except into the river, the entire Confederate garrison surrendered. The fruits of victory were copious—over 6,000 prisoners,
three generals, ammunition, supplies, and 100 pieces of artillery.

Halleck beamed. Not a single Union casualty. It was a victory
won by manoeuvre; a success which Napoleon himself could not
have better effected. The campaign, Halleck said, "exceeds in boldness and brilliancy all other operations of the war." He predicted
that Pope's movements "will be memorable in military history and
will be admired by future generations." [1]

While Pope was completing his campaign to open the Mississippi,
another of Halleck's generals made southward progress. On
March 7, Halleck had directed Curtis to advance into northwestern
Arkansas. Curtis soon saw and seized a golden opportunity to defeat
Price's men in a three-day encounter at Pea Ridge, Arkansas.[2] His
victory completed a cycle: Halleck sent three subordinates south
with general instructions, and from left to right Grant, Pope, and
Curtis reported major successes.

[1] *O.R.*, Ser. I, VIII, 634, 645, 675.   [2] *Ibid.*, 596, 610.

There could be little doubt in Halleck's mind that the general in the field was the best judge of what specific action to take, but he also realized that he alone must decide in what field the queens and rooks should act. He came to a quick Jominian decision; all forces west of the river would concentrate with Curtis, who could handle affairs there, while in the main theater all available men would join Smith's army. When all was ready, Halleck could take over and lead that army to its ultimate victory over the Confederates.

As Halleck waited for his army to accumulate at Pittsburg Landing, twenty-five miles from Corinth, he alternately prodded and cautioned his subordinates. He told Grant, directing troop movements from Fort Henry, that in no case should Smith bring on an engagement "until we can strongly re-enforce him." [3] Buell was finally on his way, as were 10,000 or 15,000 men from Missouri. Feeling that "we must strike no blow until we are strong enough to admit no doubt of the result," Halleck tried to hurry Buell, ordering him to march his force directly to the Landing. If he did not join Smith soon, the enemy might split the two Union forces, attacking first one and then the other. The next day he spurred the hesitant Buell with a command to "move on," then told Grant to stay away from any engagement with the enemy until Buell arrived. Nine days later Buell still had made little progress, and once again the exasperated Halleck urged more speed: "It is all-important to have an over-whelming force" before Corinth, he told the lethargic general. [4]

By the end of March, Halleck's force reached huge proportions. Scattered throughout Kentucky and Tennessee Buell had 101,000 men; Grant [Smith became ill and later died, so Grant took active command.] in Tennessee, 75,000; Curtis in Arkansas, 23,000; Pope at New Madrid, 25,000; and stationed throughout Missouri were more than 25,000 men. In and around Pittsburg Landing there were, counting Buell's force, over 70,000 troops. [5] Still Halleck asked for more. "Want every man we can get," he told Stanton,

[3] *Ibid.*, X, Part 2, p. 41.   [4] *Ibid.*, 77.
[5] *Ibid.*, VIII, 649.

assuring him that most of the Confederate army that just evacuated Manassas, Virginia, had arrived on his front. "It is probable that the great battle of the war will be fought in Southwest Tennessee." [6]

Despite the impending Armageddon, Halleck decided to stay in St. Louis. Pope's army was on the verge of taking Island No. 10, and would soon be available for operations on the Tennessee; Halleck would take charge of sending it to Grant. With this force, plus what he could gather in Missouri, Halleck would have 100,000 men at the Landing. Then when all was ready, when victory was assured, he would go there to direct the last great battle in the West.

The Confederates seemed content to wait for their inevitable destruction. Grant, twenty-five miles north of Corinth and the enemy, had "scarcely the faintest idea of an attack (general one) being made upon us," and was "prepared" for one if it did come. Halleck never doubted that Grant had entrenched at Pittsburg as he had neglected to do at Henry—Halleck had sent tools to the Landing for that specific purpose. When Grant said he was "prepared," Halleck took him at his word, decided the moment had arrived, and on April 5 requisitioned a gunboat for his trip up the Tennessee.

One of Halleck's friends already at the Landing, another general who did not fear a Confederate attack, looked forward to Halleck's long delayed arrival. Reviewing all the Union victories in the West, that general—William T. Sherman—declared: "Halleck has been the directing genius. I wish him all honor and glory. . . ." As he finally prepared to take the field, Halleck, too, may have thought of his honor and glory. When he came to St. Louis, the Confederates controlled parts of Missouri and Kentucky and all of Tennessee; now they were driven back into Arkansas and Mississippi, where they waited for the *coup de grace.*

But while Halleck made preparations to leave St. Louis, Johnston ruined his plan. Breaking a pattern he himself set months before, Johnston left his entrenchments at Corinth and furiously fell on

[6] *Ibid.,* X, Part 2, p. 93.

Grant. Before the battle, while the green Southern soldiers were sportingly shooting off their guns, Beauregard tried to dissuade Johnston from attacking, arguing that Grant must be aware of his approach. Johnston pushed on heedlessly, and the Federal troops were completely and inexcusably surprised. A Yankee picket who later questioned a Rebel captain learned that the Southerners "anticipated no surprise, and were surprised themselves to discover it." Grant had dug no entrenchments and his losses were heavy, but after the initial shock he managed to hold his ground. During the first day of battle, Johnston was killed leading his men and Beauregard took command. The Creole decided to halt any further attacks for that day; during the night Buell's command crossed the river and the next day Grant drove Beauregard from the field.[7]

While the contest was in progress, Halleck hurried to the scene of battle, now called Shiloh, named for a small church near Pittsburg Landing. His first thoughts were not of his men, but of the reaction in Washington. He wanted to get to Shiloh and smooth things over at once. After hearing stories that Grant was drunk during the battle and concluding that this was the cause of the surprise, Stanton asked Halleck "whether any neglect or misconduct of General Grant or any other officer contributed to the sad casualties that befell our forces." Halleck forgot his petty animosities with Grant as he turned to face the threat to his control of his army. "The sad casualties," he defiantly replied, "were due in part to the bad conduct of officers who were utterly unfit for their places, and in part to the numbers and bravery of the enemy." The unfit officers Halleck referred to were volunteers, not West Pointers. He patiently explained to Stanton: "A great battle cannot be fought or a victory gained without many casualties." He concluded simply by saying, "the enemy suffered more than we did." The North, not yet immune to long casualty lists, demanded a scapegoat; Halleck refused to give one. He told the Secretary of War: "Newspaper ac-

[7] *Ibid.*, Part 1, p. 89; Part 2, p. 65; VIII, 660; New York *World*, May 10, 1862.

counts that our divisions were surprised are utterly false," for every division had notice of the enemy's approach hours before the battle commenced.[8]

Strategically Shiloh was a draw. Halleck did not change his plans, and Beauregard merely drew back into his lines around Corinth. The Creole believed the city was still the key to the war in the West, because "if defeated here we lose the Mississippi Valley and probably our cause." [9]

Beauregard was expressing one of the two distinct Civil War strategical theories. One Northern group throughout the war maintained that ultimate victory would come only after the Union occupied key Confederate places; the other that victory would follow the destruction of the main Confederate armies. Advocates of the Jomini-inspired "places theory" argued that the Confederacy could not stand without Vicksburg, New Orleans, Corinth, Atlanta, Chattanooga, Richmond, Charleston, etc.; their opponents thought that capturing places without destroying armies was useless, because once an enemy army capitulated, his city would fall as a matter of course. McClellan, Sherman and Halleck were generals more interested in taking a place than an army. For example, in his Georgia campaign, Sherman would capture a place without destroying the enemy's army and then actually march away from that army on his route to the sea.

Halleck's Corinth campaign was planned and executed with one idea in mind—to capture Corinth. He subordinated everything else to that end and, after the Shiloh experience, entertained no idea of attacking and destroying Beauregard's army. In his *Elements,* Halleck had pronounced: "*General* battles are not to be fought but under the occurrence of one of the following circumstances: when you are, from any cause, decidedly superior to the enemy; when he is on the point of receiving reinforcements which will materially affect your relative strength; when, if not beaten or checked, he will deprive you of supplies or reinforcements, necessary to the con-

[8] *O.R.,* Ser. I, VIII, 677, 700; X, Part 1, pp. 98–99.
[9] *Ibid.,* X, Part 2, p. 403.

tinuance or success of your operations; and, generally, when the advantage of winning the battle will be greater than the disadvantage of losing it." [10] None of these conditions applied at Corinth. Before Shiloh, Halleck had been willing to fight because he felt he outnumbered the enemy. Now he felt the forces were even.

On April 14, 1862, Halleck began the preparations necessary for the twenty-five mile advance to Corinth. The country watched with interest as he made ready to take the field. The New York *World* editorialized: "He exchanges executive service in the closet for active military service in the field. If he displays the same ability in the latter sphere that he has in the former, no name will rank before his in the history of this war." [11]

His soldiers were not as impressed. As soon as they saw his high forehead and large, popping eyes, they christened him "Old Brains." [12] In an amateurish manner, he tried to make the men like him. Although it rained the entire first week he was in Tennessee, Halleck lived in a tent and found he liked it, "notwithstanding the inconveniences. . . . It will have a good effect upon the soldiers to camp out with them."

The officers were glad to see him, Halleck wrote to his wife, because "this army is undisciplined and very much disorganized." [13] Here, as in St. Louis six months before, more men and more organization were needed before he could embark on an offensive. On April 15, Halleck ordered Pope and his army to come to the Landing at once. To improve his present force, he made each corps general responsible for his own organization, discipline, and preparation for service, as well as for food, clothing and arms. A part of the organization drive required each man to carry 100 rounds of ammunition; if any soldier was found short of his quota the company captain would be arrested. After tasting some of the soldier's food, Halleck decided the large sick list resulted from haphazard

[10] Halleck, *Elements of Military Art and Science,* 132.
[11] New York *World,* April 11, 1862.
[12] Wilson, "General Halleck," *loc. cit.,* XXXVI, 549.
[13] *Ibid.,* 556.

preparation and ordered company commanders and medical officers to inspect each meal.[14] "I have been very hard at work for the last three days endeavoring to straighten things out," Halleck told his wife, "and hope to succeed in time." [15]

Philip Sheridan, a recent graduate of West Point, worked as Halleck's quartermaster to improve the commanding general's menu. He set out to make life more comfortable for his chief, even providing fresh beef every day. But Sheridan was not happy as a forager, he wanted his chance at glory. A Michigan cavalry regiment needed a colonel; Sheridan asked Halleck to let him fill the post. Halleck said he would have to wait until he could obtain the consent of the War Department, since it was opposed to having regular officers serve in volunteer regiments. Sheridan pressed, and as he later recorded, Halleck "finally resolved to take the responsibility of letting me go without consulting the War Department." When Sheridan thanked the general, Halleck told him to forget the thanks and hurry to catch the regiment, since they were just leaving on a raid. Sheridan got there in time.[16]

Halleck chose the pattern of his advance after witnessing the effect dispersal of forces had on Grant's army at Shiloh. Old Brains would keep his army concentrated to prevent Beauregard's attacking an isolated wing. He ordered that roads be repaired and constructed as troops moved forward; that pickets should always be thrown well forward to prevent surprise; that direct communication between the army commanders and himself must be maintained; that heavy artillery be established at all supply depots; and that entrenchments be used.[17]

A field commander had to face difficulties not mentioned in military texts. It rained incessantly, the whole land seemed flooded, bridges were gone, roads impassable and supplying troops arduous.

[14] *O.R.,* Ser. I, X, Part 2, p. 107.
[15] Wilson, "General Halleck," *loc. cit.,* XXXVI, 556.
[16] P. H. Sheridan, *Personal Memoirs* (New York, 1888), I, 137–39, 141–42.   [17] *O.R.,* Ser. I, X, Part 2, p. 117.

Many small streams or creeks were interspersed between Shiloh and Corinth, most of which could not be crossed without bridges because of the sudden declivities on their banks and their soft, boggy bottoms. Narrow, unimproved dirt roads, low wet ground, and numerous rains made progress almost impossible.[18]

Another obstacle was Beauregard's army, which had increased from 47,000 to 67,000, of whom 45,000 were listed as effectives, ready to fight. Halleck had an aggregate of nearly 100,000 men, but because of the excellent defensive nature of the terrain, he needed that numerical superiority. Grant thought the ground made the two forces about equal.[19]

On the afternoon of May 3, the army was ready. Before leaving, Old Brains sent a brave message to Stanton: "I leave here to-morrow morning, and our army will be before Corinth to-morrow night. There may be no telegraphic communication for the next two or three days."[20] On the fourth, Sherman's division moved to within six miles of Beauregard's works. That night and the following day heavy rains washed out bridges and tore up roads. On May 7, the weather cleared and Halleck again made some progress; Sherman left his entrenchments and advanced one-half mile.

Within two days of the start of the march the army was within six miles of Corinth. It had covered fifteen miles over extremely difficult terrain, and an early morning march would place it directly in front of its objective. But then Halleck set up a siege. He threw up earthworks all along the line, reproductions of those complicated entrenchments he had seen in France, and settled down to wait. Sherman dug from May 7 to 11, then moved 1½ miles to within 4 miles of the enemy; on May 13 he moved another 1½ miles, then dug until May 21. On that day he advanced to within 1¾ miles of Corinth. Buell was the same distance from Beauregard by May 19; on May 21 he moved one-half mile forward and a week later

[18] *Ibid.*, Part 1, pp. 664, 673, 685.
[19] *Ibid.*, Part 2, p. 421, 475; Grant, *Memoirs*, 194.
[20] *Ibid.*, Part 1, p. 665.

progressed another one-half mile. On the left, Pope had permanent fortifications at Farmington by May 17; 11 days later he moved forward 1½ miles to within 1 mile of Beauregard's works.[21]

On May 11, when the army was within easy striking distance of Beauregard, Lincoln wired Halleck: "Norfolk in our possession, Merrimac blown up, & Monitor & other boats going up James River to Richmond. Be very careful to sustain no reverse in your department."[22] For the next ten days, acting on Lincoln's suggestions, Halleck had the army dig trenches. He feared that Pope was in particular danger and when the general complained that Buell had not caught up with him and that his right flank was in the air, Halleck quickly ordered Buell to close up as soon as possible, then cautioned Pope to "avoid any general engagement." Shiloh and Lincoln's warning left an indelible impression on Old Brains; he refused to split his army to tempt the enemy into what would have been a fruitless assault. Twice Beauregard tried to attack and found Halleck's army too close together and too well entrenched.[23]

Criticism mounted as Halleck calmly besieged Corinth from three sides. To silence it, all newspaper correspondents were excluded from his camp. He sent them back to the Landing, where they could get the news—after the army approved it—from a large bulletin board. The attempt at censorship in an age when reporters felt they were entitled to print any information they discovered led to more objection. One reporter called Halleck an "irratated old maid, a silly school girl, a vacillating coquette," and another claimed he wanted to remove outside witnesses to a campaign that was turning

[21] See Buell to Halleck, May 5, 1862, in the Halleck Letter Book for a typical complaint about the weather; see Halleck's and Scott's reports to Stanton, May 5 to May 18, 1862, in the Stanton Papers for the rate of advance. The author has taken his figures from *O.R.,* Ser. I, X, Part 1, *passim,* and the *Atlas to Accompany the Official Records.* See also Bell Irvin Wiley (ed.), *"This Infernal War," The Confederate Letters of Sgt. Edwin H. Fay* (Austin, 1958), 48. Fay, in Corinth, wrote his wife on May 5: "They are within 3 ms."

[22] Roy P. Basler (ed.), *The Collected Works of Abraham Lincoln* (Rutgers, 1953), V, 210.   [23] *O.R.,* Ser. I, X, Part 1, p. 778.

into a fiasco. One correspondent, who managed to remain at camp, took a more penetrating glance at the general. "Halleck has some strong points; his love of system is one." He described Old Brains as "a born conservative who lags rather than keeps pace with his age, whose sympathies are with the past," and who was "genial and companionable" in private, yet "cold and facetious" in public.[24]

Some of Halleck's soldiers were free with their views. One perplexed officer told his wife: "I cannot imagine what our dignitaries are doing that we should lie here so long," but, he reasoned, "this is their last stronghold, and I suppose we are making sure of destroying them."[25] A soldier in the ranks agreed entirely with Halleck's policy. "Suppose Halleck should let them through his vast expansive net! . . . La me! what a croaking of critics there would be among you; 'twould resemble—the scene and sounds would—a frog pond in the spring time. . . . Halleck, it is believed, prefers the Scott: McClellan the little-loss-as-possible method of warfare, and is planning for its practice here. I belong to that school myself—the school will be glad to know." His final comment fully reflected his position in the front lines: "We've had enough of the slaughter-pen style of conquering."[26]

Halleck did favor the "Scott: McClellan" method. Careful advances, meticulous planning, and no thought of attacking the enemy characterized his siege. By May 18, when the line was within two miles of Beauregard's entrenchments, Halleck reported to Stanton: "The enemy is apparently waiting our attack upon his works." Convinced that Beauregard outnumbered him and was receiving reinforcements daily, Halleck would not deliver the attack. He believed that "Richmond and Corinth are now the great strategical points of the war, and our success at these points should be insured at all hazards." On Halleck's insistence, Thomas Scott requested

[24] B. A. Weisberger, *Reporters for the Union* (New York, 1954), 96; New York *World*, June 2, 1862. The story was written on May 26.

[25] Robert B. Athearn (ed.), *Soldier in the West: The Civil War Letters of Alfred Lacey Hough* (Philadelphia, 1957), 64.

[26] New York *World*, June 4, 1862.

50,000 men from the East to restore Halleck's numerical superiority; until then Old Brains could do nothing.[27]

As May neared its end, Halleck prepared for the last manoeuvre. It would be executed with extreme caution; its purpose was not to bring battle but to force Beauregard out of Corinth. Halleck made no effort to swing around the enemy, although he outnumbered the Confederates three to two. Beauregard's strength had increased to 75,000, but only 53,000 were considered effectives.[28] On May 27, Halleck finally resumed his gentle push against Beauregard. He ordered Buell to make a reconnaissance to "ascertain the position and strength of the enemy's works." Buell had faced these works for the better part of three weeks, but began a gradual advance on the right and left, admonishing his lieutenants to keep him fully advised of all movements.[29] Soon the advance halted and the army waited for developments. On May 29 Halleck visited Pope's camp, where he found the enemy building a concentration against the left wing. As Pope and Halleck agreed that a move to the left would bring on a general engagement, Halleck decided to move up his right and center. At 1:20 A.M. Pope reported heavy enemy reinforcements coming into Corinth. Trains were running constantly, and cheering reverberated loudly throughout the area. Ten minutes after receiving Pope's report, Halleck told Buell: "There is every appearance that Pope will be attacked this morning. Be prepared to reenforce him, if necessary."[30]

A number of explosions in Corinth at sunrise sent Sherman to Halleck for an explanation.[31] Halleck admitted his own puzzlement, but the solution was simple—Beauregard had fled, leaving little of value behind; what he could not move he burned. The cheers Pope heard each time a train ran into Corinth were for empty cars, which took the troops out. Huge "siege guns" facing Union lines were mere logs—"Quaker guns."

[27] Halleck to Stanton, May 18, 1862, in the Robert Todd Lincoln Papers; Scott to Stanton, May 6, 1862, in the Stanton Papers; *O.R.*, Ser. I, X, Part 1, p. 667.

[28] *O.R.*, Ser. I, X, Part 2, p. 548.   [29] *Ibid.*, 218.

[30] *Ibid.*, 223, 225, 228.   [31] *Ibid.*, 228.

By six A.M. Pope discovered the ruse and rushed into the city. Two hours later he had some cavalry and artillery in pursuit of the fleeing Beauregard, who retreated on the Mobile road. In the town his men found the Confederate soldiers had inscribed on empty buildings, "These premises to let; inquire of G. T. Beauregard." [32]

Halleck rode into town that afternoon wearing undistinguished clothes and a slouch hat to inspect the buildings and supplies Beauregard left. While Halleck rode around in disguise, his horse tripped on a telegraph wire and nearly threw him. Old Brains dismounted and angrily supervised the elevation of the wire to its proper height, then rode off. [33]

The pursuit Halleck tried to organize failed as his thoughts centered on Washington; he wanted to get a report to Stanton before the Secretary heard the news from an unsympathetic witness. Calling the evacuation a hasty one, he telegraphed: "In his flight this morning he [Beauregard] destroyed an immense amount of public and private property—stores, provisions, wagons, tents, etc. . . . For miles out of the town the roads are filled with arms, haversacks, etc., thrown away by his flying troops." The criticism of his failure to attack would spread throughout the country; Halleck anticipated and defied the critics: "He cannot occupy stronger positions." The Creole "evidently distrusts his army," or else he would have fought. [34]

Halleck correctly anticipated the onslaught of criticism. Newspaper reporters, still fuming from their banishment, snarled in their reports. A Chicago *Tribune* correspondent stated: "General Halleck has thus achieved one of the most barren triumphs of the war. In fact, it is tantamount to a defeat," while the Cincinnati *Commercial* reporter said the evacuation was a "triumph" for the South. [35] One of Halleck's officers agreed. Soon after entering Corinth he told his wife: "We have been outgeneralled, and there

[32] *Ibid.*, 225; William Conant Church, *Ulysses S. Grant* (New York, 1897), 145.

[33] Chicago *Tribune*, June 2, 1862.   [34] *O.R.*, Ser. I, X, Part 1, p. 668.

[35] K. P. Williams, *Lincoln Finds a General* (New York, 1948–59), III, 417.

is a feeling of intense disgust at everybody and everything that leads our Armies." In his opinion, Old Brains should have attacked. "Didn't they fool us Bad?" Two weeks later, after he more carefully examined the Confederate works, the officer altered his pronouncement. Now he considered the siege "brilliantly planned, and brilliantly executed. . . . It is a great pity that they ran, but that could not be prevented. . . . The North might have carried the Southern works, but it would have cost 20,000 to 30,000 lives. . . . This General Halleck knew, and never intended to attack them in front." [36]

Halleck himself was pleased with the results. He had his army of 100,000 concentrated at the key railroad center of Corinth, and he could move in any direction he chose. Fort Pillow on the Mississippi and the city of Memphis fell as a result of Corinth's capture, opening the river as far south as Vicksburg.

Sherman had high praise for Halleck's conduct of the campaign; he called it "a victory as brilliant and important as any recorded in history. No amount of sophistry or words from the leaders of the rebellion can succeed in giving the evacuation of Corinth under the circumstances any other title than that of a single defeat, more humiliating to them and to their cause than if we had entered the place over the dead and mangled bodies of their soldiers." Jefferson Davis agreed with Sherman.[37]

[36] Athearn (ed.), *Soldier in the West,* 74.
[37] K. P. Williams, *Lincoln Finds a General,* III, 417.

Library of Congress

HENRY WAGER HALLECK: "All agreed that when he looked at a man it seemed as though he were going literally to read him through and through. . . . It is an eye to make all rogues tremble, and even honest men look about them to be sure they have not been up to some mischief."

Library of Congress

ULYSSES S. GRANT: "With his shaggy beard and ill-kempt clothes Grant looked more like the town joke than a great soldier."

Library of Congress

WILLIAM T. SHERMAN: "Sherman alternated between fits of despair, when he often thought of suicide, and moments of extreme exhilaration."

National Archives

P. G. T. Beauregard: "The Creole believed Corinth was the key to the war in the West, because if defeated here we lose the Mississippi Valley and probably our cause."

CHAPTER FIVE

CONSOLIDATING RECENT GAINS

I do not, however, propose to pursue him far into Mississippi," Halleck said of the retreating Beauregard,[1] and thereby established a pattern for six weeks of campaigning in the West. Rather than plan offensive action, he spent his time organizing the department, improving the health of his troops, repairing railroads and obtaining new cars. The relentless heat of the Mississippi summer was conducive to that attitude.

Old Brains unobtrusively reverted to the defensive. He told Pope, who was pursuing Beauregard, to "Press the enemy as hard as you deem it safe and advisable," but warned him to watch for a surprise attack on his flanks; Halleck had done his part by deploying troops on those flanks. Pope interpreted his commander's words liberally and pushed Beauregard vigorously. He reported June 4 that the enemy had halted at Baldwyn, on the railroad line south of Corinth, and that he would attack in the morning "unless I am otherwise ordered." Halleck sped an answer that outlined for Pope the purpose of the pursuit. "The main object now is to get the enemy far enough south to relieve our railroads from danger of an immediate attack. I think by showing a bold front for a day or two the enemy will continue his retreat, which is all I desire. There is no object in bringing on a battle if this object can be obtained without one."[2] It was a perfect summary of the 18th century Jominian concept of war. Knowing that Beauregard would shortly

[1] *O.R.*, Ser. I, X, Part 1, p. 668.   [2] *Ibid.*, Part 2, p. 252.

resume his retreat, doubting that Pope could defeat his army and satisfied to free the area of the enemy, Halleck restrained the general and prevented an unnecessary battle. A few days later Old Brains abandoned the pursuit.

Then Halleck outlined his program. The army in Mississippi—the center of his line—would remain on the defensive, scattering over northern Mississippi and southern Tennessee to repair railroads and build fortifications. Curtis in Arkansas would continue his offensive and Buell would embark on an expedition into East Tennessee. Halleck himself would stay at Corinth, directing operations as he had from St. Louis. The dispersal of forces was in direct contradiction to Jomini's doctrine of concentration, but Halleck felt he had no real alternative. The huge area he had taken could not be held easily until railroad communications between strong points were improved. The intense heat and the sudden change in climate, food, and water made active campaigning nearly unendurable for northern soldiers experiencing their first southern summer. Halleck put them to repairing railroads and fortifying strong points. Even Buell's expedition was in part a railroad repairing operation. Concentration could come in the fall, after current gains had been consolidated. Knowing that Lincoln's concern for the Unionists in East Tennessee often clouded his judgment, Halleck hoped the War Department would approve his plans.[3]

Stanton and Lincoln approved, but not without reservations. "I suppose you contemplate the occupation of Vicksburg and clearing out the Mississippi to New Orleans," Stanton wired.[4] Halleck may have been amused at the casualness of the question. He could have pointed out that taking Vicksburg and clearing the Mississippi would require time, more troops and more supplies, and therefore was not being contemplated at the present. However, he chose to ignore the question and concentrate on improving his position.

To make Corinth secure, Halleck fanned out his troops. Buell

[3] *Ibid.,* Part 1, p. 671.

[4] *Ibid.,* 671. Stanton wanted Halleck to co-operate with Benjamin F. Butler, the army commander at New Orleans.

was moving along the Memphis and Charleston railroad to the east, toward Chattanooga; Pope was repairing the Mobile and Ohio road south of Corinth; Sherman was proceeding west on the Memphis and Charleston. All forces were busily engaged in getting up locomotives and repairing track. Though Halleck's men may not have shared his zeal for railroad repair, they restored over three hundred miles of track. Other troops improved the fortifications which the Confederate engineers had erected around Corinth.[5]

Halleck knew that Washington solons wanted more offensive action from the army in the West; he also knew that the slightest promise of activity in pro-Unionist East Tennessee would dispel Lincoln's objections to nonaggressive activity in all other areas. Early in June, 1862, Halleck informed the War Department that he was moving troops, despite almost insurmountable barriers, toward Chattanooga. Anticipating an onslaught from the Secretary of War, Halleck told Stanton that the Confederates would "immediately march back and attack us" if any of his troops were shifted to another arena. To further placate Washington, he added an enticing hint of occupying Atlanta: "Should Buell be able to penetrate into Georgia as far as Atlanta, he will still be in a dry and mountainous country."[6]

But Lincoln was not satisfied. He reasoned that Halleck did not need all his men to guard railroads and ordered him to detach 25,000 troops and send them to McClellan by the "nearest and quickest route." The citizens of East Tennessee were not abandoned, however; Lincoln instructed Halleck to leave Buell's column intact.[7] That was Halleck's clue; he would play on the President's anxiety as did generals before and after him. Informing Stanton that the detachment would take some time to get to McClellan, he continued in a seemingly innocent sentence: "I think, under the circumstances, the Chattanooga expedition must be postponed or a less force sent to Washington."[8]

[5] *O.R.,* Ser. I, X, Part 2, pp. 248, 278.
[6] *Ibid.,* XVI, Part 2, p. 62.   [7] *Ibid.,* XI, Part 3, p. 271.
[8] *Ibid.,* p. 279; XVII, Part 2, p. 59.

Upon receipt of the message, Lincoln hurried to the War Department and had an operator dispatch a telegram; he would be very glad of 25,000 infantry, but did not want a man "if it forces you to give up or weaken or delay the expedition against Chattanooga." This was, to the politician, "fully as important as the taking and holding of Richmond." [9]

Halleck had weathered one storm and was determined to be prepared for the next. Worried over Buell's languor—the general was making little progress toward Chattanooga—Halleck sent orders to hasten the movement. Mentioning the "very inconsiderate" order he received to send troops east, and "barely strong enough to sustain" his position, Halleck moaned that "to make other detachments was certain ruin." [10] If Buell's reading were acute, he could see that unless something were accomplished soon the Chattanooga expedition would suffer.

The threat to his command left Halleck "so much troubled and annoyed" that he barely had the heart to write to his wife. He blamed everything on McClellan, who was a "selfish" general, motivated by "ridiculous jealousies." Old Brains feared that McClellan would play on Lincoln "till he gives them a part of my army. If so, it will be almost fatal." After receiving Lincoln's order, he felt "utterly broken-hearted," and his first impulse was to resign and go back to California, yet duty to country forbade this. "I hope," Halleck ended more optimistically, "that everything will yet be right." [11]

Suddenly Lincoln made another request. This time, claiming that much of the Confederate force from Corinth was in the East and fighting McClellan, he wanted 10,000 infantry. Halleck sent a prompt refusal. His officers were "unanimous in opinion" that any detachment would necessitate the abandonment of the Chattanooga expedition or giving up West Tennessee, and Halleck himself

[9] *Ibid.,* XI, Part 3, p. 279.

[10] *Ibid.,* XVI, Part 2, p. 92. Stanton warned Halleck on June 30 that Lincoln was not pleased with "the tardiness of the movement toward Chattanooga." *Ibid.,* XI, Part 3, p. 280.

[11] Wilson, "General Halleck," *loc. cit.,* XXXVI, 556.

wanted to "earnestly protest against surrendering what has cost us so much blood and treasure, and which, in a military point of view, is worth three Richmonds." Moreover, if Lincoln needed troops, he could detach men from the idle forces in the Shenandoah Valley in Virginia, which had "no strategic importance." [12]

His arguments would ring hollow if Buell did not take Chattanooga soon, and it began to look as though he would never make it. By July 8 Halleck realized that Confederate General Braxton Bragg, now commanding Beauregard's army, was not going to sit quietly through the summer and watch Halleck consolidate his gains. Bragg left Mississippi, destination unknown. His possible objective might be Memphis, Tuscumbia, or Chattanooga. To spur Buell on, Halleck reminded him that Lincoln was dissatisfied with progress toward East Tennessee, and if the move were not hurried Bragg might head for and reach the city first. [13]

Halleck guessed right; Bragg was going to Chattanooga, and by an expeditious use of the Confederacy's limited railroads, got there before Buell. A year later Buell claimed that Halleck's policy of forcing him to repair railroads in Alabama slowed him down and was the reason for Bragg's success. The charge, although upheld by a military commission, was untrue. Buell had dallied in his movements. Halleck gave Buell orders to go to Chattanooga early in June; Bragg did not reach the city until July 22. [14]

With McClellan commanding the Army of the Potomac, Lincoln had no advisor on military affairs. Since spring the President functioned as general-in-chief of the armed forces and the results that he hoped for had not materialized. Lincoln's one big effort at tactical direction of the armies, detaching men from McClellan's army to trap the Southerners in the Shenandoah Valley, was a failure. McClellan was in trouble before Richmond, the army in the West was

[12] *O.R.,* Ser. I, XI, Part 3, p. 294; XVII, Part 2, p. 71.

[13] *Ibid.,* XVII, Part 2, p. 82.

[14] *Ibid.,* XVI, Part 1, p. 12. See K. P. Williams, *Lincoln Finds a General,* IV, chapter two, for a detailed study of the campaign and a refutation of the myth.

going nowhere, and Buell lost the race to Chattanooga. The North was fighting in a piecemeal fashion with no coordination between the armies; the Union cause needed a guiding hand. McClellan had tried and failed. Fremont, Butler, and other high ranking generals were not competent and because they were not West Pointers could not be expected to function well with Academy generals. Someone else had to be found.

Others saw Lincoln's problem and were free with advice. Pope, whom Lincoln had just called to Washington to take charge of the forces formerly operating in the Valley, told the worried President: "If Halleck were here, you would have . . . a competent advisor who would put this matter right." Stanton agreed with Pope. A prominent eastern politician, Governor William Sprague of Rhode Island, felt that the republic was in "far greater jeopardy than at any previous time during the rebellion," and that nothing could save the country "but the immediate transfer of Halleck and 50,000 men" to Washington. Sprague said Old Brains would bring the men east if he were made general-in-chief. His augury proved false—Halleck honestly felt that the war would be won or lost in the West and always refused to withdraw troops from the area. Another Washington politician wanted Halleck to take the position of Secretary of War, while James G. Blaine, congressman from Maine, felt that "increasing dissatisfaction in Congress and among the people with the supersedure of General Grant . . ." made it imperative that Halleck leave the West so that Grant could take his place.[15]

Lincoln was impressed by Halleck's activities in St. Louis, had read *Elements of Military Art and Science,* and was inclined to take Pope's advice. However, Lincoln wanted to confirm his leanings and in order to reach a final decision he consulted America's oldest and formerly foremost soldier, Winfield Scott, who was living at West

[15] Welles, *Diary,* I, 119; Sprague to Lincoln, July 5, 1862, in the Robert Todd Lincoln Papers; Frank Southwick to Halleck, July 14, 1862, Halleck Letter Book; James G. Blaine, *Twenty Years of Congress* (New York, 1884), I, 363.

Point. Halleck had been one of Scott's favorites since the young lieutenant of engineers prepared the paper on seacoast defense for him, and Scott showed no hesitancy in recommending Halleck for the job of general-in-chief.[16]

When Lincoln returned from West Point he asked Halleck to "make a flying visit for consultation" if he could do it without endangering his department. Halleck played the part of a blushing girl, flattered by the attention but determined to remain virtuous. He complained of "being somewhat broken in health and wearied out by long months of labor and care," before coquettishly concluding, "A trip to Washington would be exceedingly desirable." [17]

Halleck's hesitancy stimulated Lincoln to greater efforts. He sent Governor Sprague to Corinth to woo Halleck into getting "you and part of your force, one or both" to come to Washington; Lincoln would be "exceedingly glad" of either. Halleck replied to Washington that even if he came, he would advise only one thing: all forces in the East must be put under one head, and that head made responsible for results. The President agreed to the condition, and on July 11, 1862, Halleck became general-in-chief, commander of all land forces of the United States.[18]

Halleck did not leave for the capital immediately. Lincoln dashed off a telegram July 14 begging him to hurry. "I am very anxious—almost impatient—to have you here. . . . When can you make it?" [19] Halleck replied that he would leave as soon as he could brief Grant, the new commander of the forces around Corinth (Halleck did not appoint a departmental commander for the entire West). He hoped to begin his journey by July 17.[20]

Old Brains would not hurry. He informed his friends he was sorry to leave, for he had "studied out and [could] finish the war in the West," and neither understood nor could manage affairs in the East. Moreover, he did not "want to have anything to do with the quarrels

---

[16] T. Harry Williams, *Lincoln and His Generals*, 134–35.
[17] *O.R.*, Ser. I, XVI, Part 2, pp. 84, 88.
[18] *Ibid.*, XI, Part 3, pp. 100, 311.
[19] *Ibid.*, 311.   [20] *Ibid.*, 321.

of Stanton and McClellan." He felt that going to Washington would bring him into conflict with McClellan's friends, and protested that this was unfair, because "everybody who knows me, knows that I have uniformly supported him, and I do not wish to be placed in a false position." Halleck moaned that the officials in the capital had "no conception" of logistics and were at "the boiling point" because of McClellan's disasters. He knew his selection was a "very high compliment," yet he was "very sorry to leave, for I can be of more use here than there." He was accustomed to his own way in the West. In Washington, the hotbed of politics, the presence of the President and Congressional investigating committees made it doubtful that his freedom would remain unfettered.

Uneasiness as to his duties also made Halleck hesitate. No one knew what the functions of a general-in-chief were or should be. Did he move around from army to army, personally directing events? Did he try to give orders on the basis of reports from the field? Did he fight the war from a map in Washington? Did he have unlimited authority to appoint and discharge generals? These were but a few of the many queries already looming ahead. But he had received orders, and he had never refused honor and high office. He would not refuse now.

Before leaving, Halleck took time to say goodby to Sherman. "I am more than satisfied with everything you have done." "You have always had my respect, but recently you have won my highest admiration. I deeply regret to part from you." [21]

Sherman responded in kind. Halleck's departure caused him "heartful pain," for he could have done nothing without the "absolute confidence" he placed in his superior. Sherman knew that Halleck would be a success in the East: "You will rule wherever you go." Still he felt that Halleck's former command had greater significance than the Eastern theater; "The man who at the end of this war holds the military control of the valley of the Mississippi will be THE man." To close his farewell letter, Sherman gave a

[21] *Ibid.,* XVI, Part 2, p. 128; Wilson, "General Halleck," *loc. cit.,* XXXVI, 556; *O.R.,* Ser. I, XVII, Part 2, p. 100.

résumé of Halleck's work in expressive terms: "You took command in the valley of the Mississippi at a period of deep gloom, when I felt that our poor country was doomed to a Mexican anarchy, but at once arose order, system, firmness, and success in which there has not been a pause." [22]

It was more than a friendly tribute. As departmental commander in the West, Henry Wager Halleck was always vulnerable to criticism. Contemporaries and later historians found it easy to attribute the Western victories to Halleck's subordinates and to imply sneeringly that Old Brains hindered rather than helped their successes. They disregarded one irrefutable fact: Halleck was the most successful departmental commander in the war. All his subordinates won victories; some of them, like Pope and Curtis, found it difficult to operate without Halleck behind them. He did bring "order, system, and firmness" to the West.

His greatest contribution was efficiency. His strategy was simple —use superior numbers to force the poorly led Confederates from Missouri, Kentucky, Tennessee, and parts of Arkansas and Mississippi. Although others failed with greater advantages, Halleck succeeded because of his ability to supply eager, fighting generals with well armed and adequately provisioned troops to be used at the decisive points—Fort Donelson, New Madrid, Shiloh, and Pea Ridge. As a field commander he had shown an utter lack of imagination and audacity; the siege of Corinth looked like one of Baron Jomini's carefully drawn diagrams, and as was true of those diagrams Halleck left an escape route open. When Beauregard fled, Halleck failed to mount an effective pursuit. After Corinth his actions were decidedly conservative. But as an organizer, a supplier, a planner, in short as a manager of war, he was continually improving.

[22] *O.R.,* Ser. I, XVII, Part 2, p. 100. Sherman added: "Instead of that calm, sure, steady progress which has dismayed our enemy, I now fear alarms, hesitations, and doubt. We are all the losers."

CHAPTER SIX

McCLELLAN, POPE, AND SECOND BULL RUN

There was reason, indeed, for Lincoln to urge the western commander to Washington to assume his anomalously elevated position. McClellan was on the James River, within a few miles of Richmond, moaning that he was greatly outnumbered; Pope was south of Manassas Junction with his newly formed Army of Virginia; General Robert E. Lee, with the Confederate Army of Northern Virginia, was between them. Halleck was horrified; Jomini's first principle was concentration on important points. This situation resulted from the fumbling organization and incoherent system of the Eastern command. Without the benefit of a philosophy of military affairs, whether Jomini or other, the Eastern leaders had improvised. Halleck had applied the Jomini principles, modifying them only as the exigencies of the situation demanded, and emerged with success in the West. In the East the situation had steadily deteriorated; Old Brains prepared to apply Jomini.

Once again Halleck was expected to bring order to chaos. That meant eliminating the division between Pope's and McClellan's armies—one of the generals must abandon his position and transport his forces to the other commander. McClellan was closer to Richmond, and the popular cry to capture that city—essentially the layman's expression of a "places" theory of war—was strong. However, Halleck was displeased with McClellan's position. He was operating on exterior lines, anathema to the theorist of Jomini's school. His line of approach to Richmond was indirect rather than direct, and supplying McClellan's army appeared to be hazardous and difficult.

Halleck could hardly ignore Lincoln's attitude when he decided which army to move. The President, under the Constitution, was commander in chief of the armed forces of the nation, and Lincoln was prepared to use his vested powers. He had the ability to dominate and control men, or change their opinions by persuasion. If both of those methods failed, he would force his subordinates to take unpopular actions for which they, not he, would be damned.

Throughout the war, Lincoln would use Halleck. Confusion with regard to the powers and responsibilities of a general-in-chief made his task easier. Army regulations did not define his sphere of activity. Previous American military practice did not furnish a precedent. Washington, Dearborn, and Scott, who had been "generals-in-chief" during the country's former wars, never expostulated a theory of command and had seldom exercised their powers outside of the limits of the immediate army they commanded. During the early stages of the Civil War, when Scott and McClellan served as generals-in-chief, an identical situation prevailed. Thus Lincoln could decide for himself what Halleck could or could not do.

Halleck's services to Lincoln were invaluable. He gave the President technical advice, translated Lincoln's civilian terms into military parlance for field generals, and assumed almost all the administrative details of running the army. Politically Old Brains served Lincoln well. When the President decided to fire a general he had Halleck sign the order; thus the general's supporters blamed Halleck for the dismissal. Lincoln liked to assume a pose of weakness and simplicity and to give the impression that others were controlling him. When friends inquired about a military move, Lincoln would say, "I wish not to control. That I now leave to General Halleck," or "You must call on General Halleck, who commands." [1]

[1] T. Harry Williams, *Lincoln and His Generals*, 142–44; Basler (ed.), *The Collected Works of Abraham Lincoln*, V, 399.

But Halleck was not always a tool in Lincoln's hands. Old Brains fought for the principles he had imbibed from Mahan or Jomini, and often dissuaded the President from impractical military operations. Many of these theories Halleck modified as the war progressed, but one which he never abandoned soon became the guiding principle of the Union armies—concentration on vital points. And in the end it was the taking of a place, Vicksburg, that sealed the doom of the Confederacy.

Halleck's handling of the problem posed by the division between McClellan and Pope indicated the course he would follow in the future. McClellan's solution was simple—send more troops to the James. Pope's advice was just as short—send McClellan's men to Manassas. Lincoln had worked hard but without notable success as both commander-in-chief and general-in-chief and was glad Halleck arrived to help make the decision. He told Old Brains he had 20,000 reinforcements for McClellan and no more. Halleck must visit the Young Napoleon, find out if McClellan thought he could take Richmond with that number, and make his own analysis of the situation. If McClellan said 20,000 were not enough, Lincoln authorized Halleck to withdraw the Army of the Potomac from the James.

On July 24, 1862, the day after he arrived in Washington, Halleck boarded a steamer for McClellan's headquarters at Harrison's Landing, where his army lay huddled along the banks of the James. Many aspects of the situation indicated McClellan should be removed from the position. A majority of the country felt it would never get action from "Little Mac"; the dominant political party wanted him removed from command; the President, although he liked McClellan personally, doubted his abilities; the health of the army was poor and growing worse in an inhospitable climate. Most important, the military circumstances called for concentration.

After a day and a night on board ship, Halleck landed in Virginia. McClellan, who did not enjoy serving under a former subordinate, was there to meet him. Halleck explained that he had come to ascertain McClellan's "views and wishes in regard to future operations." McClellan had a plan ready. He wanted to take the army south of the James and occupy Petersburg, a railroad junction below Richmond, thus cutting Lee's supply line. Then Lee would have to fight McClellan on ground of the Union general's choosing. Halleck did not approve, since the operation would merely put more distance between McClellan and Pope. When McClellan finally relinquished the project, Halleck broached the real reason for his visit.

Feeling that it was a "military necessity" for the Army of the Potomac to join Pope, Halleck informed McClellan that the President had 20,000 troops available and that if the general thought he could capture Richmond with that number he could remain. When McClellan stated that 30,000 were necessary to insure "a good chance of success," Halleck reiterated that only 20,000 were on hand. McClellan then argued that shipping the troops north would have a demoralizing effect. Wouldn't it be better, he asked, to leave them where they were until more reinforcements could come to the James? Halleck, who was opposed to the James position because of its reliance on exterior lines, replied curtly that he had no authority to consider such a proposition. McClellan must take the 20,000 men and attack or ship his army back to Pope.

Even with Halleck's ultimatum, McClellan would not give a definite answer. Halleck advised him to consult with his officers and give his reply in the morning.

McClellan held the conference and received a variety of conflicting views; some of his corps commanders wanted to remain, others to withdraw. McClellan determined to try with the 20,000. Informing the General-in-chief of his decision, McClellan insisted that Halleck understand that prospects of success were not in his favor. The most he would say was that there was "a chance," and that he was "willing to try it." After all, Halleck must realize that Lee had 200,000 men, while McClellan counted only 80,000.[2]

[2] *O.R.*, Ser. I, XI, Part 3, p. 337.

After Halleck left, Little Mac realized he had not placated his superiors; "I *know* that the rascals will get rid of me as soon as they dare," he complained to a friend and bitterly commented: "Halleck remained but a few minutes (comparatively) here and saw *nothing* of the Army—departed just as wise as he came." [3]

When Halleck arrived in the capital the following day he found a telegram from McClellan, who said that the "true defense of Washington consists in a rapid and heavy blow given by this army upon Richmond," and asked: "Can you not possibly draw 15,000 or 20,000 men from the West to reenforce me temporarily?" He had confided to a cohort: "I have seen Halleck and believe that he will act with me in good faith," and was consequently stunned by a telegram Halleck sent in the wake of his letter. McClellan learned that he should send the sick in the army out of the Peninsula "in order to enable [you] to move in any direction." [4]

Writing to his wife about the episode, Halleck explained the reasons: McClellan "is in many respects a most excellent and valuable man, but he does not understand strategy and should never plan a campaign." [5] He informed Secretary Chase that all McClellan's acts were deserving of unreserved condemnation, "especially the conduct of the engagement before Richmond and the subsequent retreat to the James." [6] McClellan, in other words, was not well versed in Jomini, or rather, he favored concentration only under his own command.

The mistakes of another strategist also had to be rectified. Before Halleck's arrival in Washington, Lincoln moved General Ambrose E. Burnside's army from the North Carolina shore to Newport News, Virginia, at the eastern tip of the Peninsula. Halleck himself ordered Burnside to Harrison's Landing, ostensibly to advise McClellan, but, in Chase's opinion, "to control him." Then, to

[3] McClellan to Barlow, July 30, 1862, George B. McClellan Papers (Library of Congress).

[4] George B. McClellan, *Own Story* (New York, 1887), 473–74; *O.R.,* Ser. I, XI, Part 1, p. 76.

[5] Wilson, "General Halleck," *loc. cit.,* XXXVI, 557.

[6] McClellan, *Own Story,* 475.

hasten the concentration of troops in Northern Virginia, Halleck ordered Burnside—and his troops—back to Aquia Creek, near Washington.[7]

Meanwhile Lee left Richmond and was moving his army north. If McClellan's estimate of Lee's size was correct, or even if Lee had only 100,000 men, then Pope, stationed around Manassas, was badly outnumbered. His force did not count many more than 40,000 men and was the only obstacle standing between Lee and the northern capital. The situation was not yet critical, but was rapidly becoming so. Burnside reached Aquia Creek on Sunday, August 3; Halleck immediately sent the transports he had used back to the James River.

With them he sent a message to McClellan. "It is determined to withdraw your army from the Peninsula to Aquia Creek."[8]

In making the final decision, Halleck followed the doctrine of concentration on the vital point. McClellan wanted to combine the principles of concentration, offensive movement and manoeuvre, by sending Pope's men to the army around Petersburg, but Halleck felt that when McClellan's army was annexed to Pope's, Washington was secure from attack and the possibilities of a move on Richmond were improved.

Halleck tenaciously held to the order, while McClellan argued frantically. The movement "will prove disastrous to our cause. I fear it will be a fatal blow. . . . Here, directly in front of this army," he cried, "is the heart of the rebellion."[9] This was the crux of their disagreement, and Halleck refused to weaken. To appease McClellan, Old Brains said he had "tried every means in [his] power to avoid withdrawing [the] army. . . . It was not a hasty and inconsiderate act, but one that caused me more anxious thoughts than any other of my life." Halleck asserted that he did not know who had separated the Army of the Potomac, or why, but that he found the forces divided and wished to unite them.[10] And so the army fell back. It would be two years before it got that close to Richmond again.

---

[7] *O.R.*, Ser. I, XII, Part 3, p. 524.   [8] *Ibid.*, XI, Part 1, p. 80.
[9] *Ibid.*, 81.   [10] *Ibid.*, 82.

McClellan would obey the order in his own time, in his own way. Halleck tried to hurry him by promising that all the troops in Virginia would be under McClellan's command as soon as they were concentrated, but it did little good.[11]

There was ample cause to urge more activity; "Stonewall" Jackson and his "foot-cavalry" were mobilizing. Pope had marched south to the Rappahannock River, did not know where Jackson was, and seemed determined to blunder forward until he found the enemy. Glancing at a map, Halleck could see the possibilities Pope was presenting to Jackson. If Stonewall chose he could make a swift march through the Valley and come out on Pope's rear. Then Lee, arriving from Richmond and attacking from the south with General James Longstreet's corps, would have Pope in a vise. Halleck expected such a move and warned Pope to watch the Valley; if he saw any sign of movement there he was to "attack them in flank and give no rest."[12]

Halleck was finding much in his multifarious duties that was irksome. Cautioning and withstraining Pope, prodding the procrastinating McClellan, arguing with some politicians, placating others, giving cursory glances to the West—he felt "broken down every night with the heat, labor and responsibility." It was the beginning of a lengthy series of complaints Halleck would make about his position, usually to his wife or Sherman and always private. During the periods of stress and high excitement, he used his correspondence as a release. Instead of venting his wrath on the recalcitrant McClellan, Halleck complained to his wife. Although Old Brains admitted to her that Lincoln and his Cabinet approved "everything I have proposed," he felt there were ulterior motives behind their actions. "If any disaster happens," Halleck feared they would piously say: "We did for you all you asked." For instance, Lincoln and his advisors had urged him to remove McClellan from the Peninsula—"in other words they want[ed] me to do what they were afraid to attempt."[13]

[11] *Ibid.*, Part 3, p. 359.   [12] *Ibid.*, XII, Part 3, p. 523.
[13] Wilson, "General Halleck," *loc. cit.*, XXXVI, 557.

On August 9 the second Bull Run campaign began. Pope was at Cedar Mountain, just north of the Rapidan River, when Jackson attacked him. Halleck ordered Burnside, at Falmouth, to move up and cooperate with Pope, but his men arrived too late to have any effect on the small battle. While they marched forward, Halleck told Pope to hold Jackson in check until reinforcements could reach him. Jackson, however, had already fallen back and was waiting hopefully for Pope to make his way into a well prepared trap. Pope was about to enmesh himself when Halleck correctly divined Jackson's purpose and warned the general to "beware of a snare. Feigned retreats are secesh tactics." The next day, August 13, Halleck gave Pope definite orders not to cross the Rapidan and told his bold subordinate to "guard well against a flank movement by the enemy."[14]

Pope's victory at Cedar Mountain gave Halleck "breathing time," and allowed him to inspect the situation on the James. Acidly he reminded McClellan that he had "nearly every available steam vessel in the country" under his control and asked if it were not too much to expect that 8,000 or 10,000 men could be sent north daily. In McClellan's opinion, the General-in-chief was not a gentleman and did not act in a "candid or friendly manner."[15]

The propriety of his manners was not one of Halleck's great concerns. Pope was camped in the apex of a land triangle formed by the Rappahannock and the Rapidan, with Lee's army at the base. Halleck knew that if Lee could mount an offensive against the exposed force, which had no place to retreat, the Confederate general could annihilate them. Lee proposed to do just that; on August 18, to forestall him, Halleck ordered Pope to fall back of the Rappahannock, again warning him to be wary of a flanking operation.[16]

There was a limit to the distance the Army of Virginia could re-

---

[14] *O.R.*, Ser. I, XII, Part 3, p. 556, 564; Frank Vandiver, *Mighty Stonewall* (New York, 1956), 345; *O.R.*, Ser. I, XII, Part 3, p. 564.

[15] *O.R.*, Ser. I, XI, Part 1, p. 87; McClellan, *Own Story*, 467.

[16] *O.R.*, Ser. I, XII, Part 3, p. 590.

treat; it was imperative that McClellan's men join up. But the commander of the Army of the Potomac suddenly discovered that Richmond was almost barren of troops and wanted to force his way into the city. Halleck vetoed the proposal on the grounds that unless the Army of the Potomac joined Pope immediately, Lee might overwhelm him and capture Washington. The fate of the capital rested on Little Mac's whims. In a brief message Halleck tried to communicate the urgency of the situation: "Every moment is as important as an ordinary hour." [17] The telegram did not achieve the desired effect.

But Halleck still was the master in the giant chess game. He had twice been correct about enemy plans, once after Cedar Mountain and again when he made Pope retreat across the Rappahannock. Studying the board, he predicted Lee's new move; the enemy was trying to turn Pope's right. One of McClellan's corps, that of Fitz John Porter, was finally at Falmouth, and Halleck ordered Burnside to hurry it to Pope. Let nothing stop them, he said; if they lack supplies let them live off the country. Then he wired Pope, telling him to watch for a concentration behind him, probably at Manassas. "Do not," Halleck told the thoroughly confused general, "let them separate you from Alexandria." [18]

Soon a flood of men from the Army of the Potomac appeared in Alexandria. Halleck again showed his ability to delegate responsibility by choosing a soldier capable of handling the deluge. The officer, Herman Haupt, was a West Point graduate who left the army after less than a year of service to become a director-engineer on civilian railroad lines. Rough and brusque, Haupt tolerated no nonsense. He was running troops from Alexandria to Manassas on a single track road and determined to adhere to the schedule Halleck instituted. When General John Sturgis attempted to get his troops on cars already allocated for another corps, Haupt told him to get off. Sturgis countered by trying to arrest Haupt. The indignant Haupt appealed to Halleck, who sent a telegram giving him complete control over the roads. Haupt showed it to

[17] *Ibid.*, XI, Part 3, p. 379.   [18] *Ibid.*, XII, Part 3, pp. 620, 625.

Sturgis, whose mental powers, diluted by drinking, deluded him into thinking it came from Pope. "I don't care for John Pope a pinch of owl dung!" Sturgis exclaimed. Finally Haupt convinced the toper that the order originated from the General-in-chief. "What does he say?" stammered the flushed Sturgis. "He says if you interfere with the railroads he will put you in arrest. . . . He does, does he? Well, then, take your d——d railroad!"

Haupt did take charge of the railroad and, with Halleck's strong backing, was able to mobilize the troops. By August 24, he had sent Sturgis' division forward and was waiting for the rest of General Joseph Hooker's men to arrive. His job was not without obstacles, however. The capacity of the single track line was only 12,000 men per day; a capacity which accidents greatly reduced. Since McClellan had at last launched his withdrawal on a full scale, more men kept pouring into Alexandria and the problem of whom to transport first arose. At Haupt's suggestion and with Halleck's help they arranged a new system. Thereafter when a body of men arrived in Alexandria their commander reported to Haupt, who made the decision as to when to send them forward.[19] But despite Haupt's managerial abilities and Halleck's supervisional talents, one single track road could not get many troops to Pope in the next few days.

The strain was beginning to take its toll, but Halleck submerged the tension and emotion and presented a calm, cold front. When General Oliver O. Howard, who had been wounded on the Peninsula, went to see Halleck about rejoining his command, he waited half an hour and was then greeted with a stern look and a gruff: "Do you want to see me officially, sir?" Howard stuttered: "Partly officially and partly not." "Well, sir," Halleck sighed, "what is it?" Howard explained the purpose of his visit, and asked where he could find his command. "The adjutant general will tell you that, sir," Halleck said as he turned on his heel and walked out.[20]

---

[19] Herman Haupt, *Reminiscences* (Milwaukee, 1901), 80–81; *O.R.*, Ser. I, XII, Part 3, pp. 569, 648.

[20] Oliver Otis Howard, *Autobiography* (New York, 1908), I, 266.

Meanwhile Pope failed to heed Halleck's warnings to watch his flank. On August 27, Jackson did enter Manassas, where his "foot-cavalry" had a holiday burning stores and feasting on Yankee provisions. Halleck was in a frenzy. Jackson cut Pope's communications with Washington and the General-in-chief had no information. He was, in military parlance, completely blind. The situation was desperate but not yet hopeless. Undoubtedly Lee would attack shortly with the rest of his army. If McClellan's men could only get to Pope in time. . . .

August 28 and 29, 1862, were two of the most exasperating days of Halleck's career. He spent his entire waking hours trying to get McClellan, now at Alexandria with his army, to move. He pushed, pleaded and prodded McClellan as hard as he could, but it was not enough. After endless days, Old Brains stopped trying. He let McClellan's personality and wishes run rampant.

Halleck began with a message on August 27, predicting a great battle the next day and ordering McClellan to move General William B. Franklin's corps to the scene "by forced marches." He repeated the order in stronger terms later in the morning. At 10:20 A.M. McClellan replied that he had told Franklin to "prepare to march." Then McClellan decided that Franklin should not leave, because Washington was not safe. At 2:30 in the afternoon Little Mac made a bid for power: "I am not responsible for the past and cannot be for the future, unless I receive authority to dispose of the available troops according to my judgment." At 6 P.M. he recommended that all the troops around Alexandria should remain there, so as to protect Washington. The next morning Halleck telegrammed Franklin directly, ordering him to Manassas, but at one o'clock McClellan stated that Franklin would move only when he had enough artillery. At 4:10 A.M. Little Mac sent still another communication: "General Franklin is with me here. . . . We are not yet in condition to move; may be by tomorrow morning." Halleck, struggling to keep calm in the face of the maddening inertia, waited for a response to a wire he had sent Franklin forty minutes before, ordering him to move immediately. At 4:30, McClellan answered: "Your dispatch just received. Neither Franklin nor Sumner's corps is now in condition to move and fight a battle. It would be a sacrifice to send them out now. . . ." [21]

McClellan could have read, with profit, a sentence in Halleck's *Elements of Military Art:* "In all military operations *time* is of vast importance. If a single division of an army can be retarded for a few hours only, it not unfrequently decides the fate of the campaign." [22]

That night, August 28, Halleck told McClellan: "There must be no further delay in moving Franklin's corps towards Manassas. They must go tomorrow morning, ready or not ready. If we delay too long to get ready, there will be no necessity to go at all; for Pope will either be defeated or be victorious without our aid." McClellan replied that Franklin would march at six the next morning. That left him with 30,000 men, and he added in a sentence which must have left Halleck quaking with wrath: "If you wish any of them to move towards Manassas, please inform me."

The next morning Lee began his attack on Pope. Little Mac spent the day requesting that Franklin should go no farther; Halleck's patience finally wore out. "I want Franklin's corps to go far enough to find out something about the enemy. I am tired of guesses." [23] McClellan once again took offense at Halleck's tone. "He is not a refined person at all," McClellan felt, but he "probably says rough things when he don't mean them." [24] Meanwhile Pope was engaged in his greatest—and last—battle.

The next morning it appeared that Pope won. He transmitted

[21] Halleck to McClellan, August 27, 1862, McClellan Papers; McClellan to Halleck, August 27, *ibid* (three telegrams of the same date).

[22] Halleck, *Elements of Military Art and Science,* 63–64.

[23] McClellan to Halleck and Halleck to McClellan, August 27 to August 29, 1862, all in McClellan Papers.

[24] McClellan to Barlow, August 29, 1862, McClellan Papers.

a message claiming a great victory. "You have done nobly," Halleck congratulated, "I am doing all in my power for you and your noble army. God bless you and it!" In a more somber tone he added: "Don't yield another inch if you can avoid it." [25]

That night, however, it became evident that Pope had suffered a staggering defeat. Halleck was crushed. Pope had tipped over the chessboard and the pieces were scattered throughout the country. Until the last minute Halleck thought he controlled the game. He had stopped the enemy's queen; every move placed his own in a position to check her. Although his rooks had been ineffectual and had not entered the campaign, they were en route and when they arrived the enemy would have been overcome. But now defeat, ignominious defeat, wrought by his own pieces. His queen refused to follow directions; the rooks were glued to the board.

Before retiring that night, before sleep might blot out the horror of the upheaval, Halleck sent one more telegram. He put McClellan in charge of all troops in the vicinity of Washington and told him to look after the capital's safety. "I beg of you to assist me in this crisis with your ability and experience," Halleck cried, "I am utterly tired out." [26]

"It is my deliberate opinion," McClellan wired back, "that the interests of the nation demand that Pope should fall back tonight if possible and not one moment is to be lost." [27] When the troops neared Washington, they would come under his command.

Referring to Halleck's cry of despair, Secretary Chase later commented: "This telegram announced the surrender of Halleck to McClellan. It saddens me to think that a Commander-in-chief, whose opinion of his subordinate's military conduct is such as I have heard Halleck express of McClellan's should, in a moment of pressure, so yield to that very subordinate." [28]

[25] Pope to Halleck, August 30, 1862, Robert Todd Lincoln Papers; *O.R.,* Ser. I, XII, Part 3, p. 769.

[26] Halleck to McClellan, August 31, 1862, McClellan Papers.

[27] McClellan to Halleck, August 31, 1862, *ibid.*

[28] David Donald (ed.), *Inside Lincoln's Cabinet: The Civil War Diaries of Salmon P. Chase* (New York, 1954), 148.

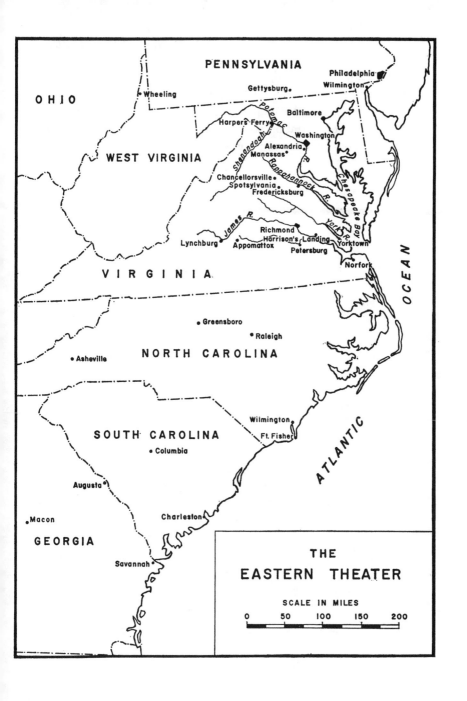

THE
EASTERN THEATER

SCALE IN MILES

0   50   100   150   200

But Halleck's surrender was not final and he would continue to fight for his strategical principles. The defeat at Second Bull Run convinced Halleck that Pope's tactics were poor, not that Jomini's theories of concentration were wrong. The struggle to introduce those theories into the army would continue.

CHAPTER SEVEN

THE GUILLOTINE
FOR UNSUCCESSFUL
GENERALS

The reverberations of Pope's defeat pounded in Halleck's eardrums. He "scarcely slept" for four nights and was "almost worn out." Two days after the battle, September 2, struggling to regain his composure, he assured his wife: "Everybody now admits that if I had not brought McClellan's army here when I did, we should have been lost." Halleck was convinced that he had made no mistakes. On September 5 he boasted: "I . . . believe I have saved the capital from the terrible crisis brought upon us by the stupidity of others. I got McClellan's army here just in time—and barely that—to save us."

But the echo of defeat would not die and at times it drove Halleck to distraction. Having no ambition and wanting to resign if he "could do so conscientiously," he expressed a desire to "go back to private life as soon as possible and never again to put my foot in Washington." [1] By the end of November he was recovering and stated in his official report: "This short and active campaign . . . accomplished the great and important object of covering the capital till troops could be collected for its defense." Bitterly he added: "Had the Army of the Potomac arrived a few days earlier the rebel army could have been easily defeated and perhaps destroyed." Halleck's strategy had not been given a fair trial.

Halleck made his official attack on McClellan three months after Second Bull Run; others had not waited that long. On August 29,

[1] Wilson, "General Halleck," *loc. cit.*, XXXVI, 558.

at the height of Pope's campaign, Stanton had written Halleck calling for a report "touching McClellan's disobedience of orders and consequent delay of support to the Army of Virginia." The wording of the request indicated that Stanton was looking for grounds on which to replace McClellan. But it was too early for a conclusive answer and moreover, Halleck was opposed to political interference with the military. He gave Stanton a short review of the reasons McClellan's men were withdrawn from the Peninsula, then said: "The order was not obeyed with the promptness I expected and the national safety, in my opinion, required." However, he hastened to add "the reasons given for not moving earlier was the delay in getting off the sick," and made no comment. "When General McClellan's movement was begun, it was rapidly carried out; but there was an unexpected delay in commencing it. General McClellan reports the delay was unavoidable." [2] Halleck could be a master of objective reporting when he so desired; Stanton could not drop McClellan on the basis of his reply.

Meanwhile, Lincoln was using the General-in-chief as a political shield. After Pope's defeat, Halleck had placed McClellan in charge of the demoralized troops streaming into Washington. When McClellan finished organizing the men in the entrenchments, Halleck asked him who had been nominated for future field command. McClellan replied that he had not designated a successor because he was willing to take command in person. Halleck informed Little Mac that his authority did not extend beyond the defenses of the capital and that no decision had yet been made as to who would lead the army when it took the field.

Lincoln, however, had decided that McClellan was the only competent general available for command. On the morning of September 2, he and Halleck called upon McClellan at the general's house. Lincoln diagnosed the situation as bad and, according to Halleck, said to McClellan: "General, you will take command of the forces in the field." McClellan later claimed that Lincoln said

[2] *O.R.,* Ser. III, II, 872; Donald (ed.), *Inside Lincoln's Cabinet,* 116; *O.R.,* Ser. I, XII, Part 3, p. 739.

Washington was lost and asked if he would take over, as a favor to the President. McClellan replied that he would. The entire occurrence came as a surprise to Halleck.[3]

But Lincoln, after making a decision that angered the very vocal Radicals in his own party, gradually changed his story until the stigma came to rest with Halleck. On the afternoon of September 2, Lincoln told his Cabinet that Halleck had agreed to McClellan's appointment and that the General-in-chief supported the President's views. On September 8, Lincoln told Secretary of the Navy Gideon Welles "that Halleck had turned to McClellan and advised that he should command the troops against the Maryland invasion. 'I could not have done it,' said he [Lincoln] 'for I can never feel confident that he [McClellan] will do anything effectual.'" Two days later the President stated that McClellan's reinstatement was "Halleck's doings." [4] And most political leaders in the capital believed Halleck decided on and gave the order.

Halleck made little effort to defend himself; there was nothing he could do. McClellan was in command and nearly everyone blamed him. Welles characterized Halleck as a man with a "scholarly intellect and, I suppose, some military acquirements, but his mind is heavy and irresolute," and many shared his opinion.[5]

Meanwhile, the initiative in the East passed to Lee, who had crossed his advance units into Maryland a few days after the battle with Pope. The day after Lincoln put McClellan in command, Halleck ordered him to organize a "movable army" to meet the enemy in the field. By September 5, Halleck declared "there can now be no doubt" Lee was crossing the Potomac in force and he told McClellan to "let our troops move immediately." [6]

---

[3] McClellan, *Own Story*, 535, 549; *Joint Committee on the Conduct of the War, Report* (3 parts, 37th Congress, 3rd session, Senate Report no. 108, serial no. 1152), I, 451.

[4] Welles, *Diary,* I, 101, 124, 134.

[5] *Ibid.,* 119; Nicolay and Hay, *Abraham Lincoln,* VI, 21; for Senator John Sherman's opinion see Rachel Sherman Thorndike (ed.), *The Sherman Letters* (New York, 1894), 164.

[6] *O.R.,* Ser. I, XIX, Part 2, pp. 169, 182.

After sending the telegram, Halleck had another thought. McClellan was taking troops out of the forts south of Washington to strengthen his force and Halleck, mindful of how Lee fooled Pope, wanted to be absolutely certain of the Confederate's intentions before exposing the capital. He warned McClellan that Lee might be trying to draw off the defense of Washington before attempting to attack the capital from the Virginia side of the Potomac. "Think of this," Halleck told McClellan. In preparing for the invasion, he also ordered the commander at Winchester, Virginia, to move his small army north to Harper's Ferry, situated at the extreme north end of the Valley and directly across Lee's supply line.[7]

Little Mac, who had moved three days before to Rockville, Maryland, a few miles north of the capital, wanted the force at Harper's Ferry withdrawn. The men were always exposed to possible capture, he contended, and he could use the reinforcements. When Halleck took no action, McClellan tried to force his hand. He called on Secretary of State William H. Seward and told him of the danger involved in leaving troops at Harper's Ferry. Seward agreed, and suggested they visit Halleck, to whom McClellan could personally repeat his statements. They went to Halleck's quarters, where they found him retired for the night. Halleck received the general and the secretary in his bedroom, where McClellan explained his objections to leaving the men at Harper's Ferry. Halleck, McClellan later recorded, "received my statement with ill-concealed contempt; said that everything was all right as it was; that my views were entirely erroneous, etc., and soon bowed us out."[8]

Halleck never gave his reasons for leaving the garrison at Harper's Ferry. He may have done it because of plain stubbornness, an explanation which McClellan believed, but he may have had one of the more penetrating insights of the war. Lee fully expected the commander at the town to evacuate; when he did not the Confederates had to detach half their army to besiege Harper's Ferry. Lee's supplies came through the Valley and he could not

[7] *Ibid:* 201; XII, Part 3, p. 800.   [8] McClellan, *Own Story,* 550.

afford to leave a hostile force of over 10,000 at the tip of the line. When Lee split his army to crush the opposition, McClellan had a golden opportunity to wipe out first one wing and then the other of the Southern army. Halleck may have seen this—he had predicted Lee's moves before. In a similar circumstance the next year he would react the same way, but both times his subordinates would fail to take advantage of the division in the Army of Northern Virginia. Although McClellan saw the possibilities at the time, he did not attack either of the exposed wings.

Excitement mounted as Lee's army marched north; Halleck was as uneasy as the rest. When Welles called to ask what the naval forces still stationed in the Peninsula should do, Halleck replied that he did not know, but thought it best to bring them north. Welles differed with the General-in-chief; he suggested leaving the ships, with a small number of troops, to menace Richmond. Old Brains "rubbed his elbow first, as if that was the seat of thought, and then his eyes, and said he wished the Navy would hold on for a few days to embarrass the Rebels." Welles noted that Halleck "seemed stupid." [9]

In fact, because McClellan did not send accurate information, Halleck was completely misjudging the situation. Halleck had to guess what McClellan was doing most of the time, and usually guessed wrong. McClellan had taken almost all the troops out of Washington into Maryland to meet what Halleck feared was only a small column. On Saturday morning, September 13, when Lee had his whole force north of the Potomac, Halleck violently criticized McClellan for "thus uncovering the capital." If Washington fell it would "throw us back six months, if it should not destroy us," the General-in-chief warned. Halleck said that McClellan always worried about Washington's safety when he was in it, but never when he was away. "Beware of the evils I now point out to you," he admonished. [10]

McClellan was better informed than his superior because by an

[9] Welles, *Diary,* I, 121.
[10] *O.R.,* Ser. I, XIX, Part 2, p. 280.

incredible piece of luck he came into possession of Lee's detailed orders. One of his soldiers found the communique wrapped around some cigars discarded by a Confederate officer. McClellan knew that Lee's force was divided, that Jackson was besieging Harper's Ferry and Lee was moving north of the Potomac in Western Maryland with Longstreet's corps. Little Mac had an opportunity few generals are fortunate enough to experience and after his own fashion he began to take advantage of it. He sent one corps of the Army of the Potomac into the gap between Jackson and Lee, while he moved in the general direction of the Confederate army in Maryland.

Halleck was ignorant of these movements. "As you give me no information in regard to the position of your forces, . . . of course I cannot advise." He feared the Southerners would recross the Potomac and cut McClellan off, a movement which he thought was always part of Lee's plan.[11]

McClellan felt he could not take the few minutes necessary to inform Halleck of his moves. He forced Lee, after an indecisive engagement that he described as a decisive victory, to take up a position near the Potomac, on Antietam Creek. His detached corps had failed to interpose between Lee and Jackson, and Lee was awaiting his subordinate near the town of Sharpsburg. McClellan, too, waited. On September 17, after most of Lee's troops were concentrated within a few miles of the town, McClellan launched his attack. It was a bloody indecisive battle, but Little Mac wired Halleck that "we may justly claim a complete victory." [12]

While the armies struggled, Halleck tried to reinforce McClellan, but because the accounts he received were "very often contradictory," there was little he could do.[13]

After the battle the wearied armies watched each other during the entire day of September 18. The next morning Lee crossed the

[11] *Ibid.,* Part I, p. 41.
[12] McClellan to his wife, September 15, 1862; McClellan to Halleck, September 19, 1862, McClellan Papers.
[13] *O.R.,* Ser. I, XIX, Part 2, p. 319.

Potomac and returned to Virginia, his army lacerated but still intact. His campaign to lift "the despot's heel" from Maryland's soil had failed.

Halleck, however, was dissatisfied with McClellan's action and bombarded him with irritating complaints. He still maintained that Lee was trying to get between McClellan and Washington, although he admitted that "his defeat may be such as to prevent the attempt." To ascertain if it had, he wired McClellan two days after Antietam: "We are still left entirely in the dark in regard to your own movements and those of the enemy. This should not be so. You should keep me advised of both, so far as you know them," and the next day he reminded Little Mac that he had received "no official information of what had taken place since the battle of the 17th." [14]

McClellan answered the next day at noon; he was north of the Potomac and had made no attempt to cross the river. The army needed more men, additional general officers, supplies, and reorganization and besides the river was rising and might soon be above fording stage. He had to stay north of the Potomac.[15] The next afternoon, Halleck again asked for his views of future movements. McClellan replied that he now had a pontoon bridge built at Harper's Ferry and felt he could safely cross the river. He proposed to concentrate at the town and march against the enemy, now camped around Winchester.[16]

Halleck, in criticizing McClellan's strategical plans, pointed out that by moving up the Valley he would expose Washington and again compel the government to keep a large force in the city. He would be operating on exterior lines. "Cannot your army move," he asked, "so as to cover Washington by keeping between it and the enemy?" [17]

[14] *Ibid.*, pp. 330, 339; for McClellan's reactions see *Own Story*, 622.
[15] *O.R.*, Ser. I, XIX, Part 2, p. 342.   [16] *Ibid.*, 353.
[17] *Ibid.*, 359. "It seems to me," Halleck said in another telegram later the same day, "that Washington is the real base of operations, and that it should not under any circumstances be exposed." A strong base of operations was basic to Jominian strategy.

McClellan did not think he could, and the generals continued
to quibble. Old Brains complained about being "left entirely in
the dark," and McClellan retorted: "I regret that you find it necessary to couch every dispatch . . . in a spirit of fault-finding, and
that you have not yet found leisure to say one word in com-
mendation of the achievements of this army, or even to allude to
them." They spent the better part of a week arguing over the
number of shoes sent to the army.[18]

Lincoln tried to restore order by paying a visit to Little Mac at
his camp; he returned with some definite ideas. McClellan should
cross the Potomac and give battle to the enemy. If he stayed between Washington and the enemy he could have 30,000 reinforcements; if he moved up the Valley, 15,000. "The President,"
Halleck said in framing the order, "advises the interior line, between Washington and the enemy, but does not order it." [19] Lincoln
was accepting Halleck's—and Jomini's—strategical views while
rejecting McClellan's.

But McClellan was in no hurry to advance in either direction.
Every day he found a new reason for inaction; for staying north of
the Potomac. "Everything would now be satisfactory if I could only
get General McClellan to move," Halleck told his wife on October 7. "He has lain still twenty days since the battle of Antietam,
and I cannot persuade him to advance an inch. It puts me all out
of patience." [20] A week later McClellan was still serenely sitting
north of the river. To add humiliation to irritation, General J. E. B.
Stuart, Lee's cavalry commander, rode his troops all the way
around McClellan's huge army without losing more than a few
horses. "The President . . . directs me to suggest," the General-

[18] McClellan, *Own Story*, 622; McClellan to Halleck, October 11, 1862,
and Halleck to McClellan, October 22, 1862, McClellan Papers.

[19] *O.R.*, Ser. I, XIX, Part 1, p. 10. Halleck ended the message: "I am
directed to add that the Secretary of War and the General-in-Chief fully
concur with the President in these instructions," which indicates that the
three men held a meeting to discuss the President's plans, and that Lincoln wanted to share the responsibility.

[20] Wilson, "General Halleck," *loc. cit.*, XXXVI, 559.

Library of Congress

ABRAHAM LINCOLN: "Throughout the war Lincoln would use Halleck. He liked to assume a pose of weakness and simplicity and to give the impression that others were controlling him."

National Archives

GEORGE B. MCCLELLAN: "The whole world seemed to be jealous of his superiority and plotting against him. He worried more about vague enemies to his rear than the real ones at his front, and never trusted anyone who did not absolutely worship him."

HERMAN HAUPT: "A West Point graduate who left the army after less than a year of service to become a director-engineer on civilian railroad lines, Haupt was rough and brusque and tolerated no nonsense."

Library of Congress

EDWIN M. STANTON: "During the excitement following Lincoln's death Stanton virtually took over the government. Among other high-handed acts, he did what the martyred President never desired—the Secretary ordered Halleck out of Washington."

in-chief wired his subordinate, "if the enemy had more occupation south of the river, his cavalry would not be so likely to make raids north of it." [21]

But McClellan would not budge. He needed more cavalry and wanted to know if he were expected to advance even if he had no horses. Halleck replied that if he could not advance because of conditions he should be able to convince Lincoln of that fact. "The President does not expect impossibilities . . ." but he did want some action before winter arrived.[22]

A week later Old Brains expressed his feelings to the governor of Missouri. "I am sick, tired, and disgusted with the condition of military affairs here in the East," he said. "There is an immobility here that exceeds all that any man can conceive of. It requires the lever of Archimedes to move this inert mass. I have tried my best, but without success." Halleck concluded by promising not to despair but to keep trying.[23]

Ultimately McClellan announced that he would move. He would follow the inside track, the line closest to Washington. Jubilantly Halleck promised 20,000 reinforcements. But before advancing, McClellan demanded more forage, food, cavalry, shoes, and indeed, anything he could think of. To one of these complaints, Lincoln posed an embarrassing question for the vacillating McClellan: "I have just received your dispatch about sore-tongued and fatigued horses. Will you pardon me for asking what the horses of your army have done since the battle of Antietam that fatigues anything?" [24]

McClellan then claimed that much of Bragg's western army had joined Lee, to which Halleck snapped: "I do not think that we need have any immediate fear of Bragg's army. You are within 20 miles of Lee's, while Bragg is distant about 400 miles." [25]

---

[21] *O.R.*, Ser. I, XIX, Part 2, p. 421.
[22] *Ibid.*, Part 1, p. 81.   [23] *O.R.*, Ser. III, II, 703.
[24] *O.R.*, Ser. I, XIX, Part 2, pp. 464, 470, 485.
[25] *Ibid.*, Part 1, p. 85.

Don Carlos Buell, who was facing Bragg, was one of the few western commanders who never saw any need for haste in war. After allowing Bragg to reach Chattanooga ahead of him, Buell stayed in Huntsville, Alabama, reorganizing and pleading for more supplies and men. Halleck was preoccupied with McClellan and tried to ignore Buell: "If you want supplies of any kind which the country affords take them on forced requisitions, causing receipts in all cases to be given. . . ." Heralding a more modern type of warfare, Halleck added: "The payment or non-payment . . . [will be] determined on hereafter." He also told Buell not to ask for more troops if he could "avoid it with safety." [26] But Buell, disregarding the warning, cried for more of everything. Lincoln told Halleck that something had to be done; a McClellan in the army was lamentable, but a combination of McClellan and Buell was deplorable.

Assuming the role of liaison between Lincoln and his subordinates, Halleck tried to warn Buell, telling the general of the President's dissatisfaction. Halleck had been asked "several times" to put someone else in command, but "I have replied that I know of no more capable officer than yourself to recommend." He concluded with a sentence calculated to motivate Buell: "Permit me, general, to say in all kindness that the Government will expect an active campaign by the troops under your command, and that unless that is done the present dissatisfaction is so great your friends here will not be able to prevent a change being ordered." [27]

To Horatio G. Wright, commander of the garrison at Louisville, Kentucky, Halleck clarified the issue: "The Government seems determined to apply the guillotine to all unsuccessful generals." Ruefully he added: "It seems rather hard to do this where a general is not in fault, but perhaps with us now, as in the French revolution, some harsh measures are required." [28] Halleck's realization demonstrated his growing insight of the necessary interrelation of war and politics in a democracy. A general who did not produce and who

[26] *Ibid.*, XVI, Part 2, p. 286.   [27] *Ibid.*, 314.
[28] *Ibid.*, 421.

had no political backing would find it difficult to keep his job. But although Halleck understood this, he did not have to condone it and he could still do his utmost to save any general about to be sacrificed on the altar of expediency.

He would even resist the move to drop Buell, who could do nothing but procrastinate and had let Bragg take the initiative from him. Starting from Chattanooga early in September, Bragg had marched straight north in central Tennessee and without pause plunged into Kentucky. In the crisis, Halleck uttered the same complaints he had brought forward during Second Bull Run and Antietam; he had no information and could therefore give neither advice nor orders to Buell. In part his claims were true. He was at the mercy of his subordinates and to a degree the role he played was in direct proportion to the amount of intelligence they gave him, but he made no extensive efforts to elicit the necessary information. Halleck's predilection for letting subordinates run their own show also allowed him to use lack of information as an excuse to refrain from giving specific orders.

He was more than willing to send out general instructions. It was obvious that Buell, who left Huntsville to follow and perhaps beat Bragg to Louisville, was moving too slowly. Bragg was almost certain to get to the Kentucky city first. Halleck chided Buell: "I fear that here as elsewhere you move too slowly. . . . The immobility of your army is most surprising. Bragg in the last two months has marched four times the distance you have." [29]

Lincoln, too, thought Buell regrettably slow. He wanted to remove him but Halleck resisted, believing "there is not a single [general] . . . in the West fit for a great command," and thinking Buell was as good as the rest, nothing would be gained by removing him in the middle of a campaign. The President listened to Halleck's arguments, rejected them, and ordered the General-in-chief to replace Buell with Thomas. On September 23, Halleck telegraphed Thomas, telling him to take command and including

[29] *Ibid.,* 530.

pertinent instructions. He then gave a message of removal for Buell to Colonel J. C. McKibbin to deliver personally.

But Halleck had won some grudging conditions from Lincoln and the orders he wrote contained important reservations; McKibbin was not to place the order in Buell's hands if the army were preparing to fight or had fought, or if Thomas were separated from Buell.

As McKibbin traveled west, Halleck continued to defend Buell. His position was immeasurably strengthened when Buell got to Louisville the next day, well ahead of Bragg. The Confederate general had stopped south of the city to partake in the inauguration ceremonies of the Confederate "governor" of Kentucky and let Buell slip into Louisville first. Because of Buell's success, and as it became evident that the city would not fall, Lincoln yielded to Halleck's insistence and decided to give Buell another chance. On September 27, Halleck told McKibbin to hold the dispatch.[30]

Halleck's loyalty to one of his old subordinates, plus Buell's own good fortune in getting to Louisville before Bragg, gave Buell a stay of execution; it was up to the general to get a permanent pardon. Bragg was still in northern Kentucky threatening Cincinnati, and much of the territory Halleck had worked for over a year to take was again in enemy hands. Old Brains tried to push Buell into a decisive battle. "There are many reasons—some of them personal to yourself—why there should be as little delay as possible," he had told Buell in September.[31] The threat of immediate dismissal was gone but prompt action was still imperative. Buell set out to find and defeat Bragg. On October 8, the two armies stumbled onto each other near Perryville and fought an indecisive engagement. Afterwards Buell proposed moving to Nashville, using that city as a base, and advancing on Chattanooga. Halleck thought he had the right idea but the wrong method. Moving to Nashville would expose East Tennessee, whereas if Buell moved south from Louisville, on interior lines, the area would be in Union hands again; therefore Knoxville, not Nashville, was his proper

[30] *Ibid.,* 537, 549.   [31] *Ibid.,* 549.

base. As Halleck had pronounced in his text on war: "We have seen that it was one of Napoleon's maxims that *an army should choose the shortest and most* direct line of operations, which should either pierce the enemy's *line of defence,* or cut off his communications with *his base."* [32]

Although he could not afford it, Buell was fast losing the respect of his one friend in Washington. Halleck liked neither his strategy nor his slowness. Had Buell gone to Nashville, he still could have gained approval from the high command by striking out immediately, but patience began to wane when he talked of stopping to reorganize. Eleven days after the battle of Perryville, on October 19, Halleck described his views and those of the administration to Buell—both the President and the General-in-chief wanted to know why "we cannot march as the enemy marches, live as he lives, and fight as he fights." Halleck proposed that Buell place his army between Bragg and Nashville and open communications with the city, or better still, live off the country. Buell complained that East Tennessee was the heart of the enemy's resources. "Make it the heart of yours," Halleck commanded: "Your army can live there if the enemy's can." [33]

But Buell showed no inclination to follow Halleck's advice and the hue and cry against him gained volume. "With one voice," the governor of Ohio said, "the army from Ohio demands the removal of General Buell." [34] Congressional elections were less than a month away and Lincoln could not afford to ignore the advice of prominent politicians. His Emancipation Proclamation, recently issued, had alienated countless conservatives, and to retain the vote which remained in that quarter he was willing to leave McClellan in command, at least until the ballots were counted. But if western politicians were going to turn against him because he maintained Buell, then the general had better be dismissed. Moreover, the North wanted some sort of military action.

Halleck knew that Buell was not ready for a major battle, but he

[32] *Ibid.,* 623; Halleck, *Elements of Military Art and Science,* 229.
[33] *O.R.,* Ser. I, XVI, Part 2, p. 626.   [34] *Ibid.,* 652.

also knew that to boost the country's morale the armies must do something. Stanton was urging that Buell be dismissed and the governor of Indiana wired that because of Buell the people of the Northwest distrusted the administration and despaired of success.[35]

On October 22, Buell sent Halleck a lengthy justification of his plans and his reasons for going to Nashville and that day moved in the direction of the city. When he received the message, Halleck relayed it to Lincoln and Stanton, whereupon the three decided to hold a conference. Meanwhile Halleck warned Buell: "To now withdraw your army to Nashville would have a most disasterous effect upon the country, already wearied with so many delays in our operations." He then convened with Lincoln and Stanton, and the three officials decided to dismiss Buell, replacing him with General William S. Rosecrans.[36]

One month and nine days after the battle of Antietam, on October 26, McClellan started to move. He began to cross the Potomac. Three days later he was still in the process. That broke Lincoln's, Stanton's, and Halleck's patience. On November 5, a few days after the fall elections, Lincoln issued an undated order authorizing Halleck to remove McClellan and put Burnside in command, "forthwith or as soon as he may deem proper." Halleck took swift advantage of the order. On that day McClellan's career ended.[37] The guillotine had fallen on two of the foremost exponents of limited, cautious, gentlemanly warfare. Halleck, one of the few remaining conservative generals, was rapidly changing some of his opinions—orders to Buell to live off the land indicated the passing of the limited war and the beginning of "total" war. Although Burnside and Rosecrans would prove to be no great improvements in terms of action, it was the dawn of a new era.

---

[35] *Ibid.,* 634.   [36] *Ibid.,* 636, 638, 639, 640, 642.
[37] Lincoln order, undated but issued on November 5, 1862, McClellan Papers; Warren W. Hassler, *General George B. McClellan: Shield of the Union* (Baton Rouge, 1957), 214; T. Harry Williams, *Lincoln and His Generals,* 177.

The Halleck-Lincoln relationship had not altered; again Lincoln gave the impression his general-in-chief made the decision to remove McClellan. So effective was the ruse that Lincoln's Illinois friend, David Davis, wrote another of the President's comrades, Leonard Swett, that Lincoln "was the last man to yield to the necessity of McClellan's removal. . . . He wished to give him every chance. Halleck . . . insisted on his removal." [38] In his own defense, Halleck told a War Department official that he had neither advised nor opposed McClellan's removal and that Lincoln issued the order without Halleck's knowledge. But McClellan was certain Halleck had been the instigator of his discharge and avenged himself years later when he recorded in his memoirs: "Of all the men whom I have encountered in high position Halleck was the most hopelessly stupid. It was more difficult to get an idea through his head than can be conceived by any one who never made the attempt. I do not think he ever had a correct military idea from beginning to end." [39]

Actually, Halleck absorbed volumes of ideas in his four months in Washington. He adjusted himself to the inevitable relationship between war and political action and learned that only successful generals could be saved from political sacrifices. He developed an interpretation of his duties as general-in-chief that had the great advantage of ideally suiting his temperament. He followed the same pattern with every commander, regardless of his ability. Halleck explained to Wright: "I have always, whenever it was possible, avoided giving positive instructions to the commanding generals . . . leaving them the exercise of their own judgement, while giving them my opinion and advice." [40]

[38] David Davis to Leonard Swett, November 26, 1862, in Harry S. Pratt (comp.), *Concerning Mr. Lincoln* (Springfield, 1944), 95–96.

[39] McClellan, *Own Story*, 137; Halleck to C. P. Buckingham, December 22, 1862, in C. P. Buckingham Papers (Illinois State Historical Society Library), Springfield, Illinois.   [40] *O.R.*, Ser. I, XX, Part 2, p. 670.

CHAPTER EIGHT

BURNSIDE
AND ROSECRANS

On November 7, 1862, the day he took command of the Army of the Potomac, Burnside outlined his plans for Halleck's consideration. He wanted to concentrate east of the Valley, give the impression he was about to attack Culpepper or Gordonsville, accumulate four or five days' supplies for the men and horses, then move by rapid march on Fredericksburg. From that Virginia city he would move straight south to Richmond, using Aquia Creek as a secondary base. Burnside claimed the movement would give better protection to Washington than an advance along the Blue Ridge Mountains. He was obsessed with the cry of "On to Richmond" and later declared the capture of the city "should be the great object of the campaign, as the fall of that place would tend more to cripple the Rebel cause than almost any other military event, except the absolute breaking up of their army." [1]

Despite the Jominian nature of Burnside's proposed advance, Old Brains did not approve the sudden change in plans. He felt that Burnside should follow through with McClellan's scheme of moving "on the interior line to Richmond" from his present position, "hugging closely to the Blue Ridge," watching its passes, prepared to fight. To convince Burnside, Halleck went to his headquarters at Warrentown on November 12. Haupt and the Quartermaster General accompanied him.

[1] *O.R.*, Ser. I, XIX, Part 2, p. 552; Edward J. Stackpole, *Drama on the Rappahannock: The Fredericksburg Campaign* (Harrisburg, 1957), 65.

The informal conference began on a discouraging note. Burnside told Halleck he did not want the command and added: "I am not fit for it. There are many more in the army better fitted than I am; but if you and the President insist, I will take it and do the best I can."

After the negative opening, the meeting deteriorated into confusion and misunderstanding. According to his subsequent account, Burnside proposed a movement to Falmouth, a city north of the Rappahannock just across the river from Fredericksburg. From Falmouth he would cross the river on pontoon bridges which the General-in-chief would provide. Halleck claimed that Burnside said he would cross the river above its junction with the Rapidan, which meant there was no urgent need for the pontoons. Still Old Brains did not like the plan, but he promised to consult Lincoln. Before he left Warrentown, Halleck ordered the pontoons sent from Berlin, a village up the Potomac from Washington, to the capital.

When Halleck returned to Washington, he told Lincoln his version of Burnside's plan. The President gave "assent" but warned Burnside: "It will succeed, if you move rapidly; otherwise not." [2]

The plan Halleck presented to Lincoln was not the one Burnside executed. The general did not cross the Rappahannock west of Fredericksburg; he steered his men straight for Falmouth. Burnside's advance corps of 30,000 reached Falmouth on November 17, but the pontoons were not in the city. Halleck had either completely reneged or chose to believe what he wished, for he took no steps to insure the arrival of the pontoons at Washington, where they could have been shipped to his subordinate. If Burnside were crossing above the Rapidan, as Halleck assumed he would be, then the pontoons were unnecessary and Halleck saw no reason for haste. Later Old Brains lamely claimed the delay was unavoidable. [3]

Burnside was not setting a pace designed to make Halleck quicken his strides. When his corps commanders reached Falmouth,

[2] Haupt, *Reminiscences,* 160; *O.R.,* Ser. I, XXI, 48, 83; XIX, Part 2, p. 579.   [3] *O.R.,* Ser. I, XXI, 48.

he wanted to cross at once. Burnside had one idea in mind and would not abandon it; he would cross on pontoons. Unless they arrived, he feared that rains would cause the river to rise and separate the army from its communications. At the time, the river was being forded by stray cows and there were a negligible number of Confederates in Fredericksburg. Longstreet's corps did not arrive until November 25; two days later Burnside's entire army was concentrated at Falmouth, and on that day the pontoons arrived. But Burnside made no attempt to cross the river for two weeks, giving Lee time to improve his already formidable natural defenses and giving Jackson's corps time to appear—unchallenged—on December 1.

After Jackson's arrival, Burnside continued to concentrate around Falmouth. Halleck contented himself with the mundane aspects of his position; shipping reinforcements daily and offering to send more pontoons if Burnside needed them. On December 4, he shifted a portion of the troops in the Shenandoah to the Rappahannock.[4]

On Tuesday, December 9, Burnside made his decision—he would cross in two days. Lee was behind entrenchments on the heights above Fredericksburg, but Burnside reasoned: "I think now that the enemy will be more surprised by a crossing immediately in our front than in any other part of the river."[5] His deduction was correct; Lee was surprised, but only at Burnside's stupidity. The Confederates let the Union men cross with only token resistance and waited anxiously for the blue infantry to begin their fruitless charges against the impregnable entrenchments.

Burnside spent the day of December 12 looking at Lee's bastion. In Washington, Lincoln was in a furor to find out what was taking place. About 9 P.M. that night, Haupt returned from Fredericksburg and went to see the President. Haupt told Lincoln the situation was dangerous; Burnside would only maim his army charging the fortifications. The President, acting swiftly, took the general and

---

[4] Stackpole, *Drama on the Rappahannock*, 86–98; *O.R.*, Ser. I, XXI, 829.
[5] Stackpole, *Drama on the Rappahannock*, 121.

went to Halleck's home. When they arrived, Lincoln shooed everyone else out of the room, then asked Haupt to give Halleck his report.

When Haupt finished Lincoln asked Halleck to telegraph Burnside orders "to withdraw his army to the north side of the river."

Halleck rose from his chair and began pacing the room, scratching his elbow and puffing on a cigar. Haupt and Lincoln watched in silence while he strode up and down, his head bent, deep in concentration.

Eventually halting directly in front of the President, Halleck squared around to face him, and then slowly, but in decided terms, pronounced his theory of command: "I will do no such thing. If we were personally present and knew the exact situation, we might assume such responsibility. If such orders are issued, you must issue them yourself. I hold that a General in command of any army in the field is the best judge of existing conditions."

An embarrassed silence settled on the room. Haupt finally broke it by diplomatically declaring the position was not as bad as he first pictured it. Lincoln sighed and said that gave him "a great many grains of comfort." [6] A chance to avert impending tragedy had come and gone; Halleck had refused to act.

Lincoln himself would not give the order to retire; the next day Burnside launched his attack. Halleck limited his efforts to asking the commander of a small garrison at Fort Monroe to create a diversion by making a demonstration on Richmond, and ordering scattered units in northern Virginia to join Burnside. [7]

Lee invited Burnside's attack with beckoning fingers which quickly turned to fists of steel. The Confederates pounded Burnside's army until it was too weary to arise for more punishment. Another battle fought, another defeat suffered.

After the massacre Burnside asserted the delay of the pontoons caused his defeat. Halleck scornfully refuted his charge. "In the first place," Halleck said, Burnside's plan "was never approved, nor

[6] Haupt, *Reminiscences,* 177.
[7] *O.R.,* Ser. I, XVIII, 479; XXI, 851.

was he ever authorized to adopt it." Both Lincoln and Halleck had
assented to Burnside's march to Fredericksburg only because they
understood he would transfer to the southern side of the Rappahannock above its junction with the Rapidan. As a *coup de
grace*, Old Brains quoted a statement Burnside made to him after
the defeat: "The fact that I decided to move from Warrentown to
this line, rather against the opinion of the President, the Secretary
of War, and yourself, and that you have left the whole movement
in my hands without giving me orders, makes me the more responsible." [8]

A formerly friendly newspaper, the New York *World,* did not
let Halleck escape so lightly. The journal decided the disaster was
Old Brains' fault and editorialized: "The hour has struck when we
must have an immediate change of measures, and of men, or the
next sound which greets our ears will be the knell of the Union."
The next day the paper commented: "The country has had
enough of the blundering pretension, General Halleck," who
"never saw a battle in his life." If the General-in-chief and the
Secretary of War "are not promptly replaced by competent men
the country is irretrievably ruined."

Two weeks later the editors learned of the pontoon controversy
and again decided Old Brains was the guilty party. "And then,"
the paper said, "after neglecting—nay refusing—to meet the expectations he had thus raised . . . General Halleck has the atrocious,
the indescribable meanness to attempt to cast the whole blame of
failure on General Burnside himself." "What, in the name of
sense," a reporter rhetorized, "is a general-in-chief for, if not to
secure the necessary concert of action among his subordinates, to
quicken their diligence, and to see that no detriment results from
their inattention to the separate operations on which the success of
a great combined movement depends." [9]

The most bitter of all the Radicals, Count Adam Gurowski,
vented his spleen on Halleck. "Mr. President," he wrote on

[8] *O.R.,* Ser. I, LI, Part 1, p. 959; XXI, 48.
[9] New York *World,* December 17, 18, 26, 1862.

January 20, 1863, "for God's sake and the country's sake read ponder [sic] an urgent and patriotic warning." Old Brains "is oderous [sic] to the country [and] to all under him who are not his spitlickers. . . . The whole country is aware that Gl Halleck has no heart in the people's cause, that he treats with contempt wounded generals; that he complained to be paid only 5000 dollars . . . that he considers himself a hireling not a patriot." Gurowski only failed to mention that Halleck had refused his application for a position on the General-in-chief's staff.[10]

After Fredericksburg, Burnside planned another move, but his corps commanders failed to see its possibilities. Two of his subordinates visited Lincoln to inform on their chief. Lincoln immediately telegraphed Burnside: "I have good reason for saying you must not make a general movement of the army without letting me know." The next day, which ushered in the new year, Burnside, suspecting some surreptitious activity by his underlings, hastened to Washington to investigate. The President revealed nothing; instead he forced Burnside to justify himself. Angrily the general said all he proposed was crossing the river above or below Fredericksburg. Lincoln, doubting that any such movement would be effective, sent for Halleck and Stanton.

While they waited for the two officials, Burnside told Lincoln that the country had lost confidence in Halleck, Stanton and himself (Burnside), and that all three should be removed. Burnside later said he gave this opinion verbally in both Halleck's and Stanton's presence, which Old Brains vehemently denied. However, Halleck later thanked Burnside for using his influence to "have me relieved from a thankless and disagreeable position, which you knew I did not wish to occupy."[11]

[10] Gurowski to Lincoln, January 20, 1863, in the Adam Gurowski Papers (Library of Congress). Gurowski's request for a position on Halleck's staff is contained in an undated letter in the same collection.

[11] T. Harry Williams, *Lincoln and His Generals*, 202–203; *O.R.*, Ser. I, XXI, pp. 941, 1006, 1007–1008.

After the fruitless conference adjourned, Lincoln sent Halleck a communique. Burnside wished to cross the Rappahannock, he said, and his corps commanders opposed the project. "If in such a difficulty as this you do not help, you fail me precisely in the point for which I sought your assistance." Lincoln wanted Halleck to visit Falmouth, examine the ground, talk with the officers, form a judgment, and tell Burnside "that you do approve or that you do not approve his plan. Your military skill is useless to me if you will not do this."

The communique's tone indicated that Lincoln expected Halleck to balk. He was correct. Upon hearing this new definition of his position, Halleck quickly dispatched a letter of resignation: "I am led to believe that there is a very important difference of opinion in regard to my relations towards generals commanding armies in the field, and that I cannot perform the duties of my present office satisfactorily at the same time to the President and to myself."

The General-in-chief had rationalized his reluctance to go to the front and convinced himself that the matter was a question of principle. Halleck felt that his interference would undermine Burnside's independence and freedom of movement, forgetting that Burnside was almost pleading for support from his superior. Ultimately both Halleck and Lincoln reconsidered and withdrew their letters.[12] The President did not mention the subject again.

Later Burnside decided to cross the river once more, this time to the west of Fredericksburg, but complained that the movement "must be made almost entirely upon my own responsibility. . . . It seems to me . . ." Burnside told Halleck, that "in making so hazardous a movement, I should receive some general directions from you as to the advisability of crossing at some point, as you are necessarily well informed of the effect at this time upon other parts of the army of a success or a repulse." [13]

Halleck sent a blistering answer. He had always advised a forward movement and still did. "The character of that movement,

---

[12] *O.R.*, Ser. I, XXI, p. 940.   [13] *Ibid.*, 945.

however, must depend upon circumstances which may change any day and almost any hour. . . . As you yourself admit, it devolves on you to decide upon the time, place and character of [any] crossing which you may attempt. I can only advise that an attempt be made, and as early as possible." The antithetical views could not be reconciled. Significantly, Lincoln endorsed and approved Halleck's message.[14]

For five weeks after the battle of Fredericksburg, Burnside rested near Falmouth. His army was torn by dissension, one symptom of which was the previous insubordinate activity of his lieutenants. Halleck sank into a fit of despair over the "exceedingly embarrassing" inactivity of the Army of the Potomac.[15]

Finally, on January 21, Burnside set out on what would become infamous as the "mud march." He tried to flank Lee out of the entrenchments at Fredericksburg, but when the rains came and churned the Virginia clay into a gooey mixture, Burnside, far from outflanking Lee, had difficulty wallowing back to his base.

The remnants of Burnside's authority over his troops shattered after the mud march. Some of his corps commanders, notably Joseph Hooker and McClellan's friend Franklin, openly criticized his generalship. In retaliation, he issued a general order dismissing them from the army, an action for which he had no authority. He wanted to publish the order, but a friend persuaded him to show it to Lincoln first. Burnside grudgingly agreed and on January 24 made the trip to Washington, where he gave the order, and his resignation, to the President, saying that Lincoln could take either. Lincoln expressed a desire to discuss the matter with his advisors and Burnside left the room. Lincoln then called Halleck and Stanton to the Executive Mansion and informed them of Burnside's action. He had already reached a decision; Burnside would be replaced by Hooker. Lincoln asked for neither the advice nor the opinion of his general-in-chief and Secretary of War, and they in turn offered "none whatever." When Burnside returned and heard Lincoln's

[14] *Ibid.,* 945. [15] *Ibid.,* XV, 656.

verdict, he announced he would sever himself from the army completely. Halleck and Lincoln combined their exhortive talents, convinced him to remain, and gave him a new assignment in Cincinnati.[16]

Although he refused to interfere with his subordinate's tactics, Halleck played an active role in army administration; throughout the war he campaigned for a more efficient, professional army. Politicians were the greatest force undermining his reforms. By November, 1862, he was constantly complaining to his friends of their schemes. He found it difficult to restrain "political wirepulling in military appointments," for it seemed that every governor, senator and representative had his own "pet generals to be provided with separate and independent commands."

The demands of state and national politicians for control of the officer corps paralleled the claims of European nobles. In Prussia and France only a few reformers—mislabeled "Jacobins" by the aristocrats—dared suggest that efficiency rather than birth be made the primary test for a commission. In the United States Halleck struggled for efficiency against a different entrenched and powerful enemy, the politicians, who wanted to include the army in the spoils system. Halleck claimed that the reason he had made legions of enemies was because he would not compromise his own convictions and insisted that competence be the only criteria for advancement. Expressing his contempt for politicians with a Biblical allusion, he said: "If they would only follow the example of their ancestors, enter a herd of swine, run down some steep bank and drown themselves in the sea, there would be some hope of saving the country."[17]

The politicians met smear with smear. One of the Radical mem-

[16] Stackpole, *Drama on the Rappahannock*, 244–50; *O.R.*, Ser. I, XXI, 998; T. Harry Williams, *Lincoln and His Generals*, 205–206; *O.R.*, Ser. I, XXI, 1009.

[17] *O.R.*, Ser. I, XXII, Part 1, p. 793; Alfred Vaughts, *A History of Militarism* (New York, 1959), discusses the problem of efficiency in European armies.

bers of Lincoln's Cabinet, Secretary Chase, told a Congressman that Halleck had "immense brain, clear powerful intellect, full knowledge of his work, but [was] cold as a stone, care[d] not one penny for the work [except] as a professional performance," and had "no more heart about it than a shoemaker who pegs away at a boot." [18]

Halleck was guilty of much, but not lack of enthusiasm for his job. Secretary Chase, who was present at most of the Cabinet meetings when Halleck fought for a reorganization of the army, knew better. Old Brains struggled relentlessly to reform the corrupt system of appointing and promoting officers. He proposed new draft laws, helped make existing ones more stringent, took volunteers out of the state governors' hands and mustered them into United States' service, minimized leaves of absence in the army, made generals reduce the amount of baggage their armies transported, and combined with Haupt to eliminate abuses in the military railroad system. Most of the reforms were designed to eliminate politicians from the inner machinations of the army. The changes took more than zeal; they required time, patience, ability and energy. All were not completely achieved, but Halleck never relinquished his program. When the South finally conceded the struggle, she surrendered to the finest army the United States had ever put in the field. Halleck, as much as anyone else, made that army.

Halleck began his reorganization drive on August 3, 1862, when he had the President read at Cabinet meeting a communication proposing a draft of 200,000 militia for nine months and urging the recruiting of 300,000 more men to fill old and form new regiments. Halleck also asked for the initiation of a board of officers to handle appointments and promotions. He condemned the government's policy of selecting officers on the basis of political power, and used as an indictment the case of a colonel who had been tried and convicted of gross misconduct, was about to be dismissed, and had gone to Washington where he received a brigadier gen-

[18] T. C. Smith, *The Life and Letters of James Abram Garfield* (New Haven, 1925), I, 241.

eral's commission. The communique gave Lincoln impetus to initiate
a new draft law and prompted him to allow the War Department
more freedom in the appointment of junior officers.[19]

During the next month, Halleck strengthened the structure of the
army, urging Northern governors to promote officers and non-
commissioned officers who had distinguished themselves in the field.
Unless men had hopes of promotion, there was no "encouragement
to a faithful performance of duty and no stimulus to deeds of valor."
Old Brains also forced regular army captains and sergeants to accept commissions in the volunteer army.[20] The change benefited
the volunteers, for in their contact with the soldiers they were able
to learn professional methods. It broadened the base of the army
and helped to eliminate petty jealousy between both branches.

Halleck helped improve the quantity as well as the quality of
the army. With Seward and Stanton he prepared an order for-
bidding changes of domicile and refusing passports until the draft
drawings were completed, fought for a larger levy of troops, and
told a member of his staff to bring volunteer regiments into Washington and the Federal army so that he, and not the state governor,
could command the men.[21] Writing to a civilian who was active
in army reforms, Francis Lieber, Halleck expressed a fear that the
governors would build up a "northern States' rights party that
would eventually overpower all Federal Authority." He had cautioned Lincoln, but "no heed [was] given to the warning," and
now "approaching danger is already visible."[22]

There was a numerical discrepancy in the army which Halleck
tried to rectify. The Army of the Potomac was supposed to number

[19] Donald (ed.), *Inside Lincoln's Cabinet*, 109.

[20] *O.R.*, Ser. III, II, 544; Halleck Circular to northern Governors,
April 13, 1862, in the State of Wisconsin Executive Department Administration files (Organization and Administration of the Army), Series
1/1/5–11, Archives Division, State Historical Society of Wisconsin,
shows that Halleck followed this policy even before he became general-
in-chief. See also New York *World,* October 3, 1862.

[21] *O.R.*, Ser. III, II, 379; Donald (ed.), *Inside Lincoln's Cabinet,* 111.

[22] Halleck to Lieber, November 23, 1862, Francis Lieber Manuscripts
(Henry Huntington Library, San Marino, Calif.).

238,464, but more than 85,000 of these men, excluding those sick and unfit for duty, were absent on various pretexts. The same ratio applied to the entire military force of 790,097 would leave 282,071 *in absentia.* In the next two years, when officers applied to him for a leave because of "sickness in family," or urgent private business," Halleck refused them, and ordered others to do the same.[23]

Halleck traversed many roads in his efforts to obtain and maintain an effective fighting force. The trains and baggage of every field corps were too large, he thought, and did nothing but impede the rate of march. Beginning on October 18, 1862, he issued general orders intermittently to reduce to "usable size and definite limitations," excess items.[24] The Army of the Potomac, which usually operated near the bountiful supply depot of Washington, was the worst offender, and Halleck never completely convinced its commanders to reduce their train.

Reorganizing the railroads for military use was the task accomplished most easily, since Halleck was assisted by his reliable subordinate Herman Haupt. Both officers talked on several occasions about the importance of a "thorough organization" of all the roads. After Halleck called Stanton's attention to the need, with no result, Haupt handed Halleck an organization plan; the General-in-chief approved it and let Haupt work out the details. The system provided Haupt with complete freedom of action and prevented any officer, whether corps commander or army general, from interfering with his operation of the railroads.[25] The military railroad system soon recovered from the fiasco at Second Bull Run to reach a timely peak of efficiency by July, 1863.

In the West during the fall of 1862, William S. Rosecrans was ably demonstrating that a change in command might have very little effect on an army. For two months after replacing Buell he

[23] *O.R.,* Ser. III, III, 55.   [24] *Ibid.,* II, 671.
[25] Haupt, *Reminiscences,* 136; Thomas Weber, *The Northern Railroads in the Civil War 1861–1865* (New York, 1952), 158.

gave no indication of making a forward movement; then he took the army to Nashville, against the wishes of both Halleck and Lincoln. Ostensibly these had been the reasons for firing Buell, but now the election was over and the political pressures were not as great. Yet if Rosecrans spent much more time reorganizing the troops, he would follow the path of McClellan, Buell and Burnside.

Halleck tried to reason with Rosecrans. When the general asked for more repeating rifles for his cavalry, Old Brains pointed out that the arms were distributed proportionally, each army receiving its share. "This rule must be followed," he said, "for we cannot 'rob Peter to pay Paul.'" Late in November, Halleck filled a requisition for more carts and drays for Rosecrans, but criticized "this piling up of impediments. . . . Take a lesson from the enemy. Move light," he advised, "and supply yourself as much as possible with provisions, animals, forage, transportations, etc., in the country you pass through." [26]

Halleck's advice was not limited to the conduct of a campaign. As he began to comprehend Lincoln's thought processes, he usually told his subordinates of the President's expectations, assuming the invaluable position of liaison between Lincoln and his generals. Typically, on November 27, he told Rosecrans that he would disappoint the government if he remained at Nashville. When a quiet week passed, Halleck warned Rosecrans that the President was "very impatient," that twice he had been asked to designate a new commander, and concluded: "If you remain one more week at Nashville, I cannot prevent your removal. As I wrote you when you took command, the Government demands action, and if you cannot respond to that demand someone else will." [27]

Rosecrans took offense at the censure and muttered that threats of removal could not affect him. Painstakingly Halleck replied, saying that although Lincoln would not reveal the reason for his anxiety over an offensive, he would hazard a guess. The British

[26] *O.R.,* Ser. I, XX, Part 2, pp. 60, 102.
[27] *Ibid.,* 117.

Parliament was about to convene and the Confederates were bringing political pressure to bear on it for a joint recognition of their country by both England and France. If, at the time Parliament met, the South could point to possession of an area that the Union held in July—middle Tennessee—it would be a major diplomatic advantage. At all other points the North had either held her ground or made advances. Thus, Halleck said, "you will perceive that your movements have an importance far beyond mere military success. It may be," he continued, "and perhaps is, the very turning-point on our foreign relations." A victory before the opening of Parliament would be of more value than "ten times that success at a later date." [28] Clausewitz, the German theorist who propounded the theory that war is merely an extension of politics, could not have presented a clearer analysis.

Soon after reading the message Rosecrans began to move. On the last day of 1862 and the second day of 1863 (the armies had rested on New Year's Day) he fought Bragg on Stone's River and forced the Confederates to fall back. When Parliament met later in the month they did not extend recognition to the South, and France would not act alone on the matter. Halleck was so busy with Burnside he did not find time to congratulate Rosecrans until January 5. When he did, the thanks were heartfelt.[29]

The outgoing year had been filled with defeats and tension, intrigues and misunderstandings. Rosecrans ushered in the new one with a victory. It was of small magnitude, but perhaps it was a significant beginning.

[28] *Ibid.*, 123.　　　　　[29] *Ibid.*, 299.

CHAPTER NINE

INTRIGUE ALONG THE MISSISSIPPI

The Mississippi River was the key to the war in the West. By seizing control of the Father of the Waters, the North would accomplish two major objectives: eliminating Louisiana, Arkansas, and Texas from the war, and freeing navigation from St. Louis to New Orleans. The resulting change in morale would hold even greater significance. If the boys in blue could pitch their tents along the Mississippi's banks the North would brim over with confidence while the South would be submerged in despair.

Just as the fabled river was the key to the war, Vicksburg was the key to the river. The only remaining Confederate railroad to the trans-Mississippi region ran through the city. There was a hairpin turn in the river below the bluff on which Vicksburg stood, making it difficult, if not impossible, to run transports by the city's guns. Halleck reduced resistance above the city; Farragut scattered the Confederates below Port Hudson, Louisiana, an innocuous fortress which would stand or fall with Vicksburg. Truly the Mississippi city was the Gibraltar of the Confederate States of America.

The administration was willing to go to any length in its efforts to open the river and take Vicksburg. The campaign began on a hot Sunday afternoon in early August, 1862, when an Assistant Secretary suggested that Halleck designate a division to march down the Mississippi, gathering slaves as it went, to free both the bondsmen and the river. Most of the Cabinet members present thought the idea sound. Shocked at the mere hint of putting guns into the blacks' hands, Old Brains told the solons they could attain their object in a less objectionable manner by putting new men into old regiments and letting them open the river; however, there were not enough troops available, and perhaps it seemed best to drop the visionary plan. Halleck told Francis Lieber that "there is in this administration, or rather I should say in the cabinet, a power of weakness,—a courage of timidity, that attempts everything and yet does nothing. Not satisfied with having so many irons in the fire that nearly all burn, new ones must be thrust in daily." This time, however, Halleck's lack of enthusiasm blunted the eagerness of Lincoln's advisors and they abandoned their proposal.[1]

Halleck may have thought he had permanently defeated the ridiculous notions of the enterprising politicians, but he did not take into account John A. McClernand's ability to sell himself to others. An erstwhile volunteer general from Illinois with a record of loyalty to the Democratic party in the state, McClernand wanted a chance to become a hero. After McClellan edged himself into the position of general-in-chief, McClernand offered profuse congratulations, then exhortations to "please give me a chance to do something."[2] When McClellan ignored the hint, the eager volunteer sniffed the political breeze and caught the prevailing aroma of Republicanism. He began to clamor for a vigorous prosecution of the war and cooperation between Democrats and Republicans.

McClernand approached the Republican governor of Illinois, Richard Yates, and persuaded Yates to take him on the governor's staff as a recruiter. Yates asked Stanton's permission, but meanwhile the impatient McClernand wrote directly to Lincoln for a leave of absence. The President showed his general-in-chief the message. Old Brains was decidedly miffed at McClernand's flagrant disregard

---

[1] Donald (ed.), *Inside Lincoln's Cabinet,* 107; Halleck to Lieber, November 23, 1862, Lieber MSS.

[2] McClernand to McClellan, November 5, 1861, John A. McClernand Manuscripts (Illinois State Historical Society Library, Springfield, Ill.).

of protocol and sent him a stinging rebuff.[3] The intrepid McClernand ignored Old Brains and continued his efforts to get to Springfield, which he planned to use as a springboard to a more glorious
position. Eventually, with Lincoln's help, his wish was granted and
on August 25, 1862, Halleck gave him orders to report to Yates in
the state capital.[4]

Entertaining no thought of rotting in Springfield while honor and
fame awaited him in another field, McClernand then cast his eye on
the most coveted enterprise on the river—capturing Vicksburg. He
wanted an independent command and left Illinois for Washington
on September 23 to begin conniving for it. Immediately upon his
arrival the capital hummed with rumors. Political correspondents of
the President talked of the proposal to give McClernand a force; one
said he would "rejoice" to see McClernand so honored. After less
than a week in the capital, McClernand obtained an interview with
Lincoln, who listened attentively. McClernand bemoaned the closing
of the Mississippi by a "small, indeed comparatively insignificant
garrison at Vicksburg," promised to open the river with a force of
60,000, after which he would move straight east and take Atlanta,
or, if the President preferred, he would head west and besiege
Texas.[5]

The idea was irresistible to the President. He needed more Democratic support for his administration and he did want the river
opened. Besides, as Halleck had once said of Lincoln, "his fingers
itch to be into everything going on."[6] On October 9 Lincoln informed Halleck and Stanton of his decision; McClernand would
raise troops in the western states and head a land and naval expedition against Vicksburg. Twelve days later Stanton drew up formal
orders. McClernand would go west and take command of the men
remaining in Indiana, Illinois, and Iowa, raising what reinforcements he could. The forces would be sent to Memphis, Cairo, or

[3] Yates to Stanton, August 19, 1862, and Halleck to McClernand,
August 20, 1862, *ibid.*   [4] *O.R.,* Ser. I, XVII, Part 2, p. 187.
[5] McClernand to Lincoln, September 28, 1862, McClernand MSS.
[6] Halleck to Lieber, February 5, 1865, Lieber MSS.

wherever else Halleck decided, before McClernand took them against the bastion of the Confederacy. The President's decision, in fact, created an independent command in Grant's department. Lincoln dictated the order in Halleck's presence, despite Old Brains' objections to the entire plan, but he did allow a minor concession: the force would remain subject to the General-in-chief's orders and would be employed "according to such exigencies as the service, in his judgment, may require." McClernand's chief of staff believed that Stanton and Lincoln, by the postscript, "opened a door for themselves to escape from all responsibility." He felt that Halleck "agreed to it [the special command] only for the purpose of obtaining the new levies to be raised by Genl. McClernand's influence in the NorthWest without any intention" of allowing McClernand to command the expedition.[7]

McClernand, however, suspected nothing and with his orders safely under his arm skipped back to Springfield. Now that he was free from their domination he would show the snobbish West Pointers what a civilian could do, and would bask in the admiring eyes of the nation. Vicksburg, with its "small, indeed, comparatively insignificant garrison," would fall into his hands before the first snowflake of winter alighted.

Halleck had not abandoned his theory that places were more important than armies and he considered the capture of Vicksburg the

[7] Stanton to Halleck, October 11, 1862; confidential order of Stanton, October 21, 1862, McClernand MSS. McClernand spoke of Halleck's objection in a letter to O. M. Browning, December 16, 1862. See also the unpublished manuscript biography of General John A. McClernand, possibly written by Adolph Schwartz, later McClernand's chief of staff, written in October or November, 1863, annotated by General Edward J. McClernand (Illinois State Historical Society Library). The facts concerning Halleck's part in the McClernand expedition have been confused. It is not true that Halleck had no information about the scheme until December, 1862. He probably knew of it from the first—at any rate he was informed of the plan by, at the latest, October 9, 1862. On the back of a Stanton to Halleck letter of October 11, 1862, referring to events of October 9, in the McClernand MSS., McClernand noted that the subject under discussion "was an expedition of land and naval forces to clear the Mississippi. . . ."

most significant object of the war. But he was more than doubtful of McClernand's native generalship. Distrusting and disliking the flashy politician who had no respect for authority, Halleck laid plans to cut the command from under him. As fast as McClernand could collect men in Springfield, Halleck ordered them down to Helena, Arkansas, or to Memphis. The recruits reported to Grant, who commanded the force in West Tennessee. McClernand thought Halleck was cooperating.

Unaware of Halleck's subterfuge, Stanton encouraged McClernand. The Secretary longed to see the general "in the field, striking vigorous blows against the rebellion in its most vital point," and promised to send Nathaniel P. Banks, another political appointee, in command at New Orleans, up the river to cooperate in the great objective of reducing Vicksburg.[8]

Halleck paid little attention to this secondary expedition. He had to prime Grant for the theft of McClernand's hard earned troops, while being careful not to relate exactly what Lincoln had ordered. Otherwise, Grant might not wish to participate in a plan which undermined the President's orders. On November 3, Halleck wired approval of Grant's plan to advance as soon as he felt strong enough, since: "I hope for an active campaign this fall."[9] Later in the week Halleck designated Memphis as the base for Grant's reinforcements. When he notified Grant, Halleck said the Tennessee city would be the depot for a joint army and navy expedition on Vicksburg. McClernand was not mentioned.[10] But by now Grant had heard rumors floating down from Springfield and asked Halleck if he were to remain still while the expedition fitted out from Memphis, if Sherman were under him, or if he were reserved for "some special service." Grant, too, was being indirect; McClernand's name did not appear. Halleck did not equivocate: "You have command of all troops sent to your department and have permission to fight the enemy where you please." Four days later he told Grant the move-

[8] *O.R.,* Ser. I, XVII, Part 2, pp. 298, 309; Stanton to McClernand, October 29, 1862, McClernand MSS.

[9] *O.R.,* Ser. I, XVII, Part 1, p. 467.   [10] *Ibid.,* 468.

ment down the river must leave Memphis "as soon as sufficient force can be collected." [11] Although Halleck thought of Grant as a "good general and brave in battle, but careless in command," [12] he preferred any professional soldier, even a careless one, to the ostentatious, solicitous McClernand.

McClernand began to suspect that Halleck was countermanding his mission and on November 20 he asked his new-found friend, Governor Yates, who was in Washington, to see Stanton to "learn the status of the enterprise." On December 1, Lyman Trumbull, another Illinois politician who had just seen Stanton, reassured McClernand: "Nothing has been . . . done to embarrass . . ." the expedition. Still another Illinois vote-getter, Orville H. Browning, rushed to the Executive Mansion, where he saw Lincoln. Browning reported to McClernand: "He [Lincoln] says so far from any purpose of superseding you existing, both he and the Secretary of War are very anxious for you to have command. . . . You are in no danger." [13]

Lincoln and Stanton may have been anxious for McClernand to have command, but Halleck forged ahead with the opposite intention. Old Brains told Grant to collect his troops at Memphis by December 20, when they would leave for Vicksburg. Two days later, he informed Grant that he could use the men as he deemed "best to accomplish the great object in view" and again gave Grant control of all the excess troops in his department.[14] The next day Grant told Halleck that Sherman would command the expedition.[15] Halleck neglected to tell McClernand the date the expedition would leave.

McClernand, meanwhile, had chosen this moment to get married; he would take his bride on his triumphal march. On December 12, the prospective bridegroom informed Stanton he was "anxiously

[11] *Ibid.,* 469.

[12] Donald (ed.), *Inside Lincoln's Cabinet,* 103.

[13] McClernand to Yates, November 20, 1862; Trumbull to McClernand, December 1, 1862; Browning to McClernand, December 2, 1862, McClernand MSS.

[14] *O.R.,* Ser. I, XVII, Part 1, p. 473.

[15] Grant to Halleck, December 8, 1862, McClernand MSS.

awaiting" the order to go forward. Lincoln received a similar request; Halleck did not.[16]

Assuming that Halleck had already given the necessary orders, Stanton was surprised when he read McClernand's note and promised to "have the matter attended to without delay." This confirmed McClernand's forebodings and he immediately wired Halleck, begging the General-in-chief to send him to command the Mississippi expedition. He then telegraphed Browning and asked his ally to confront Lincoln with the problem. "Satisfied that the President and the Secretary of War favor me as the commander of the Expedition," McClernand believed the General-in-chief was his enemy—"personal enemy and senselessly so." "My state of uncertitude is cruel," he said. "It is humiliating to the last degree. For God's sake relieve me! Learn and let me know my fate!" Then McClernand revealed his perspicaciousness: "I think I understand the General-in-chief as well as any man living. I think he designs to give the command of the Expedition to Sherman." [17]

On December 1 Halleck bent slightly under the pressure Stanton exerted upon him by stating that Grant should allow McClernand's corps to constitute a part of the expedition. The order's ambiguity gave Grant freedom of action, but it was unnecessary.[18] On December 20 Sherman took the troops McClernand had so hopefully forwarded to Memphis and set sail for Vicksburg. At the time McClernand was ceremoniously entering the state of matrimony.

The next day, with Sherman and the troops safely down river, Halleck told McClernand to take charge of the expedition. McClernand later recalled that it was "the first and only recognition and that an indirect one, which the General-in-chief had ever made of my connection with the expedition." The indirect recognition did not

---

[16] McClernand to Stanton and Lincoln, December 12, 1862, *ibid.*

[17] Stanton to McClernand, December 15, 1862; McClernand to Halleck, December 16, 1862; McClernand to Browning, December 16, 1862, *ibid.*

[18] *O.R.,* Ser. I, XVII, Part 1, p. 476.

even give the politician-soldier permission to leave Springfield.[19] On December 23, however, McClernand and his admiring bride took the train for Memphis.

When the couple arrived in Memphis they found a deserted city. The crestfallen groom dispatched two members of his staff to ride across lower Tennessee and upper Mississippi to see Grant at Holly Springs. The next day, Monday, December 29, McClernand received orders to assume command of the expedition. The same day Sherman fought the major action of the campaign. McClernand's chief of staff knew that Halleck had planned all this: "The prevailing idea among officers of McClernand's staff and indeed among some general and line officers of the expedition was," he said, "that [Sherman's expedition] was got up without proper care, and was at once sent South, to escape Genl. McClernand and capture Vicksburg before the latter could arrive and take command." [20]

Halleck had taken the responsibility of meeting intrigue with intrigue and may have enjoyed the resulting farce. But there was no time to gloat. He had disposed of the amateur only to see—for the first time—his professional subordinates in the West out-manoeuvred by the Confederates.

Grant had planned to take Vicksburg with a double thrust; Sherman would move on the fortress from the north while he came in from the east. Sherman's force did not encounter any trouble, but once he had steamed down the Mississippi he was out of contact with his superior. Grant was to march south from Holly Springs, where he had a huge supply base, then turn on Vicksburg and deliver a coordinate attack with Sherman. But as Grant moved away from his base, the Confederates seized their chance and devastated Holly Springs in an orgy of destruction. Grant had to turn back and his lack of communication with Sherman undermined his strategy. Sherman had little notion he was acting alone with the Confederates

[19] *Ibid.,* Part 2, p. 528.
[20] Unpublished MSS biography of McClernand (Illinois State Historical Society Library).

concentrated against him. When Halleck heard about the Holly Springs raid he tried to halt the entire offensive, but his message arrived too late.[21] On December 29 Sherman assaulted the bluffs above Vicksburg, suffered heavy losses and escaped without major damage only because he ceased the hopeless attack.

When Sherman started back to Memphis, McClernand, minus his bride, met the army down river, without hesitation took command, and then led the troops up the Arkansas River, capturing Arkansas Post. Grant could barely suppress his anger. He told Halleck that McClernand had "gone on a wild goose chase to the Post of Arkansas," and hinted he wanted "further information" before acting. Halleck, horrified at McClernand's abandonment of the Vicksburg offensive, wired back: "You are hereby authorized to relieve General McClernand from command of the expedition against Vicksburg, giving it to the next in rank or taking it yourself."[22]

McClernand fought back by charging Halleck with "willful contempt of superior authority, and utter incompetency for the extraordinary and vital functions with which he is charged as General-in-chief." Lincoln did not rebuke McClernand for contempt of his superior, but tried to pacify the general, telling him he was doing "well for the country and well for yourself—much better than you could possibly be, if engaged in open war with General Halleck." Lincoln had "too many FAMILY controversies—" to enter another and begged McClernand for his sake and the country's sake to devote his attention to the "better work."[23]

Other criticisms of Old Brains reached the President. The "Loyal People of St. Louis" petitioned Lincoln to remove Halleck, because "we believe him to be devoid of the military talent attributed to him by some, incompetent, . . . and [a] lukewarm supporter of that radical policy of the President in which alone we can see success for the cause of the Union." They suggested that either Fremont, Butler or Sigel replace the General-in-chief. One of Lincoln's "old and true

[21] *O.R.,* Ser. I, XXXII, Part 2, p. 40.
[22] *Ibid.,* XVII, Part 2, pp. 553–55.
[23] Basler (ed.), *Collected Works of Abraham Lincoln,* VI, 71.

friends," Isaac Arnold of Illinois, informed the President that Halleck "has lost the confidence of the people." He, too, thought either Butler, Fremont, or Sigel could do better. Even one of McClellan's aides thought Halleck's treatment of McClernand shabby.[24] Lincoln ignored the demands.

After McClernand's independent command had been eliminated, Halleck concentrated on giving his undivided support to Grant, who in turn gave his complete attention to Vicksburg. The campaign would provide the ultimate example of the Jominian principle of concentration to take a place. Halleck was prepared to bend every effort to the capture of Vicksburg—all available men in the West eventually went down the Mississippi to help take the city. Commanding generals in St. Louis, Louisville, Nashville, Knoxville, and other western cities soon learned that the General-in-chief wanted them to subordinate their activities to those taking place on the Mississippi. From November, 1862, to the fall of Vicksburg, every movement in the West was considered only in terms of its effect on Grant's offensive against the place.

Grant tried all conceivable methods to gain entry to the Confederate stronghold. He had moved to the west bank of the Mississippi where he dug canals, tried to re-route the river, and struggled to get ships on a Louisiana lake which emptied into a river which joined the Mississippi below Vicksburg, all to no avail. Throughout the winter he continued "pushing everything to gain a passage, avoiding Vicksburg." Western politicians demanded more action in the theater, but as Grant later recalled: "With all the pressure brought to bear upon them, both President Lincoln and General Halleck stood by me to the end of the campaign." [25]

Old Brains tried to enlist General N. P. Banks's help for Grant, but the general at New Orleans invented excuses and failed to comply. Banks claimed he could not help Grant because he lacked cav-

---

[24] Memorial of loyal people of St. Louis, May 10, 1863, Robert Todd Lincoln Papers; Arnold to Lincoln, May 18, 1863, *ibid.;* Colburn to McClellan, January 15, 1862 [1863], McClellan Papers.

[25] *O.R.,* Ser. I, XXIV, Part 1, p. 10; Grant, *Memoirs,* 224.

alry; Halleck pointed out that it was expensive to ship horses to New Orleans since more than half died en route and mentioned that 4,000 or 5,000 animals could be collected from the surrounding countryside. The General-in-chief told Banks he should supply himself from the neighboring plantations and cooperate with Grant. "Of such vital importance is this cooperation that nothing but absolute necessity will excuse any further delay on your part," he said sternly.[26] Two months later Banks followed at least part of Halleck's advice and supplied himself spectacularly from the area. On one day a caravan eight miles long treked into New Orleans, including 600 wagons, 3,000 mules and horses, 1,500 cattle and large quantities of food.[27]

Halleck had other managerial problems that could not be solved by confiscating enemy goods. Shipping provisions to Grant was a harassing proposition at times, since the general occasionally forgot to send the transports back to Memphis. Reminding Grant that steam vessels were scarce and their unnecessary detention at their destination created immense transportation difficulties in Memphis, Halleck alleviated the situation by pulling boats from Cincinnati, sending them to St. Louis and finally Memphis. There they were loaded and forwarded to the preoccupied Grant.[28]

As spring appeared and the land began to dry, the climax of the campaign approached. Halleck, sending Grant advice and encouragement, told the general to write more often, warned him not to let his steamers get caught when the water level fell in the bayous, and cautioned him to keep his force concentrated. The importance of the operation could not be overemphasized. "The eyes and hopes" of the North rested upon Grant, to whom Halleck confided: "The opening of the Mississippi River will be to us of more advantage than the capture of forty Richmonds. We shall omit nothing which we can do to assist you." Four days later, less rhetorically, he told Grant to get

---

[26] *O.R.*, Ser. I, XV, 671.

[27] Roger W. Shugg, *Origins of Class Struggle in Louisiana* (Baton Rouge, 1939), 185.

[28] *O.R.*, Ser. I, XXIV, Part I, p. 19, 22.

his supply transports back up river.[29] Without them, the supplies Halleck had collected would be useless.

When in April Grant indicated he was ready to halt the spade work and resume active operations, Halleck deemed the time auspicious for instruction. "The character of the war has changed very much with the last year," he commenced. "There is now no possible hope of reconciliation with the rebels. The Union party in the South is virtually destroyed. There can be no peace but that which is forced by the sword." If the North did not conquer the Confederates, Halleck said, they would conquer the North. The slave oligarchy would then make the manufacturers of the North "mere 'hewers of wood and drawers of water' to the Southern aristocrats."

In accordance with the change in war, Halleck made a change in his policy. Grant should take slaves into his lines. In Missouri in 1862, Halleck had excluded the blacks by law; he now intoned: "Every slave withdrawn from the enemy is equivalent to a white man put hors de combat." Previously he had suggested to Grant that he could support his army on the country, but Grant had replied that only horses could subsist without supplies.[30] By early May, 1863, Halleck rejected this dictum. He told a general stationed at Memphis: "We must live upon the enemy's country as much as possible, and destroy his supplies. This is cruel warfare, but the enemy has brought it upon himself by his own conduct." [31] It was a far cry from the gentlemanly war Jomini favored.

After receiving Halleck's advice, Grant outlined his plans for the General-in-chief. He hoped to run the naval fleet past the batteries of Vicksburg, march the army down the west bank of the river, transport the men over on gunboats, and then move on either Jackson, the capital of Mississippi, or the Big Black River. He promised to keep his army together and see to it that he was not cut off from his supplies, "or beaten in any other way than in fair fight." [32] Hal-

---

[29] *Ibid.*, p. 22.
[30] *O.R.*, Ser. I, XXIV, Part 3, p. 156; XVII, Part 1, p. 156.
[31] *O.R.*, Ser. I, XXIV, Part 3, p. 156.
[32] *Ibid.*, Part 1, p. 25.

leck urged Grant to give "but little attention to the occupation of the country," and later in the day wired: "In my opinion this is the most important operation of the war, and nothing must be neglected to insure success." [33]

During the night of April 17 Grant embarked. His gunboats ran the batteries with slight losses and the transports followed intermittently. Grant marched his army down the river and met the boats near New Carthage, where he reconnoitered the east bank of the river. Halleck worked on little or no information. Struggling in the dark to give some assistance, he told Banks that Grant might come to Port Hudson to help there before turning on Vicksburg. [34]

According to Lincoln it was vital that Banks and Grant open communication. In his opinion the two armies were needlessly separated. The President feared that Joseph E. Johnston, Confederate commander in Tennessee, and John C. Pemberton, in charge of the army in Vicksburg, would unite and crush first Grant and then Banks. The reasoning was sound and basically Jominian, but it did not take into account either Banks's ineptitude nor Grant's ability to hit so fast the Confederates would be too stunned for offensive opportunities. Lincoln was solicitous over Grant and Banks, but Halleck's experience at Fort Donelson assured him that as a fighter no one could surpass "Unconditional Surrender."

Grant pushed off from New Carthage just as he had from Fort Henry. On April 30 he crossed the river and for the first time since the preceding fall had his army on high, dry ground. Hardly pausing he advanced into Mississippi, in the general direction of Jackson. Again he was in an exposed position, with two Confederate armies around him. General Banks and safety lay to the South.

It was one of the decisive moments of the war. The Gibraltar of America stood serenely above the Father of Waters, daring the impetuous Yankee to attack. Her confidence seemed to seep back into the North. Perhaps Grant was too audacious; perhaps he should be ordered to join Banks. But Halleck had let Grant do as he wished at Donelson and had made a policy of not interfering with his subordi-

[33] *Ibid.*, 27.   [34] *Ibid.*, XV, 702.

nates. He could still order Grant to join Banks if he wished, but he assumed the responsibility of not intervening and left Grant's hands untied to work their artistry.

On May 11, Halleck—at Lincoln's insistence—wired Grant, who was blasting his way into Jackson: "If possible, the forces of your-self and of General Banks should be united between Vicksburg and Port Hudson, so as to attack these places separately with the com-bined forces." [35] Grant knew Halleck well enough to recognize that it was in no way a direct order. He may have recalled a previous message in which Halleck admitted: "I know that you can judge of these matters there much better than I can here . . . ," [36] and Hal-leck's promises of support no matter what he did. Grant had no qualms in disregarding the telegram and Halleck never intimated that he had been disobeyed. As Grant later admitted, the message came too late, and "Halleck would not have given . . . it if he knew our position." [37] The general headed into Jackson, turned on Pemberton, repulsing him at Champion Hill and the Big Black River, and by the end of May set up a siege of Vicksburg.

The dramatic campaign allowed Halleck to switch Lincoln's strat-egy. He now tried to get Banks to join Grant. The Democrat from New England had conducted an expedition up one of the Louisiana bayous to Alexandria, a tour which resembled McClernand's goose chase in Arkansas. Halleck irately chastized Banks: "The OPEN-ING OF THE MISSISSIPPI RIVER has been continually presented as the FIRST and MOST IMPORTANT object to be attained," he said. "Operations up the Red River [or] toward Texas . . . are only of secondary importance, to be undertaken AFTER we get possession of the river, and as circumstance may then require." He spoke of "eccentric movements" and of the exceeding disappoint-ment of the government. Halleck, who feared a "serious disaster," if

[35] *Ibid.*, XXIV, Part 1, p. 36; see Lincoln to Grant, July 13, 1862, Robert Todd Lincoln Papers, in which the President admitted: "I thought you should go down the river and join General Banks; and when you turned northward, east of the Big Black, I feared it was a mistake." Obviously Lincoln told Halleck to give the order to Grant.

[36] *O.R.*, Ser. I, XXIV, Part 1, p. 25.   [37] Grant, *Memoirs,* 274.

Banks did not join Grant, was applying what he had said in his *Elements of Military Art:* "The first and most important rule in offensive war is, to keep your forces as much concentrated as possible." [38]

Although Banks never fully complied with Halleck's wishes, he did gather a force and lay siege to Port Hudson. With the port and Vicksburg sealed, the trans-Mississippi existed no longer for Richmond; she would have to make her plans without relying upon the three western states for aid. In time their exclusion would be official, and the river would flow "unvexed" to the sea. But this would entail more concerted energy. Halleck, who had done so much to create the favorable situation, was ready to contribute his share.

[38] Halleck, *Elements of Military Art and Science,* 40–41.

CHAPTER TEN

CONCENTRATE ON
IMPORTANT POINTS

The auspicious note on which 1863 had begun would not be prolonged. Although Rosecrans' victory at Stone's River and Grant's success at Vicksburg heralded hope that the Union might win the war within the year, the North's momentum soon dwindled. Friction and inertia marked the month of June, 1863; frustration and despair furrowed Old Brains' brow.

Halleck's strategy dictated that all activities in the West would turn on events transpiring at Vicksburg, and in his thinking Rosecrans' force was closely knit into the fabric of Grant's campaign. If Rosecrans kept Bragg occupied, Johnston would be unable to draw troops from Tennessee to attack Grant's rear; Rosecrans, however, had been resting on his laurels after his battle and was thereby freeing Bragg to send troops to Mississippi, where they could unite with Johnston's men and thrust at Grant from the rear.

Efforts to activate Rosecrans only roused him to anger. In March, Halleck had sent a form letter to all important army commanders, saying that a vacant major-generalcy which existed in the Regular Army would be awarded to the "general in the field who first wins an important and decisive victory." Lincoln and Stanton had directed that the message be issued.[1] When Rosecrans read the communique he was, as an "officer and a citizen," indignant to see such "auctioneering of honor." What general, he demanded, would fight "for his own personal benefit" and not for "honor and the country?" If there

[1] *O.R.,* Ser. I, XXIII, Part 2, p. 95.

were such a man, he would gain his commission "basely," and would deserve to be "despised by men of honor." [2]

After waiting a few days, Halleck made a conciliatory reply. No one was "auctioneering honors," he said; the President was merely announcing that he would reward distinguished service in the field. No one else had replied in that manner and Grant had been so busy he did not even acknowledge receipt of the message.[3] But Rosecrans still felt that someone had cast aspersions on his integrity.

Halleck tried to divert Rosecrans' attention to the Rebels in the rear of Union lines. He told the general to change policy and make the Confederates feel the hard hand of war. Live off the land and take food and supplies from the "openly hostile" without benefit of compensation, Old Brains ordered. Apply the policy to those who took no partisan interest in the conflict; if a citizen were not pro-Union he must be against it. By necessity the most ardent Southerners would soon become Union supporters if, after the confiscation of their provisions, Rebel sympathizers lost their freedom of movement.[4]

Rosecrans, however, would not make the transition from Jominian methods to the tactics of total war. He preferred to complain about the condition of his command so that he would not be forced into a premature battle. Like Banks, Rosecrans found it easier to ask Washington for more cavalry than to scour the countryside for animals. Patiently the General-in-chief suggested that Rosecrans force the quartermasters to obtain his horses and reiterated that proportionally Rosecrans had more horses than any other general. Halleck gave his subordinate the alternative of seizing the animals from enemy country and implied that the general could define Rebel territory for his own purposes.[5]

Ignoring Halleck, Rosecrans again rang the telegraph keys with peals of complaint; from March 10 to April 20 he transmitted more

[2] *Ibid.*, 111.   [3] *Ibid.*, 138.
[4] *Ibid.*, 107.
[5] *Ibid.*, 284; Halleck to Rosecrans, April 27, 1863, Robert Todd Lincoln Papers.

than twenty requests for additional cavalry. Halleck replied that the government was "fully aware" of his wants and that daily requests would not hasten the end of the war; fighting might. Recalling Rosecrans' hypersensitivity, Halleck concluded by saying the letter was not written in "a spirit of fault-finding, but from a sense of duty to you and to the Government." [6] His tact was fruitless; Rosecrans was offended. "I regard . . ." the letter, he told Old Brains, "as a profound, grievous, cruel, and ungenerous official and personal wrong." [7]

Perhaps repenting of his misdemeanor with a shrug of his burdened shoulders, Halleck tried to halt the telegraphic onslaught and impel field action. Grant was south of Vicksburg, headed toward Jackson; he would be overwhelmed unless Rosecrans advanced. Rosecrans still claimed he needed more troops, and although Halleck tried to help, reinforcements were scarce. Grant needed every man he could obtain; Hooker was in the midst of a Virginia campaign; typically, Banks was willing, indeed anxious, to succor Grant if only he had more men. "Instead of sparing any," Halleck complained to one commander, "every general is pressing for more men as though we had a cornucopia of troops from which to supply their wants. I have tried my very best for the last year . . . to prove to generals that when we concentrate on important points the enemy must do the same." Desperately Halleck looked to Curtis; perhaps west of the Mississippi there were some unemployed men. But Curtis had already sent his spares to Grant. [8]

Two weeks later, May 18, Rosecrans was still cemented in central Tennessee and Johnston was drawing troops from Bragg. Halleck repeated his orders to Rosecrans to overcome his inertia and advance. Rosecrans replied he needed more cavalry. "I have only to repeat what I have so often stated, that there is no more cavalry," sighed the General-in-chief. Later Lincoln wired: "I would not push you to any rashness, but I am very anxious that you do your utmost,

[6] *O.R.*, Ser. I, XXIII, Part 2, p. 255.
[7] *Ibid.*, 279.
[8] *O.R.*, Ser. I, XVIII, 612; XXII, Part 2, pp. 268–69.

short of rashness, to keep Bragg from getting off to help Johnston against Grant." On June 11 the General-in-chief again reminded Rosecrans of the President's "great dissatisfaction" with his prolonged inactivity.[9]

Halleck's pen had scarcely dried when an orderly handed him an astounding document. Upon the advice of a Council of War, Rosecrans had decided to wait until Vicksburg's "fate is determined" before advancing, since military maxims dictated "not to risk two great and decisive battles at the same time." He advised "caution and patience at headquarters."[10]

The master of maxims hurled them right back at Rosecrans. Fighting one battle at a time, Halleck observed, applied to a single army, not to two armies acting independently. Johnston and Bragg had the advantage of interior lines and it was to their interest, not the North's, to fight at different times. Sneeringly Halleck remarked: "There is another military maxim, that 'councils of war never fight.'" If Rosecrans were not ready, Halleck would not order him to fight, "for the responsibility of fighting or refusing to fight at a particular time or place must rest upon the general in immediate command. It cannot be shared by a council of war, nor will the authorities here make you fight against your own will."[11]

But the "authorities" were about to make Rosecrans fight. On June 16, Lincoln began to tighten the screws. At the President's insistence, Halleck asked Rosecrans for a specific answer to the question, did he plan to make an immediate move forward? Rosecrans replied that if "immediate" meant that night or the next day, then no; if it meant four or five days, yes.[12] The answer was satisfactory. On June 24, Rosecrans wired that he would begin to move at 3 o'clock that morning.[13] The movement, however, would prove to be just another in the series of disappointments.

---

[9] *O.R.*, Ser. I, XXIII, Part 1, p. 10; Part 2, p. 369.
[10] *O.R.*, Ser. I, XXIII, Part 1, p. 8.
[11] *Ibid.*, 8.   [12] *Ibid.*, 10.
[13] *Ibid.*, 10.

While Halleck used everything short of Archimedes' lever to pry Rosecrans from his stationary position, he continued to channel reinforcements to Grant. On June 2, in the midst of Rosecrans' horse-hoarding campaign, Halleck had asked Burnside how many troops he could spare from Kentucky. Burnside's reply was evasive, but Halleck had no qualms about ordering troops away from a quiet command in northern Kentucky and directed Burnside to send 8,000 men to Grant at Vicksburg. The western general, John A. Schofield, was helpful. Upon receiving Halleck's request to donate some men, Schofield immediately replied he had six infantry regiments and three batteries of artillery available.[14]

But there were few Schofields among Halleck's subordinates. Banks, who had started toward Vicksburg, could not bear to leave the Pelican state without at least one more attempt. Stopping north of Baton Rouge, he lay siege to Port Hudson. Halleck sent "dispatch after dispatch" ordering the general to join Grant, and could not understand why he refrained. The Port Hudson operation was a glaring violation to the principle of concentration and in "direct violation" to orders. He told Banks the manoeuvre was "so opposed to military principles I can hardly believe it true," and added he had so often demonstrated "the peril of separate and isolated operations, that it would be useless to repeat them."[15]

But Banks had found a Louisiana town receptive to his advances and ignored the General-in-chief. On June 4, Halleck remarked that he hoped Banks had relinquished his project and sent Grant his force, since it was obvious that the moment Vicksburg fell Port Hudson would follow.[16] Banks paid no attention.

Despite Banks' obstinate refusal to help, Grant's investment of Vicksburg was by now complete. Halleck had scraped together more than 20,000 reinforcements for the besieger, enabling Grant to de-

---

[14] *O.R.*, Ser. I: XXIV, Part 3, pp. 376, 384; XXIII, Part 2, p. 384; XXII, Part 2, p. 306.
[15] *O.R.*, Ser. I, XXIV, Part 1, p. 40; XXVI, Part 1, p. 534.
[16] *Ibid.*, XXVI, Part 1, p. 535.

tach Sherman's corps to the Big Black River to watch Johnston. While deathbound with cancer years later, Grant still recalled with gratitude Halleck's efforts on his behalf.[17]

Halleck never felt compelled to pressure Grant. He knew that "so long as we can gain success, the interference of politicians in military matters can be resisted; but on the first disaster they press upon us like a pack of hungry wolves." [18]

Halleck did not expend his energies solely on Rosecrans and Vicksburg. Mindful of his army reforms, he searched for a lawyer who could establish a uniform set of instructions for armies in the field.

Such a man was Francis Lieber, a Prussian liberal who had fought against despotism at Waterloo and for liberty in Greece, taught in the deep South from an antislavery podium, advocated prison reform and tried to codify international law. In 1862 Halleck had requested a copy of one of the lectures Lieber had given on the laws of war. Before Lieber could send it, he had rushed to visit one of his sons who had been wounded at Fort Donelson. The professor and Halleck met on this trip and became firm and lasting friends. Halleck did not forget the scholar when he went to Washington.[19]

Old Brains had been pondering over the legal status of guerillas during a civil war and was pleased to learn that Lieber had been studying the question. He encouraged Lieber to write a treatise on the subject since "it had now become an important question in this country and should be thoroughly investigated. I know of no one who can do it as well as yourself." Lieber responded to the compliment with a sixteen page pamphlet about guerillas, distinguishing between the types and treatment for each. Halleck ordered five thousand copies printed and distributed to the army.[20]

---

[17] *O.R.*, Ser. I, XXIV, Part 3, pp. 249, 452. Grant, *Memoirs*, 280.

[18] Halleck to Schofield, July 7, 1863, John M. Schofield Manuscripts (Library of Congress).

[19] Frank Freidel, *Francis Lieber: Nineteenth-Century Liberal* (Baton Rouge, 1947), vii, 324.   [20] *Ibid.*, 329.

Since the North was in legalistic confusion during the war, there were other areas where Halleck needed the professor. The government's official policy, that the Southern states had not withdrawn from the Union, meant that the Confederate armies were mere rebellious mobs and were therefore not protected by established rules of civilized warfare. But Union generals could not slaughter every captured Confederate, or their own men would receive similar treatment when they were seized. Halleck hoped for a solution that would allow the government to maintain its position while providing for just treatment of prisoners on both sides. The government had attempted to institute a system of exchange, but bickering over the status of Negro troops defeated it, and consequently the large numbers of prisoners in northern and southern camps increased.

Factors other than legality were bound to the problem. The Northern populace needed a heavy diet of propaganda to sustain their fighting spirit and the government had to cater to them. The Confederacy's inadequate prison camps, which were neither designed nor intended for great bodies of already dirty, hungry men, were the *soup du jour* on the propagandists' menu.[21]

Halleck contributed his share of atrocity stories. In his annual report for 1863, he said that the North treated Rebel prisoners with "consideration and kindness," while the Confederates stripped Union officers of blankets, clothing and shoes even in winter, confined them in "damp and loathsome prisons," fed them on "damaged provisions, or actually starved [them] to death." Others were murdered "by their inhuman keepers," and the "horrors of 'Belle Isle' and 'Libby Prison' exceed even those of 'British Hulks' or the 'Black Hole of Calcutta.'" Southerners applauded these "barbarous" acts as a "means of reducing the Yankee rank." Laws of war justified retaliation and the "present case seems to call for the exercise of this extreme right," he concluded.

But while advocating retaliation, Halleck looked for a means of

[21] *O.R.,* Ser. II, VI, 523; Freidel, *Lieber,* 331; for a survey of prison systems and war propaganda see William B. Hesseltine, *Civil War Prisons, A Study in War Psychology* (Columbus, Ohio, 1930).

ameliorating the situation. He hoped the Confederates would "abandon a course of conduct which must forever remain a burning disgrace to them and their cause," [22] and he asked Lieber to help the North find a practicable solution to this and other phases of the conflict. Spying and property rights, the distinction between insurrection, civil war, and rebellion—all needed definition. In November of 1862 the conscientious Lieber had written Halleck that a committee to formulate a code of war ought to be established, suggesting that the General-in-chief be chairman. A few weeks later, Old Brains asked Lieber to visit Washington for a month. Lieber arrived to find that Halleck had appointed him to a special board, created by the War Department, to suggest amendments for the Rules and Articles of War and devise a code of regulations for field generals. All members of the committee, except Lieber, were army officers.

Lieber did most of the work and supplied most of the initiative, although he called on Halleck and others for ideas. The task was time-consuming and not until February, 1863, was it accomplished. By then Halleck thought the section on parole and exchange of prisoners so important and essential that he edited Lieber's rough draft on the topic and had it printed and distributed as General Orders No. 49. Lieber complained that "it will never be known whence this came," and humorously added, "I shall not even be made Major General."

In March, Halleck suggested that Lieber add a belated section on civil war, rebellion and insurrection. Halleck reduced the outpouring from six pages to a few paragraphs and issued them as General Orders No. 100.

Entitled "Instructions for the Government of Armies of the United States in the Field," it was the basis for all subsequent army codes. In part propaganda, in part good military law, the code was general enough to allow great variations in interpretations. Halleck said it was a statement of "general principles which apply only in absences of a special agreement," while Southerners denounced it for legaliz-

[22] *O.R.*, Ser. II, VI, 523.

ing crime—any slave, according to the code, who escaped to the Union lines was "immediately entitled to the rights and privileges of a freeman." Yet "our little pamphlet . . . short but pregnant and weighty like some stumpy Dutch woman when in the family way with coming twins," as Lieber called it, had ordered some of the chaotic questions of the war.[23] Again Halleck had delegated authority to the correct person.

Halleck's actions showed the tenacity of Jomini's influence upon his thinking and his personal commitment to order and system. Clausewitz believed total war could not nor should not be limited; the Prussian said that restrictions on violence—such as General Orders 100—were "hardly worth mentioning."[24]

Old Brains' efforts at organization did not terminate with general orders. In his report for 1862 he appealed for reforms; let the armies learn to subsist from the country; eliminate the sutlers and have the armies supply those goods which the peddlers sold; revise the penal code for expediting courts-martial; create more artillery and cavalry officers; put more men in the engineering regiments; finally, send cavalrymen whose horses were a liability back into the infantry, where the men could be an asset.[25] Eventually, the Army adopted most of his proposals. The fact that Halleck could not compell his commanders to execute the reforms if they did not so desire was a retarding element. In March, however, he was at least able to discontinue commanding a general's authority to grant leaves of absence.[26]

While Halleck supervised Lieber, reinforced Grant, pushed at Rosecrans and argued with Banks, he did not neglect the army nearest the capital. The new leader of the Army of the Potomac, Joseph Hooker, known to the country as "Fighting Joe," knew Old Brains

[23] Freidel, *Lieber,* 331–34; *O.R.,* Ser. II, V, 306–307; Lieber to Samuel Ruggles, March 16, 1863, Correspondence of Francis Lieber (Library of Congress); *O.R.,* Ser. II, V, 671–82; Freidel, *Lieber,* 334–37; *O.R.,* Ser. III, III, 1037.

[24] Carl von Clausewitz, *On War* (London, 1956), I, 2.

[25] *O.R.,* Ser. III, III, 1037.   [26] *O.R.,* Ser. I, XXV, Part 2, p. 125.

in California, where he borrowed money from Halleck and never repaid it.[27] Halleck's opinion of Hooker had not risen as he watched the general intrigue for his position, but fortunately for both they had little official contact. Halleck had not suggested Hooker for the command and rarely corresponded with him; Hooker received his orders from, and sent his reports to, Lincoln.

During February and March, Hooker reorganized the Army of the Potomac, as each of his three predecessors had done, making notable improvements in the cavalry. Although involved with Rosecrans and Grant, Halleck found time to send a suggestion. Since Lee had detached Longstreet to southeastern Virginia, Halleck told Hooker he should attack the weakened Army of Northern Virginia.[28] But Hooker was planning his own manoeuvres and did not even reply to the General-in-chief's message.

Hooker had devised a plan to cross the Rappahannock and envelop Lee at Chancellorsville; it was an exact duplicate of Alexander the Great's battle at Jhelum. Like the Macedonian, Hooker feinted crossing up and down the river, got the bulk of his men across without Lee's discovering the movement, and had a sizeable force still at Falmouth which could make an uncontested crossing as Hooker broke Lee's left flank. But Hooker was not facing a Porus, and certainly he was no Alexander. After fording the river he lost his nerve and allowed Lee to send Jackson around to his flank. When Jackson delivered a crushing blow on an unsuspecting Union infantry corps, Hooker fell completely apart and the victory was Lee's.

During the battle, Halleck tried to get General John Dix, sixty-five-year-old veteran of the War of 1812, to move from his base at Fort Monroe toward Richmond and Lee's rear. Halleck reinforced Dix with 4,000 men, but the veteran ran no risks, and Old Brains' efforts came to naught.[29] After Hooker's loud boasting about what he would do to "Bobbie Lee," everyone looked rather ludicrous.

[27] Gamaliel Bradford, *Union Portraits* (Boston, 1914), 42.
[28] T. Harry Williams, *Lincoln and His Generals*, 211; *O.R.*, Ser. I, XXI, 1009; XXV, Part 2, p. 158.   [29] *O.R.*, Ser. I, XXV, Part 2, p. 682.

After the battle at Chancellorsville, Lee began another invasion of the North and again threw the capital into an uproar. On June 5, when Lee had his movement well underway, Hooker sent a plaintive call to Washington. He proposed to attack the Confederate troops still south of the river, but like Burnside wanted definite orders. Lincoln replied that he had given Halleck the problem and then added: "I would not take any risk of being entangled upon the river, like an ox jumped half over a fence and liable to be torn by dogs front and rear, without a fair chance to gore one way or kick the other." [30] Wanting to avoid Lee, Hooker proposed an entirely new plan. While Lee menaced northward he would take the Army of the Potomac south of the Rappahannock and capture the undefended Richmond. Hooker was operating under the theory that a place, rather than the enemy army, was his true objective.

The President rejected this proposal. Lincoln pointed out that the entrenchments surrounding Richmond would retard Hooker for twenty days; meanwhile Lee would ravage the North. He told Hooker to follow Lee on the inside track, "shortening your lines while he lengthens his. If he stays where he is, fret him and fret him." When Lincoln asked if Halleck concurred, the General-in-chief responded, "I do so fully." [31]

But beyond seconding Lincoln's view, Halleck did little. Instead he played Cassandra, predicting disaster but doing nothing to avert it. He warned a captain of engineers at Pittsburg of the possibility of a raid on the city and lamely advised that he make "preparations." [32]

Halleck did give orders to those troops in the Eastern theater well removed from the formidable Lee. He tried to employ Dix's force by suggesting to him that he interpose on Lee's supply line to slow his movements. Dix might capture Richmond and "at least [he would] find occupation for a large force of the enemy." Two weeks later Halleck would regret the wording of his telegram, for Dix would claim that any operations in the vicinity of the city would "threaten Richmond," while Halleck maintained he meant an actual

---

[30] *Ibid.,* XXVII, Part 1, p. 31.   [31] *Ibid.,* 35.
[32] *Ibid.,* Part 3, p. 32.

attack on the Confederate capital's defenses.[33] Again Halleck's vague orders, which most of his western generals were pleased to receive, were rejected by a stubborn eastern general.

Old Brains gave his only definite orders of the campaign to Robert Schenck, Ohio political general situated in the Valley. He told Schenck to concentrate all the troops in the Valley at Harper's Ferry, for "that place must be held." [34] The city was on Lee's supply line, and if Schenck remained there Confederate movements would be drastically curtailed. Halleck also hoped Lee would stop to besiege the city, in which case the north would be spared invasion and Hooker could fight Lee in Virginia, but he did not relate his outline to Hooker and when the general asked about Harper's Ferry, Halleck evasively replied he did not know enough about the situation to forward any orders.[35]

But Halleck knew enough to know the situation was bad. On June 11 he had ordered the outpost at Winchester, commanded by Robert Milroy, a political appointee, to fall back to Harper's Ferry.[36] Milroy serenely disregarded the order and Lee, moving through the Valley, captured his division. When Milroy blamed his misfortune on Halleck's prejudice against non-professionals, Lincoln came to Old Brains' defense. He reminded the disobedient Milroy: "You hate West Point generally, and General Halleck particularly; but I do not know that it is his fault you were at Winchester on the 13th, 14th and morning of the 15th—the days of your disaster." However, Lincoln failed to inform his Secretary of the Navy of the facts, and when Welles heard of Milroy's capture he knew at once who was at fault: "Halleck sits, and smokes, and swears, and scratches his

[33] *Ibid:* 111; XXVII, Part 1, p. 17.

[34] *Ibid.,* XXVII, Part 3, p. 124.

[35] *Ibid.,* 125. Halleck told Schenck to put every man into the Harper's Ferry defenses, without delay and gave advice on how to set up the defense. Then he said: "Should the place be besieged, it will soon be relieved." Halleck hoped that Lee would halt to take the city, and that Schenck could hold out long enough to allow the Army of the Potomac to get to the scene. See also *O.R.,* Ser. I, XXVII, Part 1, p. 47.

[36] Basler (ed.), *Collected Works of Abraham Lincoln,* VI, 308.

arm . . . but exhibits little military capacity or intelligence; is offusticated, muddy, uncertain and stupid as to what is doing or to be done," he added to the growing list of Halleck condemnations in his diary.[37]

More bad news soon gave "Father Neptune" Welles similar occasion to froth. On June 16 Halleck told Hooker that Harper's Ferry itself was surrounded. Schenck reported he could not hold out much longer and asked for relief. "He can hope for none," Halleck told Hooker, "excepting from your army." The telegram was neither an order nor a clear description of the situation. Bemused and befuddled, ignorant of even Lee's position, Hooker forlornly asked that "it might be made the duty of some person in the telegraph office in Washington to keep me informed of the enemy's movements." [38] Lincoln finally realized the disastrous results emanating from the confused command system and the failure of his own efforts to direct Hooker. In lucid language Lincoln told Hooker he was placing him under Halleck. Lincoln claimed that he had not "intended differently, but as it seems to be differently understood, I shall direct him to give you orders and you to obey them." [39]

The President did not reckon with Halleck. Lincoln wrote his message to Hooker in the War Department while Halleck watched. Fifteen minutes later Halleck sent his first message to Hooker under the new system. He said, in part: "You are in command of the Army of the Potomac, and will make the particular dispositions as you deem proper. I shall only indicate the objects to be aimed at." [40]

Since it was obvious he would receive little aid or encouragement from Halleck, and since fighting Lee was hardly an appealing prospect, Fighting Joe looked for an escape. He demanded that the garrison at Harper's Ferry be removed and when Halleck refused, Hooker asked to resign. Lincoln had appointed Hooker, Halleck claimed, and the General-in-chief could do nothing about relieving him. Old Brains referred the dispatch to the President, recommend-

---

[37] *Ibid.;* Welles, *Diary,* I, 331.
[38] *O.R.,* Ser. I, XXVII, Part I, pp. 45, 47.
[39] *Ibid.*   [40] *Ibid.*

ing General George G. Meade for the post. That day Lincoln ended
Hooker's sojourn as commander of the Army of the Potomac and
began Meade's tour of duty in the position.[41]

June, 1863, did not end on an auspicious note for the North. Lee
was roaming at will through Pennsylvania; Grant's siege moved
into its sixth week and Pemberton still held firm; Rosecrans had
failed to bring Bragg to battle; Banks was settled down before Port
Hudson, apparently oblivious to the rest of the war; and the General-in-chief was obstinately refusing to dictate to the eastern commanders. The dawn of the first day of July, however, revealed a
clear, bright sky.

[41] *Ibid.,* 60; Clarence Edward Macartney, *Grant and His Generals* (New
York, 1953), 161.

CHAPTER ELEVEN

GETTYSBURG AND VICKSBURG

Halleck, a thoroughly practical soldier not inclined to pessimistic musing, still may well have wondered on July 1, 1863, if the North would ever win the war. Indeed, would it even be able to hold its capital? Studying his map and plotting the spread of Lee's army over the rich farm land of southern Pennsylvania, Halleck had cause to despair.

One ray of hope was the reliability of the new commander of the Army of the Potomac. General Meade, West Point class of 1835, was seeped in the traditions of the old army. He had distinguished himself in the battles of Palo Alto and Monterey during the Mexican War and remained in the service after the conflict. During the first two years of the Civil War he served as a brigade commander in the Army of the Potomac, suffering a severe wound at the Seven Days' battle. Returning to active duty he broke the Confederate right wing at Fredericksburg and played no part in the disaster at Chancellorsville. In Washington he was known as a "safe" general who had not been implicated in Hooker's intrigues. Meade excited neither antagonism nor hatred; perhaps for that reason he held his job longer than any of his predecessors. His most salient characteristic was a violent temper, which had led his soldiers to dub him "the old snapping turtle."

In only one respect did Halleck's instructions to the new commander deviate from his previous pattern. Meade would not be "hampered by any minute instructions . . . ," and his army was free to act as Meade deemed proper, excepting that he should fight if

Lee approached either Washington or Baltimore. Halleck then introduced the unique condition. Meade could control all troops in the sphere of his operations; the garrison at Harper's Ferry was under his direct orders.[1] Since Lee had advanced to the Susquehanna River in Pennsylvania, Meade was assuming a difficult command; this strong evidence of the government's faith in him might foster his confidence.

When on June 28 the insecure Meade inquired if he could withdraw a portion of the garrison at Harper's Ferry Halleck replied he could "diminish or increase it" as he wished. When Meade ordered the evacuation, however, the commander at Harper's Ferry rebelled. He stated that the withdrawal would necessitate destroying valuable property, which he could very easily defend. Halleck then shifted his position—supporting Meade in the abstract was one thing, but actually withdrawing troops from Harper's Ferry another—and said that the village "should not be abandoned, but defended." [2] Meade bypassed Halleck and appealed to Stanton, who maintained that Meade's judgment was correct. The garrison destroyed the property and began to march out of the village, leaving the bridge intact. Halleck was irate. Since Lee had crossed north of Harper's Ferry, the Federal troops were not in danger of capture. They would be needed there if, and when, Lee fell back to Virginia. Harper's Ferry would block at least one avenue of Lee's escape, and it constituted a threat to his supply line. Meade had wanted the 11,000 men at the garrison for reinforcements; Halleck thought their strategic position precluded their availability for the army in the field. He stopped the evacuation after the old snapping turtle swam off with half of the troops.[3]

While Halleck and Meade bickered, Lee was winning the race for

---

[1] *O.R.,* Ser. I, XXVII, Part 1, p. 61.

[2] *Ibid:* 63, 69; Part 3, p. 428.

[3] *Ibid.,* Part 1, p. 15. Halleck stated that the order to evacuate was "based on erroneous representations," and "was not known in Washington until too late to be countermanded. It was, however, not entirely executed when General Meade very judiciously directed the reoccupation of that important point."

the Susquehanna. Meade ambled along behind, nipping at his heels, trying to annoy the Confederate so that Lee would turn and attack. Although he had lost communication with Meade, Halleck tried to help. He wired the commander at Harrisburg, Pennsylvania, a city on the north bank of the Susquehanna directly in Lee's path, and told him to build impediments in the enemy's line of march.[4] The following day, July 1, Lee moved east to strike at the irritating Yankee and the battle of Gettysburg began.

Although Halleck's hands were tied due to the break in communications, he managed to order the commander at Harrisburg to march south and attack Lee's rear.[5] Then he and the President settled down to a long, tense wait. Hour after hour they paced the telegraph office, seizing any scrap of news that arrived. Anxiously, impatiently, Halleck waited for telegraph operators to catch up with Meade.

That night Halleck learned the general's battle plans. Advanced corps of both armies had fought an indecisive action during the day, and Meade had decided to erect a defensive line south of Gettysburg. Halleck approved the tactical arrangements but he feared that strategically Meade was too far east. He sent Meade thoughtful advice which did not propound to be an order. Lee might turn the army's left flank, Old Brains pointed out, interpose on Meade's supply line and entrench between the Union army and Washington. Then Meade would have to attack Lee, not vice versa. Manoeuvre had been the key to Lee's previous victories and Halleck saw no reason for the Virginian to discard the Jomini method in favor of a direct attack.[6] Longstreet proposed that precise plan to Lee, but his chief decided—over Longstreet's protest—to fight where he found the enemy.

On the second day of July, Lee launched his attack. The Union line bent but did not break. On the third, the great commander tried once again. He failed.

---

[4] *O.R.*, Ser. I, XXVII, Part 3, p. 433.

[5] *Ibid.*, 473.

[6] David Homer Bates, *Lincoln in the Telegraph Office* (New York, 1907), 155; *O.R.*, Ser. I, XXVII, Part 1, p. 71.

Over 1,000 miles away, northern farm boys were winning another victory over the people who had refused them the use of the Mississippi River. Old Brains, beginning with the capture of Fort Donelson, had been an active manager of the Vicksburg campaign. He had taught, supplied, and reinforced Grant, dumped McClernand, and diverted political attention in Washington away from the Mississippi. In Pemberton's surrender to Grant on July 4, Halleck could take a personal pride. The Father of Waters, in the words of a westerner who loved it as only a boy reared on the frontier could, now flowed "unvexed to the sea."

Halleck gave Grant unbounded praise. The campaign, he told Grant, "in boldness of plan, rapidity of execution, and brilliancy of results, . . . will compare most favorably with those of Napoleon. . . . You and your army have well deserved the gratitude of your country, and it will be the boast of your children that their fathers were of the heroic army which reopened the Mississippi River." Halleck said of his protégé in his official report: "No more brilliant exploit can be found in military history." On July 7, he recommended Grant for a major generalship and Meade for a brigadier generalship in the Regular Army, saying that Meade "seems the right man in the right place." [7]

The taciturn Grant was less verbose than Halleck but his simple words of appreciation fully acknowledge his debt to Halleck: "I feel under many obligations to you, general, for the interest you have taken in my welfare and that of the army I have the honor to command." [8]

After Gettysburg, Halleck tried to insure the annihilation of Lee's army. He ordered the forces at Harrisburg to fall on Lee's left flank, those at Cumberland, Maryland, to push into Virginia and prepare to attack the retreating Confederates, and gave Meade command of all the forces in the vicinity to utilize in the pursuit. [9] Lee retreated through Maryland to the Potomac above Harper's Ferry, where high

[7] *O.R.,* Ser. I, XXIV, Part 1, p. 6, 63; Part 3, p. 498.
[8] *Ibid.,* 587.
[9] *O.R.,* Ser. I, XXVII, Part 3, p. 507; Part 1, p. 79.

water prevented a crossing. The Confederates established a strong defensive position and waited for the river to recede. Meade was indicating his pursuit would be inactive. He had suffered terrific losses at Gettysburg and wanted to refit and reorganize his army before attacking Lee, whose army, as he well knew, had not been routed.

Halleck, however, tried to force Meade to fight. Reminding Meade that Lee had no artillery ammunition left, he said that the Confederate general should be punished. "You have given the enemy a stunning blow at Gettysburg. Follow it up and give him another." The next day, July 7, he again urged an immediate attack, but on July 9 Halleck told Meade not to be influenced by "any dispatch from here against your own judgment. Regard them as suggestions only. Our information here is not always correct."[10] Meade could now disregard Halleck's orders with impunity.

Halleck spoke from the platform upon which he stood throughout his tenure as general-in-chief: "To order a general to give battle against his own wishes and judgment is to assume the responsibility of a probable defeat. If a general is unwilling to fight, he is not likely to gain a victory."[11] But Lincoln had ordered Halleck to make Meade press the pursuit and destroy Lee, and Old Brains did urge Meade on, promising him full support, and sending more reinforcements. Then he told Meade to postpone a general battle until he could martial all the reserves entering his army, and until the concentration was complete. When they arrived, Meade should hurl them upon the enemy.[12]

After further delay, however, Halleck fired a barrage of messages, orders, and telegrams in his effort to have Meade attack Lee. When one subordinate complained he could not send Meade reinforcements because he lacked transportation, Halleck told him not to stop for "trifles at this crisis, but prove yourself equal to the emergency." Then he told Meade not to call a council of war, since they were proverbially against fighting. "Do not let the enemy escape," were his

[10] *O.R.,* Ser. I, XXVII, Part 1, pp. 82, 85, 88.
[11] *O.R.,* Ser. I, XXIX, Part 2, p. 277.
[12] *O.R.,* Ser. I, XXVII, Part 3, pp. 567, 633; Part 1, pp. 88, 89.

final words.[13] But the burst of activity came too late; Meade let the enemy escape. In driving Lee from Pennsylvania, he reminded Lincoln of "an old woman trying to shoo her geese across a creek." [14]

After Lee crossed the Potomac, Halleck told his subordinate to pursue and lacerate the Army of Northern Virginia, keeping between the enemy and Washington and living off the country. He told Meade that Lincoln was greatly dissatisfied because of Lee's escape and he expected an "active and energetic pursuit" immediately.[15]

Lincoln was not the only dissatisfied northern official, although he was one of the few to blame Meade instead of Halleck for Lee's escape. Lincoln told Welles he had not interfered because "Halleck knows better than I what to do. . . . It is better that I, who am not a military man, should defer to him, rather than he to me." In his reverence for the President, Welles, as always, did not question his statement. He vituperated: "I have been unable to see, hear, or obtain evidence of power, or will, or talent, or originality on the part of General Halleck. He has suggested nothing, decided nothing, done nothing but scold and smoke and scratch his elbows." [16]

The country, too, was discontented. Later when a rumor circulated that Halleck was going to leave his desk for the field, one paper's invective read: "The public, which has appreciated the dashing and soldierly qualities of Halleck, will look to his new career with an interest not unmixed with a generous apprehension that his notorious daring may lose him to the country." A congressman sneered: "Put Halleck in the command of twenty thousand men, and he will not scare three setting geese from their nests." The incorrigible Radical, Adam Gurowski, jeered: "As for Jomini-Halleck and Lincoln, Lee knew their mettle." He then wrote Lincoln: "If this noble generous devoted and reliable and sacreligiously butchered people is doomed to be handled after such as McClellan by such

[13] *Ibid:* Part 3, p. 678; Part 1, p. 92.
[14] T. Harry Williams, *Lincoln and His Generals,* 271.
[15] *O.R.,* Ser. I, XXVII, Part 1, p. 92.
[16] Welles, *Diary,* I, 371, 373.

as Halleck; return to McClellan Mr. President; McClellan is the less destructive of the two." [17]

Old Brains did not even attempt to rebuke his accusers. He told one general he made it a rule "never to notice newspaper abuse," and retained his reaction from the public because he believed it was his duty to remain silent—taking arms against the sea of troubles would neither improve his position nor strengthen Lincoln's. He simply wrote Grant: "I sincerely wish I was with you again in the West. I am utterly sick of this political hell." [18]

Meade, too, wanted to be relieved and he seized upon Halleck's message conveying Lincoln's displeasure as an excuse to resign. Halleck told him to interpret the telegram as a stimulus, not a censure, and refused to accept the resignation. Two weeks later Halleck wrote an unofficial letter to lift Meade's morale. Old Brains told the snapping turtle the fight at Gettysburg met "with the universal approbation of all military men . . ." and he might "well be proud of that battle." Casually turning Meade's attention to subsequent events, Halleck mentioned that the general should not have been surprised at Lincoln's disappointment, for the President thought Lee's extermination a certainty—thus he felt "no little impatience at his unexpected escape." Halleck spoke of Meade's "superior generalship," and concluded forcefully: "I need not assure you, general, that I have lost none of the confidence which I felt in you when I recommended you for the command." [19]

Two days before Halleck dispatched his letter, Meade had partially recovered and asked if Halleck wanted him to reoccupy the Shenandoah Valley, which Lee had abandoned. The proposal seemed to

[17] *Wilkes' Spirit of the Times,* May 6, 1865; Adam Gurowski, *Diary 1863–1865* (Washington, 1866), 19, 297; Gurowski to Lincoln, undated, Gurowski Papers (Library of Congress).

[18] *O.R.,* Ser. I, XXXII, Part 2, p. 407; XXIV, Part 3, p. 498. Halleck told Sherman: "I cannot say to the public I approve this and I disapprove that. I have no right to say this, as it might embarrass the execution of a measure fully decided on. It is my duty to strengthen the hands of the President as Commander-in-Chief, not to weaken them by factious opposition."

[19] *O.R.,* Ser. I, XXVII, Part 1, pp. 93, 104.

come from McClellan's pen. Halleck rejected the idea, telling
Meade that "Lee's army is the objective point." [20] With the statement, and by later actions, Halleck showed that he was modifying
one of Jomini's precepts to meet the situation in the East. The armies
were fighting over a small area and no one place had any over-
whelming economic or strategic importance. Lee could have shifted
his base of operations away from Richmond much easier than Pemberton could have from Vicksburg, or later, Johnston from Atlanta.
The capture of Richmond would be a moral victory; that of Vicksburg added powerful economic and strategic advantages. Halleck
recognized this when he maintained that the fall of Vicksburg was
worth "forty Richmonds," and he was beginning to see that in the
East, Lee's army, not Richmond, was the true objective.

But Lee's army was to enjoy a long period of quiet. On July 29,
Lincoln told Halleck he had no desire to force Meade into battle. In
language he learned from his general-in-chief, the President said he
was "unwilling" that Meade "should now get into a general engagement on the idea that we here are pressing him." At 2:30 that
Wednesday afternoon, Halleck told Meade to discontinue a pursuit
that had never really been mounted.[21]

For a variety of reasons, Meade did not get fired after out-pro-
crastinating McClellan. He had no entrenched political enemies; he
had won a more dramatic victory at Gettysburg than McClellan at
Antietam; he had not fanned Halleck's hatred; and above all there
was no one remaining to replace him.

The Army of the Potomac would not fight again that year. The
civilians turned soldiers could enjoy a long overdue vacation and
rest while their managers repaired the machinery. Halleck took the
lead in the restoration. He told Meade to collect all the forage and
provisions left in northern Virginia, clean out the guerillas operating
behind Union lines, and to cut down on his transportation. On
August 7, Halleck drastically reduced the trains of the superflu-
ously supplied Army of the Potomac. Knowing that his action

[20] *Ibid.,* 101.
[21] Basler (ed.), *Collected Works of Abraham Lincoln,* VI, 354.

"would be considered 'niggardly,'" Halleck still maintained: "One thing is certain, we must reduce our transportation or give up all idea of competing with the enemy in the field." Napoleon, he remembered, had calculated the effective strength of an army by multiplying its numbers by its mobility. Ten thousand men who could march twenty miles a day were worth 20,000 who could only cover ten miles a day.[22] The "impedimenta" of the Army of the Potomac was too large, but Halleck's treatment of the symptom did not cure the disease. The army operated in tempting proximity to the fountainhead of wealth, Washington, whose storehouses were easily accessible. Needlessly so in Halleck's eyes, Meade's army would remain the best equipped in the service.

In the West, after Vicksburg, Halleck followed the same trail he had plotted the year before. Because of the vast distances in the area he thought of the war there as one of position, of securing and holding places followed by concentration of forces. Halleck answered the question of how to employ Grant's army in terms of temporary dispersion—just as he had done after Corinth, Halleck again consolidated his gains.

Halleck returned the Ninth Corps to Tennessee and ordered re-inforcements down to Banks. Grant had suggested leaving his army intact and moving on Mobile, but Halleck thought it would be "best to clean up a little" first. He wanted Arkansas and Louisiana cleared of "organized rebel forces," Johnston's army disposed of, and Vicksburg and Port Hudson remolded "so as to be tenable by small garrisons." Then Grant could use the Mississippi as a base of operations, either to go to Mobile or into Texas.[23]

Halleck purposely neglected to inform Grant at the time, but he knew that the Mobile operation, according to Washington solons, was definitely a poor relation when held up to the stern criterion of economic necessity. There were long ignored, but still powerfully felt forces in Washington which made an invasion of Texas impera-tive. As early as 1861 political leaders in the cotton factory states of

[22] *O.R.*, Ser. I, XXIX, Part 2, p. 13.
[23] *O.R.*, Ser. I, XXIV, Part 3, p. 542.

the northeast had been angling for an advance into the Lone Star State. Governor John Andrew of Massachusetts outlined to the Assistant Secretary of the Navy the historical and military reasons. "Texas we virtually bought," Andrew said, and she had no right to secede—besides, she "flanks the whole rebellion." As an afterthought Andrew alluded to the possibility of obtaining cotton bales from the Confederacy through Texas.[24]

Soon after he entered Washington, Halleck had sensed the undercurrents, and in August of 1862, ordered Grant to exert himself and "see that all possible facilities are afforded for getting out cotton." In November, 1862, Halleck had discussed with Banks the operations which would take place after the Mississippi was opened. The primary objective would be to ascend the Red River, "and thus open an outlet for the sugar and cotton of Northern Louisiana." [25] From the Red River, Banks could invade Texas.

Lincoln added his voice to the clamor: "I believe no local object is now more desirable" than a movement into Texas, he told Banks.[26] Lincoln was neither greasing the palm of the greedy cotton speculator nor seeking employment for the needy factory workers in Massachusetts; he wanted to get his own special brand of Reconstruction marketed in as many states as possible before Congress refused them the commodity. He also feared Napoleon III's puppet, Maximilian, in Mexico. Both he and Seward wanted to substantiate their remonstrance to the second-rate reincarnation of Bonaparte by flying the United States flag in Texas.

Halleck was theoretically opposed to the scattering of the forces, and Jomini's principle of concentration on vital points in this case meant Mobile rather than Texas. Old Brains had stated in *Elements:* "Converging lines of operation are preferable, under most circumstances, to diverging lines." [27] Once again, however, his theories

[24] *O.R.,* Ser. I, XV, 412.
[25] *Ibid.,* 590. For an excellent discussion of the entire situation, see Ludwell H. Johnson, *Red River Campaign: Politics and Cotton in the Civil War* (Baltimore, 1958).
[26] *O.R.,* Ser. I, XXVI, Part I, p. 659.
[27] Halleck, *Elements of Military Art and Science,* 53.

underwent modification to meet the exigencies of the situation. He adjusted his thinking to the political demands and in July of 1863, after Port Hudson followed Vicksburg's fall, ordered Banks to clean out southwestern Louisiana and prepare for an expedition into Texas. He promised reinforcements from Grant. But Banks had already tried to invade the Lone Star State; he did not want to fail again and proposed instead an expedition against Mobile. Halleck appreciated the importance of the Alabama port, but said there were "reasons other than military" for his other refusal; "On this matter we have no choice, but must carry out the views of the Government." [28]

On July 30, Halleck began sending Banks reinforcements, and the general launched another abortive attempt to invade Texas. For a year Banks would try to pitch a tent on Texas soil, but "Nothing Positive's" own indecision, hesitation, and the general lack of efficiency precluded any chance of success. Once again the country reverberated with criticism.

But Banks at least had been willing to move, which was more than Halleck could get from Meade. The old snapping turtle had found a quiet pool of backwater and resisted all efforts to push him back into the swift current of battle. By mid-September his reorganization was complete, and Lincoln told Halleck it was time to pressure Lee again. "Of course," the President added, "my opinion is not to control you and General Meade." [29]

If Banks were guilty of indecision in Louisiana, Halleck added the evil of excessive caution in Washington. Meade was incapable of forming his own plans; Halleck would not plan a campaign for him. Instead he sent contradictory messages that served only to infuriate Meade. On September 15 Halleck asked his subordinate to discover the condition of affairs in Lee's army. There were, however, no reinforcements available so "no rash movements can . . . be ven-

---

[28] *O.R.*, Ser. I, XXVI, Part 1, pp. 652, 675, 835; XXXI, Part 3, p. 376; New York *World*, September 26, 1863; Fred Harvey Harrington, *Fighting Politician: Major General N. P. Banks* (Philadelphia, 1948), 151–57.

[29] *O.R.*, Ser. I, XXIX, Part 2, p. 187.

tured." Still there were rumors that Lee had sent a corps to Bragg in Tennessee, and Halleck told Meade that, if Lee were weak, he should make him weaker.[30]

On September 19 Halleck sent Meade some figures the President had been pondering. Lincoln had heard it said throughout the war that three men on the offensive were barely equal to two on the defense, and decided that since Meade was on the defense anyway, why could he not drop down to 40,000 and use the spare 50,000 somewhere else. In other words, Meade could stand on the defense against Lee's 60,000 with 40,000 as well as with 90,000.[31]

Meade ignored Lincoln's mathematics and remained at full strength in his sedentary position. At Lincoln's insistence, Halleck made an attempt to implement action. He wanted to know if Lee was steadily shifting troops to Bragg, and to make his request emphatic, he relied on military history: "When King Joseph wrote to Napoleon that he could not ascertain the position and strength of the enemy's army, the Emperor replied: 'Attack him and you will soon find out.'" By then it was October and Longstreet's corps had gone west. Almost from habit, Halleck continued to urge Meade to fight. Lincoln was so anxious for a move he did what Halleck never dared; he promised that if Meade would fight "the honor will be his if he succeeds, and the blame may be mine if he fails." Halleck forwarded the note to Meade without comment. Two days later, after Meade complained he did not know where Lee was, Halleck again alluded to the dialogue between King Joseph and Napoleon.[32]

Meade was thoroughly exasperated. He retorted that if Halleck gave him orders he would obey them, but he insisted "on being spared the infliction of such truisms in the guise of opinions as you have recently honored me with, particularly as they were not asked for." Again he reqtested to be relieved. Once more Halleck became a pacifier. He had not repeated truisms to give offense, but to convey the wishes of the Government. If he had "used words which were

---

[30] *Ibid.*   [31] *Ibid.,* 206.
[32] *Ibid.,* 278, 332, 346.

unpleasing," he sincerely regretted it.[33] To another general Halleck expressed different feelings. The Army of the Potomac, he said, fought well when attacked, "but all its generals have been unwilling to attack, even very inferior numbers. It certainly is a very strange phenomenon." [34]

It was the closest Halleck ever came to recognizing the difference between his eastern and western commanders. In general the Eastern officers had an unconscious, unmitigated fear of Lee; those in the West held their opponents in contempt. But Old Brains did not follow his observation to its logical conclusion; he treated both sets of officers exactly the same. Cautioning Grant to keep his forces together during the Vicksburg campaign worked to the Union's advantage; cautioning Meade profited the Confederates.

[33] *Ibid.,* 347, 354.   [34] *Ibid.,* 277.

CHAPTER TWELVE

RESPONSIBILITY AND ODIUM

It has been said that you are as inactive as was General Buell," Halleck chastized Rosecrans, "and the pressure for your removal has been almost as strong as it [was] in his case."[1]

Old Brains felt justified in comparing Rosecrans and Buell; Rosecrans had done almost nothing since the first day of the new year. In June, after repeated threats from Halleck, Rosecrans had forced Bragg south of the Tennessee River, but since the brief excursion his army remained immobile. While Grant took Vicksburg, Rosecrans serenely watched and waited and did nothing. Any cooperation that had existed between the two armies was gone—if Halleck could not create some the war in the West would degenerate rapidly into a series of small, independent battles.

Other factors made an advance imperative. Control of Chattanooga would give the north a springboard pointing toward the interior of the south; Bragg's army was the second strongest Confederate army and must be crushed; East Tennessee had to be redeemed. The President, Halleck told Rosecrans on July 25, had "repeatedly promised" relief to the citizens of East Tennessee and they must be freed. "The pressure for this movement at this time is so strong that neither you nor I can resist it," he admonished.[2]

Rosecrans did resist the pressure and moreover took offense at Halleck's tone. With a long, weary sigh Old Brains seated himself

---

[1] *O.R.*, Ser. I, XXIII, Part 2, p. 552.
[2] *Ibid.*, 554.

to explain once again his motives to the exasperating, puerile Rosecrans. "In other words, general," Halleck patiently summed up, "while I am blamed here for not urging you forward more rapidly, you are displeased at my doing so." Then, on August 4, Halleck threw the whole weight of his position behind an order to Rosecrans. The general should advance "without further delay," and was to report daily until he had crossed the Tennessee River.[3] Remembering Halleck's previous assertions that he would never interfere in local matters, Rosecrans asked if the order were intended to remove his "discretion as to the time and manner of moving."

Halleck spat out an answer: "The orders for the advance of your army, and that its movements be reported daily, are peremptory." The object, Halleck explained two days later, was stated in "plain and unequivocal terms"—Rosecrans should execute it. As for "discretion," Rosecrans was free to employ what means and follow which roads he chose, and if he sincerely desired to implement the wishes of the government he would "not stop to discuss mere details." Halleck did not interfere in "such matters."[4]

Rosecrans tried another dodge—enemies in the War Department prevented him from accomplishing anything. Nonsense, Halleck scoffed. Everyone in the capital admired Rosecrans, although the intensity of his brilliant star was diminishing. War Department officials were irritated with his penchant for writing telegrams and his almost total lack of any other form of activity. Halleck told the general the officials were saying Rosecrans did "not draw straight in the traces," but was "continually kicking out or getting one leg over."[5]

Eventually yielding to the pressure, Rosecrans dropped his pen, picked up his sword, and moved straight for Bragg. In a series of intricate manoeuvres he proved his ability as a manipulator of troops—at least non-combatant troops—and gained control of Chattanooga without a battle. Highly irritated at Washington's attitude and determined to prove his mettle, Rosecrans hardly paused.

[3] *Ibid.*, 592.   [4] *Ibid.*, 592, 597.
[5] *Ibid.*, 601.

Drawing from a new found source of energy, he pushed after Bragg, who had retreated into Georgia.

Satisfied that action had finally come, Halleck tried to help. During the burst of activity he ordered Burnside to start reinforcements to Rosecrans, told Grant to move to Tuscumbia, Alabama, where he could operate on Bragg's flank, and drew men from other fields.[6]

The reinforcements did not arrive in time. On September 19 at Chickamauga Creek Rosecrans caught up with Bragg, who in fact was waiting in ambush. Bragg was in the process of receiving his reinforcements, almost a corps from Lee's army, and launched his attack at dawn. For one of the few times in the war the Confederates outnumbered the Federals. During the battle Halleck tried to get Burnside to move on Bragg's right from his new headquarters at Knoxville, but to no avail.[7]

When the battle at Chickamauga turned against him, Rosecrans fled back to Chattanooga with some of his troops. Others, under Thomas, stayed on the field and repulsed several Confederate attacks before withdrawing.

The blue infantry would soon learn that retaining the city was a more formidable task than repulsing Confederate dashes on solid entrenchments; the soldiers could fight men but not starvation. Bragg initiated a siege of Chattanooga, spreading the wings of his army to engulf Rosecrans on three sides. The open end, to the north, was mountainous country through which it was impossible to send supplies, Halleck and Lincoln, however, determined to hold the city; "It keeps all Tennessee clear of the enemy," Lincoln said, "and also breaks one of his most important Railroad lines." Chattanooga itself was a convenient springboard for invasions either north or south. The President had learned from his general-in-chief the value of places in the West. "The details must of course be left to General Rosecrans," Lincoln continued in language borrowed from Halleck, "while we must furnish him the means, to the utmost of our ability." Halleck tried to build up a concentration, marshalling

6 *Ibid.*, XXX: Part 1, p. 35; Part 3, p. 643.
7 *Ibid.*, Part 1, p. 130.

reinforcements to Chattanooga from Grant, Burnside, and Sherman; still he feared they would arrive too late to be effective.[8] But his professional mind was exhausted—he had run out of ideas.

Civilian strategists were about to instruct West Pointers on one aspect of modern war. On Wednesday night, September 23, Halleck joined an urgent conference at the War Department. Stanton, Seward, Chase, Halleck, Hooker, Lincoln and three lesser officials were present. Their entire agenda was the problem of transporting the maximum number of reinforcements to Chattanooga in the minimum amount of time. Rosecrans had wired Washington, saying he could hold out for only ten more days.

Stanton opened the conference by interrogating Halleck—he wanted to know how many men Burnside could send to Rosecrans.

"Twenty thousand in ten days," Halleck replied.

"How many in eight days?" Stanton asked.

"12,000."

"When will Sherman's army reach Rosecrans?"

"In about ten days. . . ."

"Are any more available elsewhere?"

Hardly any, Halleck replied. Then, as midnight approached, Stanton placed his proposal before Lincoln. He would send 30,000 men from the Army of the Potomac to Rosecrans on the railroads. He said they could be there in five days.

"I bet that if the order is given tonight, the troops could not be got to Washington in five days," Lincoln rejoined.

Ignoring the President's skepticism, Stanton said that if the government took complete possession of the railroads they could ship 30,000 cotton bails in that time—why could not 30,000 men go as well? If not 30,000, Stanton continued, then at least 20,000.

A general discussion followed. Although they failed to realize it, the officials had reached a critical stage in the history of war. Twice the Confederacy had used her limited railroads for large troop movements, but the North had not even made the experiment. In

[8] Rosecrans to Halleck, September 20, 1863, Robert Todd Lincoln Papers; Lincoln to Halleck, September 21, 1863, *ibid.*

the argument the civilians advocated the innovation while the soldiers stuck to precedent—it couldn't be done, they maintained. Lincoln listened to and sided with his general-in-chief.

After two hours of fierce debate, Halleck, Hooker and Lincoln, with reservations, surrendered. At 2:30 in the morning Halleck wired Rosecrans: ". . . 14,000 or 15,000 men from here will be in Nashville in about seven days." Then he sped the necessary orders to Meade. It was a tribute to the new efficiency of the military railroads—an efficiency Halleck helped create—that the Washington civilians could afford to entertain the idea. It was a greater tribute that the engineers needed little more than the allotted seven days to make the move.[9] The science of war had taken a large step forward.

Old Brains, in fact, was still trying to help Rosecrans in the usual manner. He urged Grant to send all available forces to Chattanooga, while he continued to push at Burnside, whom he had long since ordered to leave Knoxville and go to Rosecrans.[10] But Burnside had halted en route to rest, missing the battle of Chickamauga, and still did not dare move. Halleck had refused to issue orders to Burnside when the bewhiskered general led the Army of the Potomac, but now that Burnside was in the West, he sent a ringing declaration: "You must go to General Rosecrans' assistance, with all your available force, . . . The orders are very plain, and you cannot mistake their purport. It only remains for you to execute them." [11] A month later, with a half-starved army, Burnside was still in Knoxville.

But before Burnside could be saved Bragg had to be eliminated. Since Grant was currently unemployed, Halleck and Lincoln decided to utilize his talents. On October 16 Halleck told the hero of Donelson and Vicksburg to repair to Louisville; there he would

[9] Donald (ed.), *Inside Lincoln's Cabinet,* 201–204; Festus P. Summers, *The Baltimore and Ohio in the Civil War* (New York, 1939), 167; Kamm, *Civil War Career of Thomas A. Scott,* 165; *O.R.,* Ser. I, XXIX, Part 1, p. 150; Halleck to Meade, September 24, 1863, Edwin M. Stanton MSS.
[10] *O.R.,* Ser. I, XXX, Part 3, p. 923.
[11] *Ibid.,* 906.

meet an officer from the War Department bearing his instruction. They were orders to assume command of all the departments and armies in the West, including Rosecrans'. Grant could retain Rosecrans or replace him as he wished. He was free to make any other changes he deemed advisable. Grant used his power at once, relieving Rosecrans in favor of Thomas before he arrived in Chattanooga.[12]

After a year of incessant hesitation and delay, climaxed by an ill-conceived and mismanaged battle, there was a new commander in Tennessee. There was also a different command system, similar to the old arrangement under Halleck. Grant could take command of any army in the West whenever he chose and direct the whole; the possibility of one army waiting for another to conclude a battle before mobilizing was lessened, if not removed.

A minor problem confronting Grant was Burnside's besiegement. Longstreet had left Bragg and was surrounding Burnside in Knoxville while Bragg continued to engulf the Federal Army at Chattanooga. Halleck wrote Grant that he outnumbered Bragg and should encounter no difficulty defeating him, provided he obtained supplies. Reassuringly, Halleck concluded: "You have never complained before, I doubt that you will have to now." [13]

On November 5, when Grant took command in Chattanooga, Halleck again reviewed the situation with him and scribbled some more suggestions. Since Burnside could barely feed the troops he had, no more men should be sent to Knoxville and although Sherman was marching toward Chattanooga, it was inadvisable to concentrate more soldiers than necessary in the city because it also was plagued by a food shortage. Instead of allowing Sherman to join him, Grant should send him on a raid to Atlanta, Bragg's supply depot. If Sherman could destroy Atlanta, Bragg would have to retreat.[14] The plan was an expression of the Jominian idea of manoeuvre and of Halleck's belief that, in the West, places were more important than armies; Old Brains would

---

[12] *Ibid.*, Part 4, p. 404.   [13] *Ibid.*, XXXI, Part 1, p. 667.
[14] *Ibid.*

prefer the capture of Atlanta to the destruction of Bragg's army. Grant, however, decided against Halleck's strategy and refused to change Sherman's orders.

After his arrival in Chattanooga, Grant quickly opened a "cracker line" into the city. On November 24, he proved that he did his best work if not hampered by binding instructions from the General-in-chief. He attacked and completely routed Bragg.

Halleck and Lincoln sent brief congratulations; both messages concluded with a request to look after Burnside. The next day Halleck related the victory to one of Lincoln's recent perfunctory proclamations: "I congratulate you and your army on the victories of Chattanooga. This is truly a day of Thanksgiving." [15] Much like a father looking after his errant boy, Grant went to Burnside's relief soon after the battle. Bragg had retreated south into Georgia, and Longstreet, threatened by a rear attack from Grant's army, had to lift the siege.

During the rest of the winter, the North pushed no active engagements. Meade continued to watch Lee despite Halleck's habitual protests. Old Brains wanted to send Sherman to Banks, who was again gadding about northern Louisiana, but Grant rejected the idea. Instead Sherman operated in Alabama and northern Mississippi, mainly to keep his men in marching condition.[16]

With active operations suspended until spring, Halleck turned his attention to winning the peace as well as the war. He had increased his own importance—and that of the military—through his contact with Lincoln. Now Halleck wanted to use the army's newly gained stature and make it the architect of reconstruction.

During the summer of 1863, Halleck had asked Sherman for his views on reconstruction, saying the North's "ultimate and complete success" depended on the manner in which the peace was made. He felt that the task was formidable, but thought Lincoln could accomplish it if he would "consult opinions of cool and discreet men, who are capable of looking at it in all its bearings and

[15] *Ibid.,* Part 2, p. 25.
[16] *Ibid.,* XXIX, Part 2, p. 495; XXXI, Part 3, p. 458.

effects." Lincoln was displaying a disconcerting tendency to refuse advice on reconstruction; Halleck wanted to force West Point opinion on him. Although he claimed to be against political interference in military matters, he was now advocating military interference in politics. Hopefully he told Sherman: "I think he [Lincoln] is disposed to receive the advice of our generals who have been in these states and know much more of their condition than gassy politicians in Congress." Halleck requested the same opinions from Grant, McPherson and other officers "as I may wish to use them with the President." [17]

Sherman replied that he deemed it "very unwise at this time, or for years to come, to revive the State governments. . . ." Halleck agreed. The rebellion must be put down by armed force; there could be no "compromise and offers of peace, as proposed by Northern copperheads. The conquered territory must . . . be governed by military authority" until the states were fully reconstructed.[18] But in his eagerness to impose his opinions on the President, Halleck had misjudged Lincoln's disposition to receive them. When Halleck presented Sherman's letter to Lincoln, the politician made it clear he did not want any advice on the subject, and Old Brains' dream of a reconstruction directed by the military vanished.

Despite the failure of their plan for reconstruction, Halleck and Sherman continued to correspond and compliment each other. Much had happened since their parting in July, 1862, when "Cump" had told Old Brains that no one could replace him in the West. A new galaxy of stars had risen: Sherman himself, Grant, Thomas, Sheridan, McPherson. Yet, in December of 1863, Sherman could tell his brother: "Halleck has more capacity than anybody in the army. Grant has qualities Halleck doesn't, but not such as would qualify him to command the whole army. The war hasn't developed his equal as a commander in chief." [19]

[17] Sherman, *Memoirs,* I, 363.
[18] *Ibid; O.R.,* Ser. I, LII, Part 1, p. 717.
[19] Sherman to Senator John Sherman, December 20, 1863, John Sherman Manuscripts (Library of Congress).

Halleck confided in his friend and subordinate. When Congress created the new rank of lieutenant general, he told Sherman that everyone knew Grant would be chosen for the post and implied he would also become general-in-chief. Old Brains said he would "welcome [Grant] to the command, glad to be relieved from so thankless and disagreeable a position." Since he had taken it against his will, Halleck would gladly relinquish the post.

"The great difficulty in the office of General-in-chief is," Halleck said, "that it is not understood by the country." As his pen flew across the page, he poured months of frustration into a single sentence: "The responsibility and odium thrown upon it does not belong to it." His true position, as Halleck viewed it, was military advisor to the Secretary of War and the President. Although he told Lincoln and Stanton when he disagreed with them, he regarded it as his professional duty to "faithfully carry out their decision." The West Point cadet had not dissipated his training: "As a good soldier, I obey the orders of my superiors."

In strengthening the hands of the President, the General-in-chief was compelled to refrain from saying publicly "I approve this and I disapprove that," since "it might embarrass the execution of a measure fully decided on." Halleck trusted history to "vindicate or condemn" his "opinions and plans." He had previously told Sherman: "If I do not survive the war, sufficient materials for a correct understanding of my acts are on record and will be found by the future historian who seeks the truth." [20]

But Halleck's self-proclaimed interpretation of the duties of a general-in-chief did not explicate all its ramifications. It could not. Just as his evolving opinions on war symbolized the transformation of American military thought, his era as general-in-chief was transitional. Halleck stood between the old and the new and tried to balance one against the other.

In the strategical field Halleck made great, although unoriginal, contributions. Halleck was Jomini's high priest in America; ever since the 1840's and the publication of *Elements of Military Art*

[20] *O.R.*, Ser. I, XXXII, Part 2, p. 407; LII, Part 1, p. 717.

and Science, Halleck had intoned Jomini's concepts of war. And the Swiss Baron's ideas had dominated the thinking of the professional soldiers of the era; both Confederate and Union generals emphasized concentration, holding places, interior lines, and battles of manoeuvre rather than slugging contests. Sometimes they seemed to be more concerned with following Jomini's principles than they were with success.

Halleck, who knew Jomini best, was better able to modify his teachings to meet changing situations than some of his fellow professionals. Until July, 1862, when he came to Washington, Halleck seldom had questioned the propriety of beginning his offensives from a strong base of operations, and directing the offensives against places rather than the enemy armies. But he soon learned that the war in the East, where the armies did most of their fighting in a 100 mile area between Richmond and Washington, was of a different nature. Taking a place, Richmond, would not materially hasten the end of the war, since Lee could easily shift his base of operations. Moreover, if the Union army moved into Richmond, Washington would be unprotected and Lee would take the Northern capital. This "swapping Queens" would benefit neither side. McClellan, Burnside and Hooker had not agreed; they had been willing to abandon Washington any time Lee left Richmond unprotected. But Halleck and Lincoln had overruled them, for they realized that the war in the East must be one of concentration against Lee's army and that the Confederate army, not Richmond, was the true objective.

Lincoln tended to feel the same way about operations in the West, but here Halleck refused to abandon his Jomini, and he soon convinced Lincoln that operations in that theater were of a different nature. Old Brains had expressed the difference when he calculated that one Vicksburg was worth forty Richmonds; he felt almost as strongly about Nashville, Chattanooga, Atlanta, and other Western cities. With the vast distances involved, no army could operate without a strong base of operations, and as the Union armies progressively captured and held the Southern cities they left the Confederates "up in the air." The Western Confederate armies were never really defeated; they merely disintegrated as it became increasingly difficult to supply them. This Halleck saw, and he made Lincoln see it. Halleck's successful influence on the President's thinking would best be demonstrated during Sherman's march to the sea, when Lincoln did not stop the general from marching away from an enemy army and toward a place.

Halleck had also brought reform and efficiency to the army. His diplomacy had helped generals work at their optimum. But the essence of his invaluable service was the coordination he had brought where none had existed. Shifting reinforcements with the least possible friction and waste, he synchronized operations and speeded the ultimate victory. He was, in short, the manager of the Northern effort—the man who brought about the professionalization of the army, supplied it, gave it rules and regulations while serving as the military liaison with the civilian government.

On March 9, 1864, after Halleck saw Grant appointed lieutenant general in the Regular Army, he requested that Grant be made general-in-chief of the army, a request with which Lincoln soon complied.[21] Like his subordinate, Lincoln was not oblivious to history's judgments, and he explained to his private secretaries why he let Halleck go. He had wanted Old Brains to take "the full powers and responsibilities of general-in-chief," which Halleck had done until Pope's defeat, Lincoln said, "but ever since that event he has shrunk from responsibility whenever it was possible." [22] That made Halleck responsible for withdrawing McClellan from the Peninsula and for Pope's defeat, but not for the victories at Antietam, Gettysburg, Vicksburg, nor Chattanooga.

Sherman took a different view of the matter. Although his prophecy that "the man who won the Mississippi would be THE man," came true, Sherman still believed "Halleck has more reserve book-learning and knowledge of men than Grant, and is therefore better qualified for his present post; whereas the latter, by his

---

[21] Halleck to Stanton, March 9, 1864, Robert Todd Lincoln Papers; see also T. Harry Williams, *Lincoln and His Generals*, 301.

[22] T. Harry Williams, *Lincoln and His Generals*, 305.

honesty, simplicity, candor and reliance on friends, is better suited to act with soldiers." [23]

It was a shrewd analysis of both Grant and Halleck. Despite his constant mutterings about the politicians, Old Brains liked the interplay of intrigue and political strategy, power and politics, and office seeking—the excitement that Washington generated. He enjoyed being on the inside ring of the big circus; Grant did not, and after barely stopping in the city long enough to shake Lincoln's hand and look up into his face, he left for the field and Meade's army, where he stayed until the end of the war. He traveled with the Army of the Potomac while acting as general-in-chief. Halleck switched his title—he became chief of staff—but not his residence nor his duties. He stayed in Washington and did exactly what he had been doing for the past two years.

[23] M. A. DeWolfe Howe (ed.), *Home Letters of General Sherman* (New York, 1909), 287.

CHAPTER THIRTEEN

CHIEF OF STAFF

Old Brains' new position as chief of staff to the Army, Hooker decided, was "very much like a fellow marrying a woman with the understanding that he should not *sleep* with her." Hooker expressed the feelings of many of his fellow officers. There was uncertainty about the responsibilities of the new office. Was Halleck, next to Grant, the ranking officer in the Army? Could he, in the name of either the General-in-chief or the President, give orders to commanders in the field? Was he the directing head of the various bureaus and departments in Washington?

General Orders No. 98, which Lincoln issued to create the new command system, did not clarify the issue. Grant was general-in-chief, but the Head Quarters of the Army were "in Washington, and also with Lieutenant General Grant in the field." Lincoln did not explain how the Head Quarters could be in two places, under one man, at the same time. He did, however, appoint Halleck "Chief-of-staff of the Army, under the direction of the Secretary of War and the Lieutenant General commanding," and indicated that his headquarters be in Washington. Lincoln added that Halleck's orders should be "obeyed and respected"; evidently he wanted Halleck to run the "Head Quarters" in Washington and Grant those in the field. Halleck told Lieber that he would have preferred to command the Western army, but "I am perfectly willing to labor wherever the Prest., Secty of War & Genl Grant decide that I can be most useful. As the latter has determined to remain in the field some one must be here to attend to the vast amount of military-administrative duty connected with the war Dept & Head Qrs of the Army." And Grant, according to his chief of staff, had "great confidence and friendship for the General-in-chief, and would without regard to rank be willing at all times to receive orders through him."[1]

The final solution of the command problem the army solons agreed upon—unofficially and never formally—was a practical rather than a theoretical one. The command system became a loose, working arrangement that could change for any emergency. Grant and Halleck defined Old Brains' duties as essentially those he had fulfilled as general-in-chief, compounded with new and important additions to meet the Army's needs.

Halleck was not the celibate Hooker envisioned. He distributed reinforcements to the armies with his usual skill, coached generals in the field, directed the maintenance of supply lines, secured sufficient provisions to flow through them, coordinated diverse civilian and military enterprises, and tried to raise the level of the army from amateur to professional. Halleck had gained experience for all these duties as general-in-chief; it required little effort to re-orient himself.

He also assumed a new and demanding role. From the spring of 1864 until the end of the war Old Brains acted as liaison between Lincoln and Grant and between Grant and the departmental commanders. Halleck translated Grant's desires for Lincoln and at Grant's request processed an enormous amount of reports, demands, and plans received by the War Department from field generals—he boiled them down and sent their essences to the new general-in-chief. In one sixty word telegram Halleck informed Grant of the movements in four departments and transmitted a request, which he had already fulfilled, from another.[2] When Sherman began his campaign against Johnston, he sent daily reports to Halleck, who re-

[1] Hooker to Chandler, Z. Chandler Manuscripts (Library of Congress); Basler (ed.), *Collected Works of Abraham Lincoln*, VII, 239; Halleck to Lieber, March 14, 1864, Lieber Collection; K. P. Williams, *Lincoln Finds a General*, V, 374.　　[2] *O.R.*, Ser. I, XXXIII, 878.

duced them to a sentence and forwarded them to Grant.[3] The General-in-chief, in turn, sent his orders to Halleck, who reworded and forwarded them to the departmental commanders. A highly capable administrator, Halleck adequately directed army affairs and still found time to translate Jomini's life of Napoleon. Without Halleck in the army, Grant would have found it impossible to travel with Meade in Virginia.

The arrangement of Grant in Virginia and Halleck in Washington evolved slowly, painfully. In the spring of 1864 Halleck told Grant he would go wherever the General-in-chief desired, for he was "willing to serve anywhere and everywhere." But Halleck was cognizant of his own abilities and services, and was reluctant to leave the Capital: "Just at the present crisis," he observed, "it might not be well to derange the machinery here. There must be some military head here to keep things from getting into a snarl." Someone, Halleck stated, had "to make the different bureaus act in concert and with promptness"; it was "impossible" for Stanton or his assistants to "attend personally to these matters." [4] To Halleck's delight, Grant decided that Old Brains should stay in Washington. The results were beneficial both to the Army of the Potomac and the General-in-chief himself. The personal cooperation between Halleck and Grant—which began with the Vicksburg campaign—moved to a larger scene.

Grant's decision to direct the Army of the Potomac created an ideal situation in the East. With Grant at its head, in fact if not in name, the Northern army became an effective, hard-hitting force. Unlike many of the eastern generals, Grant had no fear of Lee and no qualms over encountering him in battle. Unlike McClellan, Burnside, Hooker and the others, he made his decisions quickly and executed them swiftly. Halleck, who could never rouse the Army of the Potomac to action, supplied it with provisions and reinforcements, duties for which he was best suited. Confident of having his orders fulfilled, Grant was free to concentrate on Lee.

---

[3] See *ibid.*, Part 4, *passim.*   [4] *Ibid.*, XXXVI, Part 2, p. 328.

Grant began his tenure as general-in-chief with high hopes. He planned an offensive for 1864 in which all the armies would cooperate, with the two principal forces making a double thrust into the Confederacy. Sherman would move south from Chattanooga against Atlanta; Grant would hammer at Lee to prevent the Confederate from shipping reinforcements to Georgia and to annihilate the Army of Northern Virginia. Halleck devoted his energies to reinforcing the two armies and keeping the General-in-chief informed of Sherman's moves. At first the concept and the system worked well. Ultimately the idea of cooperation failed and then, more by accident than design, was restored.

Halleck tried to anticipate Grant's desires, keep both the Army of the Potomac and Sherman well supplied, and leave Grant free from unnecessary worry. He had a pontoon bridge constructed at Fredericksburg before Grant needed it; he had 20,000 reinforcements ready for the western army before Sherman requested them.[5] Grant relinquished all details of running the army to Halleck as he engaged Lee in a death struggle. On May 5, after crossing the Rapidan, Grant received Lee's attack in the Wilderness, a forlorn area near Chancellorsville, and by May 7 had repulsed the assaults. Contrary to the custom of the Army of the Potomac, Grant then continued to march south instead of retreating across the Rapidan. By May 11 he had again come to grips with Lee, this time near Spotsylvania Courthouse. His losses were tremendous. Busily establishing a hospital at Fredericksburg, Halleck anxiously asked Grant to inform him of the position and condition of the army so that he could anticipate its demands.[6] Grant's reply was brief and lucid—he needed fresh supplies of provisions and ammunition and proposed "to fight it out on this line if it takes all summer."[7]

Halleck constantly sent Grant encouragement and, more important, reinforcements. On May 12 Halleck promised 10,000 men within a day with 4,000 to follow. Without prompting Halleck assured Grant he could shift the supply base at Belle Plain south when-

---

[5] *Ibid.*, XXXVIII, Part 4, p. 25.   [6] *Ibid.*, XXXVI, Part 2, p. 628.
[7] *Ibid.*, 627.

ever Grant required. The North had complete control of the sea and with the aid of the navy Halleck could move a supply depot without fear of enemy raids.[8] Three days later Halleck rounded up more reinforcements and sent them on to Belle Plain. He simplified his own and Grant's problems by providing each of the "6,000 splendid infantry" with five days' rations and 150 rounds of cartridges. Halleck estimated that 30,000 more troops could join the army within a few days.[9] By May 21 Grant had forced Lee closer to Richmond and was ready to shift his supply depot—Halleck handled the transfer with customary calm and lack of friction. He sent detailed instructions to the Engineer, Quartermaster, Commissary, Medical and Railroad departments, then delegated the authority to the departmental heads.[10] The new base at Port Royal was soon in functioning order.

The arrangement was working well. In May, Halleck shipped Grant nearly 50,000 men,[11] and by June 2 stated he had "nearly exhausted" all possible resources of volunteers. However, he managed to scout up "six or eight good regiments of 100 days' militia," and sent them on to Grant.[12] The General-in-chief realized he could not stay in the field without Halleck's efforts in Washington, and wired his appreciation: "The promptness and rapidity with which you have forwarded re-enforcements have contributed largely to the feeling of confidence inspired in our men and to break down that of the enemy."[13] Years later, when sneering at Old Brains was the vogue, Grant chose to omit the compliment from his *Memoirs*.[14] The omission's significance could not be mistaken, for Halleck never stopped the flow of reinforcements. By June 15, he had ordered 5,000 more boys to the field, making a total of 55,178.[15]

In mid-June, Grant abandoned his intention to fight it out "on this line if it takes all summer," and, stealing a march on Lee, shifted his army south of the James River. When General William F.

8 *Ibid.*, 652.   9 *Ibid.*, 782.
10 *Ibid.*, Part 3, p. 770.   11 *Ibid.*, 655.
12 *Ibid.*, 478.   13 *Ibid.*, 206.
14 Grant, *Memoirs*, 425.   15 *O.R.*, Ser. I, XL, Part 2, p. 47.

"Baldy" Smith, in local command, hesitated outside the city for two days, Grant reluctantly relinquished his hopes of taking Petersburg, a railroad junction south of Richmond, before Lee could bring up his army. Grant settled into another siege, and Halleck once again with customary facility changed Grant's base of supplies.

After two years of unnerving tempest, Halleck was in his element—administration. Yet newspaper editors decided he was dissatisfied. Rumors that Old Brains was about to resign flitted around Washington. "Trouble with the lieutenant general [Grant] is said to be at the bottom of the matter," the New York *World* announced.[16] Sherman had read the "mischievous paragraph" and having once persuaded Grant to remain in the army, turned his hortatory talents on Halleck. "You possess a knowledge of law and of the principles of war far beyond that of any other officer in our service," Sherman told his superior. "Stability is what we lack in our Government, and changes are always bad," he continued: "Stand by us and encourage us by your counsels and advice. I know Grant esteems you, and I assure you I do." [17]

Halleck replied that stories about quarrels between the President, Secretary of War, General-in-chief and himself were all "bosh" and that Sherman would be happy to learn there was "not a word of truth in them." The relations between Grant and Halleck were "not only friendly and pleasant, but cordial"; for the others, there had not been the "slightest difficulty, misunderstanding, or even difference of opinion between any of the parties." Halleck assured Sherman that he had no intention of resigning as long as his "services [could] be useful to the country." His only grievance was one he had held as general-in-chief. He could not retaliate for the "malicious stories" in the newspapers. "Of course my position here both as General-in-chief and as Chief-of-staff has been a disagreeable one from which I can receive no credit, but," he received, "sufficient abuse to satisfy any ordinary ambition." He boasted that he had become "utterly callous" to criticism, yet forlornly concluded that

[16] New York *World,* April 20, 1864.
[17] *O.R.,* Ser. I, XXXII, Part 3, p. 469.

Grant "very wisely keeps away from Washington, and out of reach of the rascally politicians and shoddy contractors who infest every department of the Government and abuse everybody who will not grind their axes."

Halleck struck back by attacking the political generals who invaded the private domain of West Pointers. "It seems but little better than murder to give important commands to such men as Banks, Butler, McClernand, Sigel, and Lew Wallace," he railed to Sherman. Banks' operations in Louisiana were "about what should be expected from a general so utterly destitute of military education and military capacity."[18]

As general-in-chief, Halleck had worked actively and sometimes successfully to eliminate political soldiers; as chief of staff, he utilized his position to hasten the pace. Halleck had previously informed Sherman he wanted to combine the Department of the Arkansas, under West Point graduate Frederick Steele, and the Department of the Gulf, under Banks, and thereby dump the politico. But because of political considerations, Lincoln refused to allow the merger. Banks controlled numerous votes in New England. Moreover, Halleck needed to produce a man of stature to replace the amateur. Old Brains had thought of Sherman for the replacement, but rejected the idea since Sherman's talents were needed in the field.[19] He had asked Grant to restore Buell to a command.[20] Politically, however, Buell was a featherweight; thus his chance for command in a presidential election year was eliminated.

The General-in-chief would contribute to the stockpile of ammunition Halleck was building against Banks. Grant wanted a professionally led army and wanted the general removed by any means, except one which involved soiling his own hands. Halleck, who was already so caked with intrigue that no amount of scrubbing could launder him, could do Grant's dirty work just as he had done Lincoln's. Banks had pushed up the Red River toward Shreveport with an impressive force, but on April 8 and 9 he was utterly

[18] *Ibid.*, XXXIV, Part 3, p. 332.   [19] *Ibid.*, XXXII, Part 3, p. 289.
[20] *Ibid.*, 322.

routed by a makeshift Confederate army at Sabine Cross Roads. Grant received the news on April 22 and gave Halleck his ammunition. Smugly he wired: "Banks has had a disaster. I have been satisfied for the last nine months that to keep General Banks in command was to neutralize a large force and support it most expensively." He hinted that General Joseph Reynolds, a West Pointer, should be placed in command. When Halleck showed the telegram to Lincoln, however, the President stipulated in endorsement that Grant "must delay acting on it for the present." [21]

But Halleck did not delay action. His first move was to force Banks out of the field. Grant hastily sketched out the orders he wanted transmitted to Banks, saying that the general should leave the troops under the senior officer in his army and go to New Orleans himself.[22] To make the order unequivocally indicate that Banks should leave the field, Halleck changed the wording slightly, then forwarded the message.[23]

On April 29, three days after ordering Banks back to New Orleans, Halleck cautiously outlined the situation to Grant. Halleck thought Lincoln would yield "very reluctantly" to Banks' removal if Grant insisted upon it as a "military necessity." Lincoln's hesitancy resulted from Banks' "many political friends," who would demand for the New Englander a command equal to that of the Department of the Gulf. At this time Halleck might have faltered were it not for the Secretary of War's entrance. When the Chief of staff informed Stanton of his and Grant's manipulations he found the Cabinet member eager to participate. Stanton advised requesting that Grant submit "in definite form precisely the order" of removal he desired. Halleck knew that this request, if successful, would accomplish a double purpose. It would give the removal the authority of Grant's name and absolve himself and Stanton of the blame.[24] But the General-in-chief did not want to be so intimately implicated and made no reply to Halleck's telegram.

A desperate chief of staff explained to Grant why the removal

[21] *Ibid.*, XXXIV, Part 2, p. 252.   [22] *Ibid.*, 279.
[23] *Ibid.*, 293.   [24] *Ibid.*, 331.

could not be effected without his official support. Banks was a "personal friend" of Lincoln's and had "strong political supporters in and out of Congress." Using the methods of the politicians he had so vociferously denounced and utilizing his position as liaison between Grant and Lincoln, Old Brains told the General-in-chief that Lincoln would "act immediately" if Grant sent him a request for Banks' removal. Admitting that he had "no authority" for so saying, Halleck said that it was his opinion, "formed from the last two years' experience . . . that to do an act which will give offense to a large number of his political friends the President will require some evidence in a positive form to show the military necessity of that act," for Lincoln "must have something in a definite shape to fall back upon as his justification" if he fired Banks.[25] After reading the letter Grant decided that it was time to comply with Halleck's request, and formally made his recommendation to Lincoln. On May 7 Halleck informed his West Point classmate, General Edward Canby, that the Departments of the Gulf and Arkansas were now in his command.[26]

Grant did not direct Halleck's relentless activities only toward Banks—there were other amateurs in high command who must be eliminated for the benefit of the army. On the agenda was General Butler, who commanded a force on the James River, east of Richmond and south of Lee's army, at the beginning of Grant's campaign and from whom Grant expected assistance. The General-in-chief thought Butler might possibly interpose between Lee and Richmond or even take Richmond. Though he was dubious, Halleck sent reinforcements to the political general in accordance with Grant's orders. During the campaign Butler allowed a small Confederate force to "bottle" him at Bermuda Hundred, south of the James River, and he did little to influence the fighting. Highly dissatisfied, Grant told Halleck to send an investigating committee to Bermuda Hundred. Halleck gladly sent the "smelling committee," as Butler dubbed it, and they reported that Butler "has not [the] experience and training to enable him to direct and control movements in

----

[25] *Ibid.*, 409.   [26] *Ibid.*, 491.

battle." They suggested that "Baldy" Smith be given the virtual command.[27] Grant noted the report but took no immediate action. Encouraged by the Banks episode, Halleck decided to push the General-in-chief. He was worried about the demands politicians were making for Butler and wanted him removed at once. There were two vacant major-generalcies in the Regular Army; Butler had been nominated for one. Halleck moved swiftly but cautiously. He asked Grant to advise Stanton that Meade and Sherman be elevated to the positions—Halleck did "not wish to see these vacancies left so long unfilled, lest outside political influences may cause the President to fill them by the promotion of persons totally unworthy." Halleck whispered to the General-in-chief that "influences have been exerted in favor of a man utterly unfit to hold any commission in the army," and hinted at conspiracy by the politicians. To counter it he pleaded that Grant hasten the appointment of Sherman and Meade, for after his "splendid victories almost anything . . ." Grant asked would be granted.[28]

But again Grant did not want to become so deeply involved and did not answer. Hopefully Halleck tried an envelopment, suggesting that Grant bring Butler's command into the Army of the Potomac. He did not "like these divided commands, with the enemy intervening," and "would rather use them altogether under your own eye." [29] Again Grant would not comply, so on May 23 Old Brains reminded Grant of the vacancies for major generals, said he tried to get Sherman and Meade appointed but failed, and remarked: "There is some obstacle in the way and I can't remove it." He professed to be ignorant of "outside influences," before proceeding to explain to Grant what they were. The names of Butler and General Daniel Sickles, a Democrat from New York City, had been "strongly urged by politicians, in order they say to break down

[27] William D. Mallam, "The Grant-Butler Relationship," *Mississippi Valley Historical Review* (September, 1954), XLI, 260; *O.R.*, Ser. I, XXXVI, Part 3, pp. 177–78. The two man committee consisted of Montgomery C. Meigs and John G. Barnard.

[28] *O.R.*, Ser. I, XXXVI, Part 3, p. 145.

[29] *Ibid.*, 148.

'West Point influence.'" All this, Halleck concluded, was *"entre nous."* [30]

Finally, when in early June Butler failed in two attempts to take Petersburg, Grant decided to remove him. Once again he would let Halleck do the dirty work. Grant told Old Brains that although Butler was "always clear in his conception of orders and prompt to obey," he nevertheless wanted the politician out of the area. Half the message was consumed with praise of Butler; the other half clearly intimated that Butler must go and that Halleck would have to handle the delicate task. [31] Halleck joyfully embraced Grant's opinions and launched a smear campaign. In his reply to the General-in-chief, Old Brains spoke of Butler's "total unfitness to command . . . , and his generally quarrelsome character." Halleck was horrified at Grant's suggestion that Butler be sent West: "If we send him to Kentucky there would be an insurrection in that State." Butler would try to supersede Sherman, Halleck said, "by using against him all his talent at political intrigue and his facilities for newspaper abuse." He suggested banishing Butler to New England, where a department of sorts could be created, or putting Smith in command of the forces in the field—the same suggestion the "smelling committee" had made. [32]

Butler did not waste any time in beginning his counterattack. Knowing that Halleck's spare time was devoted to translating Jomini's life of Napoleon, he commented: "Now there is General H., what has HE to do? At a moment when every true man is laboring to his utmost, when the days ought to be forty hours long, General H. is translating French books at nine cents a page; and, sir, if you should put those nine cents in a box and shake them up, you would form a clear idea of General H.'s soul!" [33]

Halleck withstood the assault and continued to maintain his position, until on July 6 Grant decided to remove Butler from the

[30] *Ibid.,* 115.   [31] *Ibid.,* XL, Part 2, p. 558–59.
[32] *Ibid.,* 598.
[33] George Agassiz (ed.), *Meade's Headquarters 1863–1865* (Boston, 1922), 193.

fighting area and ship him off to a quiet post in North Carolina. Grant asked Halleck to "obtain an order" placing Smith in command of Butler's troops.[34] Eagerly the Chief of staff prepared the order.[35] Meanwhile Butler caught wind of the scheme and rushed to Grant's headquarters at City Point. Shamefacedly the General-in-chief said the order had been a mistake and assured Butler he would ask Halleck to recall it, which he did.[36] Butler gleefully told his wife he was still in charge and would soon have a more important command.[37] Eventually Grant suspended the order and Halleck relinquished all hope of disposing of Butler.[38] Grant was learning, as indeed almost every officer in the Union Army learned, how to play politics. He gave Butler the impression that Halleck had instigated the attack while he, Grant, supported the general. Butler believed him, castigated Halleck, and finished a letter to Grant: "I can see no reason why I cannot always subscribe myself, as I do now, Most truly your friend." [39] Lincoln himself could not have done a more efficient job of shifting blame. The Chief-of-staff resumed his preoccupation with administration.

When Grant began his extensive spade work around Petersburg, an injudicious withdrawal from the Shenandoah Valley by one of his own generals started a chain reaction which nearly proved fatal. General David Hunter, the same Hunter who commanded at St. Louis for the brief interlude before Halleck had arrived there, had taken charge of the Valley in 1864. A sixty-two-year-old anti-slavery fanatic, he had commanded the first regiment of blacks in the Federal service. Now, after a short campaign marked by his burning of Lexington, he retreated to the Ohio River and broke his communication with Halleck.

Meanwhile Lee, who had decided to lift Grant's siege with the old

[34] *O.R.,* Ser. I, XL, Part 3, p. 31.   [35] *Ibid.,* 59.
[36] *Ibid.,* 122.
[37] T. Harry Williams, *Lincoln and His Generals,* 323.
[38] *O.R.,* Ser. I, XL, Part 3, p. 122; see also Mallam, "Grant-Butler Relationship," *loc. cit.,* XLI, 262.
[39] Mallam, "Grant-Butler Relationship," *loc. cit.,* 264.

expedient of a raid down the Valley, sent General Jubal Early with a detachment of infantry and cavalry to repeat Stonewall Jackson's magic. By June 19 Early was in possession of Staunton and Lexington, between Washington and Hunter's latest position. Early grasped his opportunity and pushed forward toward Harper's Ferry. By July 5 Halleck was growing alarmed. He told Grant that the Federal forces had withdrawn to the north side of the Potomac before Early's force, estimated at between 20,000 and 30,000. Halleck thought the figures were "probably very exaggerated," but if Early had one-half that number there was no effective force to stop him. Halleck had stripped Washington and Baltimore of troops to reinforce Grant. He suggested that Grant send his dismounted cavalrymen back to Washington—they could obtain horses in Maryland.[40]

The situation worsened the following day, July 6. Now the invasion appeared to Halleck to be "of a pretty formidable character." Anxiously he asked Grant for the dismounted cavalry and hoped the General-in-chief could send a "good major-general to command in the field. . . ."[41] Halleck scraped together 10,000 men and advanced them to the Monocacy, a small stream east of Harper's Ferry and north of the Potomac.[42] After receiving Grant's permission, he augmented the force by rerouting some 20,000 men whom Canby was sending from New Orleans to Fort Monroe, directing that they be forwarded to Washington. Early was across the Potomac raising havoc in Maryland and causing "considerable alarm" in Washington.[43] The Chief of staff needed more troops. "If you propose to cut off this raid and not merely to secure our depots," he wired Grant, "we must have more forces here."[44] The fact that Lew Wallace, an amateur soldier and embryonic novelist, was the only general available to command on the Monocacy did not lessen Halleck's fears.

Because of the rapid succession of events, Halleck soon found he

[40] *O.R.*, Ser. I, XXXVII, Part 2, p. 59.
[41] *Ibid.*, 79.   [42] *Ibid.*, 100.
[43] *Ibid.*, 119.   [44] *Ibid.*, 119.

did not have time to check with Grant before acting. On July 9 Early attacked Wallace at Monocacy and at the end of the day the future author of *Ben Hur* wired Halleck that he was fleeing the scene of the battle with "a footsore, battered, and half-demoralized column." Wallace informed the Chief of staff: "You will have to use every exertion to save Baltimore and Washington." [45] Halleck in turn ordered Wallace to rally his forces and "make every possible effort to retard the enemy's march on Baltimore." He then began a search for any men who could carry a gun and stand in the defenses of Washington. He ordered an examination of the hospitals in Philadelphia and directed that "all convalescents capable of defending the forts and rifle-pits" be sent to the Capital. [46] While Halleck engaged in stop-gap measures, Grant gave him encouragement and advice. He told Halleck to send troops south of Early while allowing the raiding party to continue marching north. Grant's object was to destroy the enemy, not merely to drive him south of the Potomac. [47] But as Early turned toward the capital Halleck, with only convalescents to defend the city, demanded more troops of Grant. The General-in-chief detached the Sixth Corps to Washington, contributing to the success of Lee's strategy; he had relieved Federal pressure on Richmond.

Before the Sixth Corps could arrive, Early was in front of Washington; Halleck ordered the clerks to shoulder rifles and go to the lines. He directed that every officer and man who left his post be shot. With a reassuring note he cautioned a young captain at Fort Lincoln: "Hold your post firmly. The enemy in your front is not in large force, and re-enforcements are moving out." [48]

Halleck was demonstrating that he, too, would hold his post firmly. In the midst of a panicked populace, he could remain calm, assume responsibility, and give directions and encouragement to his men. His measures were neither highly imaginative nor overly bold, but they were effective. With the help of freshly bandaged soldiers and pasty-faced clerks he held Early—who fortunately was

---

[45] *Ibid.*, 145.
[47] *Ibid.*, 134.
[46] *Ibid.*, 153.
[48] *Ibid.*, 226.

not overly bold himself—long enough to allow General Horatio Wright and the Sixth Corps to arrive and to repulse the Confederates. When he reported to Grant, Halleck also repeated a hint which he had made previously. Since Early had 24,000 men, Lee must be very weak. Grant ignored the embarrassing hint.[49]

Two officers, members of the Sixth Corps, gave a good indication of Grant's attitude. At breakfast on July 11 "they ridiculed the suggestion that any considerable force had been detached from Lee's army and sent northward without the knowledge of General Grant." Lee had "quite enough to do" around Richmond, and "Washington . . . was in no more danger than Boston." [50] The General-in-chief's feelings were about to have dangerous repercussions.

Grant had originally set the objective of the campaign as the destruction rather than the repulse of Early. In accordance with his wishes, Halleck ordered Wright to continue pursuit of the Confederate general until Grant indicated otherwise.[51] But Grant was in Virginia and unaware of the actual situation in Washington; he told Halleck on July 16 he wanted Wright and the Sixth Corps to return to City Point, Virginia. Now that Early was south of Hunter's position, Grant wanted Hunter to take up the pursuit.[52] Halleck thought Wright's withdrawal a hasty and unwise interference on Grant's part, but although he felt justified in giving orders during an emergency, Halleck did not want to give directions after the General-in-chief had indicated his wish. However, before sending Wright back to City Point, Halleck registered his protest: "In my opinion," he told Grant, "raids will be renewed as soon as he leaves; but you are the judge whether or not a large enough movable force shall be kept here to prevent them." [53]

Halleck's prophecies proved correct. Immediately upon discovering that Wright had left the field, Early turned north once again and

[49] *Ibid.,* 221, 257.

[50] L. E. Chittenden, *Recollections of President Lincoln and His Administration* (New York, 1891), 404.

[51] *O.R.,* Ser. I, XXXVII, Part 2, p. 337.

[52] *Ibid.,* 350.   [53] *Ibid.,* 413.

lunged toward Pennsylvania. Hurriedly Grant gave Halleck permission to send Wright back into the field and said that since it took so long for dispatches to go from City Point to Washington, Halleck should give orders "to meet pressing emergencies." [54] Again the loosely constructed command system was proving better able to adapt itself to an emergency situation than one based on formal lines. Halleck used his discretion, sent Wright out to the Monocacy and ordered Hunter, finally moving closer to the capital, to cover it and Baltimore.[55] On July 28 Halleck outlined the tactical dispositions he desired the generals to make, ordered Hunter to give battle if Early crossed the Potomac and to initiate an active pursuit if the Confederates retreated. Halleck hoped that "this time Wright's forces will not be withdrawn." [56] On the morning of July 30 a Confederate raiding party managed to move into Chambersburg, in southern Pennsylvania. Halleck soon learned it was only a small force of 1,000 men and scraped together what reinforcements he could find in Washington and hurried them to Hunter.[57]

Halleck was finding that directing active operations in the field was a difficult task. He did not know where Early had his main body, but did know the Confederate presently had "at least" 30,000 men. To concentrate his men and place them in a central position Halleck ordered Hunter east of South Mountain and consequently closer to Baltimore. Grant was sufficiently aroused by Halleck's reports—and the situation—to send one of his best subordinates, Philip Sheridan, to Washington. The General-in-chief wanted Sheridan placed in command of all troops in the field, "with instructions to put himself south of the enemy and follow him to the death." [58]

Halleck showed the telegram to Lincoln, who scribbled a response. The President asked Grant to look over his dispatches from Washington and "discover, if you can, that there is any idea in the head of any one here of 'putting our army south of the enemy,' or of 'following him to the death' in any direction." [59] Lincoln's insinua-

[54] *Ibid.*, 451.
[55] *Ibid.*
[56] *Ibid.*, 482.
[57] *Ibid.*, 511.
[58] *Ibid.*, 527, 558.
[59] *Ibid.*, 582.

tion was misguided. If the President himself had reviewed dispatches from capital headquarters, he would have discovered that it was Halleck who had originally ordered an active pursuit of the enemy, and Grant who had prevented it when he ordered Wright back to City Point.

On August 3 Sheridan arrived in Washington and held a conference with Halleck. He had advanced notably since that day in 1862 when Halleck promoted him from quartermaster service to the colonelcy of a cavalry regiment. Now Sheridan, bustling with importance, wanted to create a military division of the departments of Pennsylvania, Washington, Maryland, and West Virginia, with himself in charge of the whole. Halleck approved and with Grant's permission gave Sheridan his wish. Halleck and Sheridan also agreed that the time had come to lay waste the Valley, where crops were being harvested and most of them sent to Richmond for provisions. On August 6 Halleck told Sheridan to "assume general command of all the troops in the field." [60] A new regime was about to enforce its will on the Shenandoah.

While Grant continued his war of attrition by digging in the south of Richmond and matching wits with Lee in the Valley, Sherman was quietly but effectively making his way toward Atlanta. During his campaign Sherman reported to Halleck, who forwarded the gist to Grant. Other than sending supplies and reinforcements to Sherman before his campaign commenced, Halleck made no attempt to influence the general's moves. From the Chattahoochee River, north of Atlanta, Sherman wrote on July 9 that he needed "advice and encouragement" from his old friend. "Write me a note occasionally and suggest anything that may occur to you, as I am really in the wilderness down here." [61] Halleck replied that he had sent no "encouragement or advice" because Sherman needed neither: "Your operations thus far have been the admiration of all military men; and they prove what energy and skill combined can accomplish, while either without the other may utterly fail."

[60] *Ibid.*, XLIII, Part 1, p. 709.   [61] *Ibid.*, XXXVIII, Part 5, p. 91.

Also, Halleck did not want to make suggestions without Grant's sanction. Although the General-in-chief was "free from petty jealousies," he had men about him "who would gladly make difficulties between us." The Chief of staff would take his orders from Grant; "The position is not an agreeable one," he philosophized, "but I am willing to serve wherever the Government thinks I can be most useful."

Then Halleck, who had given up direction, but not criticism, of Union strategy, speculated on the outcome of his superior's moves. *"Entre nous,"* he told Sherman that he feared Grant had "made a fatal mistake in putting himself south of James River." Petersburg was strongly fortified and must fall before Richmond—Halleck doubted that Grant could take it. Moreover, with Grant's army south of Richmond, Lee was free to detach large raiding parties to attack Washington. "I hope we may have full success," Halleck concluded, "but I find that many of Grant's general officers think the campaign already a failure. Perseverance, however, may compensate for all errors and overcome all obstacles." [62] The criticism was well founded. Ostensibly the campaigns of Grant and Sherman hinged on one another; Grant was to occupy Lee so he would not be able to make detachments to Johnston. Lee had made a detachment, but fortunately to the Valley—an easier task, to be sure, but still he might have sent Early to Johnston. If he had then Grant's entire campaign, with its tremendous losses, would have been a failure.

Lee's concern with Richmond rather than Atlanta had worked in the Federals' favor. On September 2 Sherman moved into Atlanta after John Hood, Jefferson Davis' replacement for the retreating Johnston, abandoned the city. Two days later Sherman confessed to Halleck: "I owe you all I now enjoy of fame, for I had allowed myself in 1861 to sink into a perfect slough of despond, and do believe I would have run away and hid from dangers and complications that surrounded us." [63] Halleck replied that he had watched Sherman's movements most "attentively and critically" and did not

[62] *Ibid.,* 150. [63] Lewis, *Sherman,* 412.

"hesitate to say that your campaign has been the most brilliant of the war." [64] It had also been conducted on the best Jominian principles. Sherman had concentrated on the decisive point and outmanoeuvred his opponent.

The brilliance of the campaign, as Halleck implied, was more due to Sherman than the command arrangement. Grant made the general plan while Halleck reinforced the army; Sherman made the important decisions independently. The links of the chain of command had never been welded—they did not have to be. With subordinates like Sherman and Halleck, Grant could afford to allow them to make the right moves in particular circumstances. The system was ideally suited for the Union top command.

[64] *O.R.*, Ser. I, XXXVIII, Part 5, p. 856.

CHAPTER FOURTEEN

TOTAL WAR

A transformation had taken place. It culminated when Sherman took Atlanta and deliberately and relentlessly destroyed it. The shackles of Eighteenth Century limited warfare had been broken. From his Washington headquarters Old Brains sent his highest approval. "We have tried three years of conciliation and kindness without any reciprocation," Halleck told Sherman: "I would destroy every mill and factory within my reach which I did not want for my own use." Halleck approved taking or annihilating anything that could possibly be of service to the enemy. He sanctioned a type of warfare abhorrent to Jomini and balked only at burning private homes, which was "barbarous." [1]

Just as Halleck's abilities had grown throughout the war, so too had his bitterness increased. The bombardment of Fort Sumter had torn him from a lucrative law practice, position and social prestige. He had discarded much of value to come to Washington, but with a reasonable degree of certainty he expected to gain greater prestige in the eyes of his country. After all, he had been the only American contributor to the lofty theoretical aspects of war. But rather than earning the country's great respect he received its derision. His sacrifices had been made in vain. Halleck progressively looked at the Southerners with increasing hatred. They, who had started the war, became the object of his vituperation. The new attitude both contributed to and made easier his transformation into an advocate of

[1] *O.R.,* Ser. I, XXXIX, Part 2, p. 503.

total war, a subject on which Sherman was about to hold introductory classes.

By September, Sherman was well into the interior of Georgia with a huge veteran army and several courses of action open to him. After trying unsuccessfully to catch Hood's battered but intact army, Sherman showed no inclination to pursue the Confederate, maintaining he would never find Hood and that he could do more good on a raid of his own toward the Atlantic coast. Grant, who usually went after armies rather than places and saw little difference between the Eastern and Western theater, objected to any movement south until Hood was destroyed. Although Halleck agreed with Sherman, he thought the objective of his march should be the Gulf, rather than the Atlantic coast. All the courses presented various possibilities and drawbacks and all presented difficult supply problems for Halleck.

Grant, who would finally have to assume the responsibility for any decision, Halleck, who would handle the administrative work, and Sherman, who would execute the move, exchanged ideas before reaching a conclusion. On September 26 Halleck said the line for Sherman to follow was through Montgomery, which would open the Alabama River. This course would prevent Confederate raids into Mississippi, Tennessee and Kentucky, while depriving the Southerners of the grain, iron and coal of Northern Georgia, Alabama, and Mississssippi. Another advantage was that Hood's supplies would be cut and his raiding power limited.[2]

Sherman preferred to march to Savannah because it would cut off a larger slice of Confederate territory. On October 1 he telegraphed the General-in-chief and proposed sending Thomas and his corps back to Nashville while taking the rest of the army to Savannah, or Charleston, "breaking roads and doing irreparable damage." He would cut loose from supply lines and live off the countryside. Thomas could remain on the defense and restrain any serious damage Hood might do.

Every proposed movement save one was based on Jomini's teach-

<hr>

[2] *Ibid.,* 480.

ings; Sherman would leave a strong base of operations in his rear, would operate on interior lines, would "fight battles" of manoeuvre rather than blood fests, would keep his army concentrated, and would aim at cities rather than the enemy army. He had only abandoned, as had Halleck, Jomini's implicit gentlemanly war that refrained from striking at civilians. And showing his appreciation for one of the cardinal tenets of war, Sherman concluded: "We cannot remain on the defensive." [3]

Halleck saw the telegram as it passed through Washington on the way to Grant's headquarters at City Point. Assuming his right to comment, he composed a lengthy letter to Grant the next day. He criticized the Jominian plan in Jominian terms. The Chief of staff carefully weighed the advantages of each alternative; a movement down the Alabama River, an advance to Mobile, a drive to Pensacola or a march to Savannah. Halleck agreed with Sherman's basic premise—the veteran army could not remain idly on the defensive —but he disagreed with the tactical plans. The route from Atlanta to Mobile was closer to the sea and therefore to awaiting supplies. It was less directly exposed, would leave a smaller force in Sherman's rear, and would not open Kentucky and Tennessee to raids from Confederate cavalry. Canby's New Orleans force could be used if Sherman went to Mobile; it would be useless if he went to Savannah. Montgomery and Mobile were more important cities than Augusta and Savannah, and the area around the Alabama River was of more value than that on the Georgia coast. If Sherman went to Savannah, Hood would receive the bounty of a harvest which unobstructed slave labor was reaping at that moment. All the advantages made it logical for Sherman to march to Mobile in preference to Savannah, Halleck reiterated. He had "taken every possible means to obtain correct information on the subject," and presented his conclusions "only after a thorough examination and the most mature consideration." Halleck was not writing to influence Grant's decision, he said, but to inform and "simply to urge . . . an early decision."

[3] *Ibid.*, Part 3, p. 3.

The Chief of staff considered it imperative that he know Sherman's route immediately. Canby was demanding ships to transport his command to Mobile (where Farragut had recently captured the harbor but not the city in a naval battle), which would tie up all available transportation. If Sherman were going to Savannah it would be a waste to send troops to Mobile, and the ships could be used elsewhere.[4]

The casualness of the command arrangement was proving to be a boon. On October 4 Grant wired Halleck, giving his approval of Sherman's idea of a march to the sea; he did not say which route Sherman would follow. He had wanted Sherman to connect with Canby after taking Atlanta, but since Halleck had drawn the Nineteenth Corps from Canby (for the defense of Washington), it was impossible to carry out the plan. But plans could change as fast as the situation. Grant, like Halleck, would not attempt to dictate to his subordinates—especially one he trusted so implicitly as Sherman. Moving either to Mobile or to Savannah would cut off Confederate food supplies, Grant said, and intimated Sherman could do as he wished.[5] The situation, ideal for Sherman, who had complete freedom of movement, made Halleck's task difficult. Wherever Sherman emerged he would need to have a huge supply base awaiting him. It would be Halleck's responsibility to create the depot and he did not know where Sherman wanted it. But Grant trusted Halleck as much as he did Sherman, and although Halleck would constantly complain about his position he was equal to the task. Grant, Halleck and Sherman complemented each other perfectly. A lesser man in any of the three positions and the system, based on personality rather than formality, probably would have folded.

Like Halleck, Grant would have to wait until Sherman started south to learn his destination, but he did not have to overcome the supply problem. On October 12 the General-in-chief ordered Halleck to load transports with 200,000 rations of grain, 500,000 ra-

---

[4] *Ibid.,* 25.   [5] *Ibid.,* 63.

tions of provisions and 300,000 rounds of ammunition. Knowing that Sherman's preference was a move to Savannah, Halleck asked permission to send the supply-laden ships directly to Hilton Head, a Union base in South Carolina near Savannah. Grant wanted the transports to rendezvous at sea; Halleck said that shipping the supplies directly to Hilton Head would save demurrage expenses and that if plans were changed the stores could be readily transferred.[6]

Then Halleck changed his mind and responded to Sherman's freedom of movement by compromising. On October 31 he ordered the Quartermaster General to send one-half of the supplies for Sherman to Hilton Head, the other half to Pensacola.[7] Four days later Halleck suggested to Grant that Canby should be ordered to march for the Alabama River, rather than be sent to the Georgia coast, as Grant desired. When the General-in-chief expressed doubts as to Canby's ability to do so, Halleck demonstrated the advantages of the proposed move. "Considering the uncertainty of Sherman's movements," Halleck said, an expedition into Alabama would accomplish a double purpose. It would relieve pressure on Sherman's rear and would destroy supplies that otherwise would go to Hood.[8] Grant approved, and on November 7 Halleck composed and forwarded to Canby his instructions. Canby was to strike out from the Mississippi River into Alabama, with the general objective of destroying enemy communications and, "if possible," threatening Selma, Alabama. He was to give what help he could to both Thomas and Sherman. Thomas was facing Hood and Sherman was operating in Georgia, destination unknown. "Possibly," Halleck finished, "he [Sherman] may strike Montgomery and Selma."[9] The orders were neither thorough nor complete and left Canby, like Sherman, a free agent. They did, however, provide strategical cooperation between the three western armies. The next day Halleck told Sherman, who was about to depart, that abundant stores were collected at both Hilton Head and Pensacola, "with transportation

[6] *Ibid.*, 267.
[7] *Ibid.*, 529.
[8] *Ibid.*, 658.
[9] *Ibid.;* XLI, Part 4, p. 463.

to any other required points" ready. "I think," the Chief of staff concluded, "you are now free to move as soon as you choose." [10]

Halleck arranged for cooperation on the Atlantic as well as the Gulf Coast. On November 13 three days before Sherman left Atlanta "for the interior of Georgia or Alabama," Halleck ordered the commander of the small forces at Hilton Head to make a demonstration on the Charleston and Savannah Railroad, smashing it if possible. Halleck thought Sherman would probably emerge on the Atlantic coast, but was still uncertain and concluded: "You will learn more of his movements from rebel papers than from here." [11] But no matter where Sherman went, he would find a friendly force protecting his flank.

Sherman plunged into the interior of Georgia and left the government ignorant of his movements. Wrecking havoc wherever he went, Sherman directed his army toward the Atlantic coast, bringing economic warfare's implications home with a vengeance to the people of Georgia. Almost a month later, in mid-December, he appeared before Savannah. The Confederates tried to defend the city, but obviously they would not be able to stop the besieging Yankee.

Sherman's march proved a boon to the Army of the Potomac. He had destroyed Lee's granary in the process of his movements, and was now aiding his general-in-chief—who a few months before had been fighting to keep Lee from detaching forces to confront Sherman. Cooperation, from the small force in North Carolina to the largest armies, was restored all along the line.

After the war, Grant claimed he was in favor of Sherman's plan "from the time it was first submitted to me," and that Halleck was "very bitterly opposed to it, and . . . appealed to the authorities at Washington to stop it." [12] It was hardly an accurate statement of the facts. Halleck had approved the plan from its inception, but kept the emphasis on a march to the Gulf rather than to the Atlantic coast.

On December 18 Halleck congratulated his friend, who would

[10] *Ibid.*, XXXIX, Part 3, p. 697.   [11] *Ibid.*, XXXV, Part 2, p. 328.
[12] Grant, *Memoirs*, 500.

officially take Savannah on December 21. He said Sherman's march would "stand out prominently as the great one of this great war." He proposed another raid through the Confederacy as soon as Savannah fell, but recalling his recent difficulties and confusion added: "I will not anticipate." Then, thinking of the war in its entirety and the city which he, along with the rest of the North, considered the cause of the nation's and his own personal tragedy, Halleck bitterly remarked: "Should you capture Charleston, I hope that by some accident the place may be destroyed, and if a little salt should be sown upon its site it may prevent the growth of future crops of nullification and secession." [13]

While the suspense of Sherman's movements harassed Halleck, he had to contend with other problems. Halleck was trying to create an efficient and economically sound War Department. His position, although at times anomalous, was vital to army organization. Few, if any, could have attended as effectively to the details so essential to the defense of the country. Supply problems, forage for horses, clothing for troops, ammunition, guns, communication routes, all were within Halleck's immediate sphere of activity. Despite persistent attacks of hay fever, which caused his eyes to tear so profusely that he could "hardly see to write," he fulfilled his duties with energy and skill.

When $50,000,000 of unpaid requisitions for cavalry embarrassed the treasury, Halleck took active measures to attack the basic cause of the managerial defect. He created and headed a cavalry bureau, concerned with the organization, equipment, inspection and uses of cavalry. He discovered during the winter that although the Armies of the Potomac and the James, as well as Sheridan's and Sherman's, were adequately supplied with cavalry, the local quartermasters were purchasing more horses. He strongly urged that the army cease the purchases and practice the "greatest economy." Grant had hardly given his approval when another problem appeared. After an extensive study of the situation, Halleck concluded

[13] *O.R.*, Ser. I, XLIV, 741.

that there would not be enough forage for the horses in the spring. Since many farmers sold their hay crop early to pay for local taxes used in raising bounties for volunteers, the supply was short. Lack of transportation for what little forage was available compounded the shortage and in general complicated Halleck's dilemma. He suggested a further reduction in the cavalry force.[14] Halleck's foresight in the matter was setting a precedent for later army administrators who would estimate the amount of oil available before deciding how many tanks to include in a campaign.

Although skeptical about instituting military innovations, Halleck did not hesitate to diverge from the past in administrative duties. In February of 1865, Grant demanded that Halleck find some way to pay the troops. Halleck's reply was couched in the spirit of modern war and tempered by his training as a businessman. He realized that most army officers and Congressmen wanted any available money in the treasury to go to the Pay Department in preference to the Quartermaster's, Commissary's, and other departments, but protested against the policy. Since the Quartermaster was already $180,000,000 in debt, manufacturers would not furnish cloth, tailors make clothes, shoemakers produce shoes, nor railroads transport troops and supplies until they received some of their claims. Western railroad employees, for instance, were threatening to quit unless they received at least a part of their pay. By paying the troops, their supplies would cease, leaving them without food, clothing, and ammunition. "We must equalize and distribute the Government indebtedness in such a way as to keep the wheels going," Halleck lectured.

Demonstrating his knowledge of the interrelation between military and monetary matters, Old Brains ventured a solution. If Grant could win a major victory, confidence in the inflated Union currency would be restored and businessmen would be convinced that the war was nearly over. As a result they would be more inclined to accept government bonds and greenbacks, or paper money. Meanwhile, it would be better to have troops go without pay than without

[14] *Ibid.,* 715; Ser. III, IV, 229.

ammunition. Just as Grant saw that to save lives in the long run he must sacrifice some at present, so Halleck recognized that at this point supplies were more essential than pay to the troops.[15]

Amid a sea of organizational problems and astride a wave of suspense over Sherman's moves, Halleck also had another struggle. While Sherman headed seaward, Thomas was the only obstacle between Hood's army and the North; if Hood defeated or skirted Thomas and crossed the Ohio River, he could cause major damage, principally to morale. Thomas had to spread himself thinly enough to prevent Hood from slipping around his flank, yet had to remain concentrated enough to withstand an attack. Although the situation was resplendent with possibilities for Hood, Thomas, whose head-quarters were in Nashville, refused to become excited. A meticulous soldier, lacking imagination but possessing perseverance, Thomas seemed incongruent in a war filled with romantic generals. Refusing to budge from his position on the left flank at Chickamauga, Thomas had saved the Union army from total defeat that day and earned the sobriquet, "Rock of Chickamauga." His men preferred to call the forty-seven-year-old warrior "Old Pap," because of his kindly paternal qualities. Grant had seen Thomas operate in the West but was estranged from him personally. The impetuous General-in-chief probably did not understand the scrupulous soldier. Halleck had remarked: "Thomas is . . . a noble old war horse. It is true that he is slow, but he is always sure." [16] Thomas' slowness would prove to be highly irritating to Washington officials before his sureness assuaged their anxiety. During the interim, Grant would try to dismiss him as "slow," Sherman would comment on his "provoking, obstinate delay," while Halleck alone shielded him for the benefit of his country.[17]

Neither the Chief of staff nor the General-in-chief maintained close communications with Thomas, nor did they interfere with his

---

[15] *Ibid.,* Ser. I, XLVI, Part 2, p. 561.
[16] *Ibid.,* Ser. I, XXXVIII, Part 5, p. 856.
[17] *The Union Army* (Madison, Wisconsin, 1902), V, 192.

tactical arrangements. Instead Grant contented himself with sending him irksome telegrams urging more action, while Halleck confined his activities to getting reinforcements to Nashville, a task
which demanded all his talents.

Like a dark cloud General William S. Rosecrans again appeared
on Halleck's horizon and almost prevented Halleck's obtaining reinforcements for Thomas. Rosecrans had garnered the command at St.
Louis, replacing Schofield, whose removal as head of the Department of Missouri was demanded by the Radicals after Schofield
had aligned himself with a conservative faction. The new department head did not please Halleck.[18]

On October 26 Grant told Halleck that Rosecrans must send all
available troops to Thomas. "This ought to be done without delay,"
Grant continued: "He has 6,000 or 8,000 troops around St. Louis
and within a few hours travel of it, that can start at once." Halleck
made significant changes before transmitting the order to Rosecrans.
The Chief of staff had not been notably successful in obtaining
action from Rosecrans during the preceding year, but Halleck felt
he knew "Old Rosy" better than Grant, and decided that a brusque
order would produce only hurt feelings. Using his discretion, Halleck reworded the telegram and told Rosecrans that all available
troops "should be brought to St. Louis and prepared to assist General Thomas in West Tennessee." He neither mentioned a specific
number nor used the phrase "start at once." Instead Halleck told the
sensitive general the troops should be "prepared to assist" the "Rock
of Chickamauga." [19]

It was an honest effort, but a mistake nevertheless. His attempt to
handle Rosecrans with gentleness backfired. By November 1 Hood
was crossing the Tennessee River and it was imperative that reinforcements get to Thomas, who gave no indication of moving
against the audacious Confederate. Rosecrans, however, had shown
no inclination to forward the reserves. Rectifying his error, Halleck
did not mince words as he wired: "Grant directs that all available
troops in St. Louis and vicinity be sent immediately to General

[18] *O.R.*, Ser. I, XLI, Part 3, p. 468.   [19] *Ibid.*, Part 4, pp. 263, 274.

Thomas." [20] Rosecrans replied the next day. He wished to know what route Halleck wanted the troops to follow, if they should take artillery, ammunition, and regimental trains with them, and if they should go in "driblets" or *en masse*.[21] The telegram heightened War Department officials' exasperation. Thomas was gingerly collecting troops in Nashville and watching Hood make his way, unopposed, through Tennessee. "This looks like the McClellan and Rosecrans strategy of do nothing and let the enemy raid the country," Stanton growled. An infuriated Halleck told Rosecrans the troops could follow any route so long as they reached Nashville in the shortest possible time.[22]

Meanwhile, Halleck encouraged and advised Old Pap. Thomas should put reinforcements coming in from the western states into the garrisons and place veterans in the front. A division had been ordered from St. Louis to his headquarters, Halleck said, along with other spare troops in the vicinity. Halleck anticipated little cooperation from Rosecrans, but Grant in desperation had sent his chief of staff, John Rawlins, to St. Louis to expedite the movement. Halleck had told Rawlins to send "all the troops you can lay hands on . . ." to Thomas "with the least possible delay," and awaited results. Rawlins was a good choice. In St. Louis, where as Grant's personal chief of staff he spoke with Grant's authority, he was the embodiment of action. One day after he arrived Rawlins had started 9,000 men to Old Pap from St. Louis, added detachments from Cairo, Springfield and Alton, Illinois and Paducah, Kentucky, talked with Rosecrans, and requested permission to return.[23] Old Rosy must have wondered dazedly what happened.

The General-in-chief had more surprises for Rosecrans, and the Chief of staff had more help for Thomas. On November 25 Grant asked Halleck to urge Lincoln that Rosecrans be removed from the Department of the Missouri. Halleck was anxious to make the request, thus dooming Rosecrans, who had little political support. On December 2 Major General Granville M. Dodge became com-

[20] *Ibid.*, 390. [21] *Ibid.*
[22] *Ibid.*, 400. [23] *Ibid.*, 429, 439.

mander of the Department.[24] A Massachusetts resident who graduated from a military academy in Vermont, Dodge was expected to
give Thomas more assistance, since he had recently been a member
of Old Pap's army. Halleck took advantage of the appointment to
get Thomas more men. There were 6,000 troops in St. Louis and
requisitions for $20,000 to construct new barracks for them. Halleck
considered the money a waste, for St. Louis, he commented, "is in no
more danger of an insurrection than Chicago, Philadelphia or New
York." Halleck proposed that 5,000 of the troops be sent to
Thomas. Grant wired Dodge the same day, ordering him to send the
5,000 men to Nashville.[25]

Halleck had sent "every available man" from all western departments to Old Pap. The Government had done all it could to
supply Thomas' demands and wants, Halleck told Grant, implying
it was time for the Rock of Chickamauga to move out against Hood.[26]

Viewed from Washington, Hood looked more of a threat than
ever. He had delivered an all-out attack on a part of Thomas' army
at Franklin on November 30, driving the Union advance forces
back to Nashville. Hood followed the Union detachment and was
facing Thomas with something over 30,000 men; Thomas had
about 55,000. Actually Hood's army was weakened and demoralized, in no condition to accomplish anything. To the capital,
however, it appeared a formidable force, and Halleck and Grant began to plead that Thomas attack immediately.

Old Pap would not advance until every button on every private
had been secured and every Springfield loaded. Moreover, he was
building up the largest and most efficient cavalry force in the
war, under General James Wilson, and refused to move before
Wilson had every cavalryman mounted. Halleck was peeved.
Though he could understand delay, he could not abide waste of
supplies. He had sent Thomas 22,000 horses since late September,
and the number was already reduced to 10,000. "If you wait till
General Wilson mounts all his cavalry," Halleck chided Thomas,

[24] *Ibid.*, 782.   [25] *Ibid.*, 797, 799.
[26] *Ibid.*, XLV, Part 2, p. 28.

"you will wait till doomsday for the waste equals the supply." Bitterly Halleck compared Thomas to Rosecrans, and warned that Old Pap would end up in the same condition, with more animals than he could feed. Lincoln and Stanton, who did not realize Hood's battered army could not take the offensive, feared Thomas would allow the Confederate to slip away and raid into Kentucky. They complained to Grant, who sent several sharp dispatches to Thomas with no result.[27] Tiring of inaction, Grant reverted to the old method of removing a general who did not jump when his superiors (hundreds of miles away) cracked the whip. On December 7 he recommended that Thomas be relieved and that Schofield, now a corps commander in Thomas' army, replace him.[28]

When Halleck saw Grant's recommendation, which was addressed to Stanton, he composed a short dispatch to the General-in-chief. With Lincoln's approval, Halleck told Grant if he wanted Thomas relieved he must give the order. No one in Washington would interfere. "The responsibility, however, will be yours, as no one here, so far as I am informed, wishes General Thomas' removal." [29] Halleck's dispatch cooled Grant, and he replied that he only wanted Thomas reminded of the necessity of action. Grant would not relieve him until he received more information from Nashville.[30] Halleck had, for a day at least, prevented a hasty and unwise action. Instead of merely executing Grant's recommendation, he had taken the responsibility for delaying the order. The rest was up to Old Pap. Hood faced him from entrenchments south of Nashville; a simple attack would dislodge and repel the Confederate.

But Thomas was not ready and when by 11 A.M. of the following day, December 9, Grant had received no news of an assault, he ordered Halleck to relieve Thomas at once. Again Halleck rose to his defense. Soon after reading Grant's telegram, Halleck received a dispatch from Thomas, who set out to attack that morning but was halted by a sleet storm. He would attack as soon as the weather cleared. At 4 P.M. Halleck transmitted the news to Grant, and

[27] *Ibid.,* 15, 17, 55, 70, 97, 114. [28] *Ibid.,* 84.
[29] *Ibid.,* 96. [30] *Ibid.*

asked if the General-in-chief, in view of developments, still wished Thomas replaced. Halleck held the removal order, being personally responsible for it until Grant could reply. Grant agreed to suspend the order "until it is seen whether he [Thomas] will do anything." [31] Unaware of all the activity, Thomas sat out the storm. Halleck, who for three years had been Grant's self-proclaimed mentor and had continually but usually unsuccessfully urged caution upon the bold general, had finally succeeded in forcing Grant to take his advice.

After saving Thomas, Halleck gave him encouragement, advice, and explanations. The reason Grant wanted an immediate attack, Halleck told him, was connected with the whole scheme of the war. While Hood occupied a threatening position in Tennessee, Canby was obliged to retain large forces on the Mississippi in order to protect navigation. Grant wanted these forces to cooperate with Sherman, and every day's delay by Thomas interfered with Grant's plans. Thomas replied he would attack the next day. [32]

But the impetuous Grant's patience was at an end. He hurried to Washington, planning to continue on to Nashville to relieve Thomas personally. Before leaving, however, he conferred with Lincoln, Stanton and Halleck. The President emphasized Halleck's long maintained theory that the field general was a better judge of conditions than officials in Washington. Still Grant insisted on removing the general and prepared to start for Nashville. Halleck watched in silent despair; there was nothing more he could do. Then, dramatically, word came that Thomas had attacked. A disgruntled Grant remarked: "I guess we won't go to Nashville." [33]

Thomas' battle at Nashville was a complete vindication of Halleck's thinking. In an attack that was a model of planning and exe-

---

[31] *Ibid.*, 114, 115.   [32] *Ibid.*, 180.

[33] Bates, *Lincoln in the Telegraph Office*, 315–18; T. Harry Williams, *Lincoln and His Generals*, 343–44; Grant, *Memoirs*, 550. Grant had tried one other method of relieving Thomas—he sent General John Logan to Nashville with orders to supersede Thomas. Logan arrived in Nashville and refused to deliver the order. Once again Grant's wish was overruled.

cution, he completely smashed Hood's army and sent it retreating pell-mell into the south. Grant sent Thomas an ungracious dispatch while Lincoln wired one filled with praise. Halleck contented himself with urging Thomas to make a "hot pursuit" of Hood's army.[34] It was hardly necessary. Using Wilson's cavalry to full advantage, Thomas hit again and again at Hood's defenseless men and ruined the Confederate army. Old Pap had engineered and fought the most complete victory of the war. He may have been excessively slow, but he was certainly sure.

The Nashville campaign revealed both strengths and weaknesses of the new command arrangement. With Grant as general-in-chief, the North possessed a commander willing to make decisions and execute them; with Halleck as chief of staff the Union had found a brilliant administrator. The stress of the system was on personality and when, as in Thomas' case, Grant's personal judgment went awry, the system had to lean on its inherent checks and balances. Halleck's refusal to take a completely subordinate role saved Thomas. Once again the right men were in the right places. The success of the system was best indicated by Lincoln's withdrawal from the picture. He trusted the men he had promoted—and the system he helped create—so implicitly that he voluntarily reduced himself to exercising only an occasional veto. The North had learned from its mistakes.

[34] *O.R.*, Ser. I, XLV, Part 2, pp. 195, 295; Basler (ed.), *Collected Works of Abraham Lincoln*, X, 315.

CHAPTER FIFTEEN

VICTORY

Thomas' victory brightened the situation for the Northern high command. Lee now commanded the only sizeable Confederate army in existence—the North had two forces, Thomas' and Sherman's, with which the generals could do literally what they wished. Sherman might march through South Carolina and North Carolina to join Grant, or take transports from Savannah directly to City Point. Thomas was resting in the West with a successful army and almost no opposition. He too could march where he pleased, or have all or part of his force join Grant. The possible alternatives were happy ones for Lincoln and Grant, but any decision reached would create more work for Halleck. If Sherman marched north he would have to be supplied, if Thomas shifted part of his troops east, transportation would have to be arranged, and Halleck would administer all the activities. But the duties would not be difficult; he had learned to handle them almost unconsciously. With Confederate resistance down to a minimum the command system was ideally suited for the situation. Grant would make the decisions, Halleck would handle administration, while Sherman and Thomas would carry them out. There would be little wasted effort or confusion.

After Sherman took Savannah, Grant's inclination was to bring his army to City Point by sea. Halleck argued that Sherman should make his next move "another wide swath through the center of the Confederacy." Sherman agreed, contending that a march through the Carolinas was "as much a direct attack upon Lee's army as though we [were] operating within the sound of his artillery." Grant finally concurred and early in 1865 Sherman left on another march of destruction. Halleck sent supplies to Savannah and after Sherman shoved off shifted his attention to aiding the general with other methods. He told Lieber not to worry about Sherman. "Lee and Johnston combined cannot hurt" such an army, he said: "I first organized that army & know it well. It was trained very differently from the Army of the Potomac. Its general never had 75 wagons to carry the luggage of his Head Qrs, nor were its officers ever permitted to take their wives with them in the field." [1]

During the fall of 1864 the Navy Department had proposed to Halleck a scheme for capturing Wilmington, North Carolina. The Chief of staff rejected the plan, but sent the Assistant Secretary of the Navy down to City Point to confer with Grant. "I think," Halleck told Grant before the official arrived, "we have more irons now than we can keep from burning." [2] Grant, however, approved a joint land and naval expedition against Fort Fisher, which guarded Wilmington harbor. The expedition would give employment to troops otherwise remaining idle, and would close the last open Confederate port. Then to everyone's consternation, Butler, who still commanded the department in which Wilmington was located, asserted his right to lead the land forces and give general direction to the whole expedition. He would take a "torpedo ship," a vessel filled with explosives, run it up to the side of Fort Fisher, detonate it, and dramatically lead his troops through the resulting holes. In December Butler made his try and failed miserably. Halleck and Sherman, who had been exchanging bitter telegrams prophesying failure for Butler, were amused. Halleck sarcastically exclaimed: "Thank God, I had nothing to do with it, except to express the opinion that Butler's torpedo ship would have about as much effect on the forts as if he should —— at them." [3]

---

[1] Halleck to Lieber, March 5, 1865, Lieber Collection; *O.R.,* Ser. I, XLVII, Part 2, p. 3; Lewis, *Sherman,* 471.
[2] *O.R.,* Ser. I, XLII, Part 2, p. 624.   [3] *Ibid.,* XLVII, Part 2, p. 3.

Seven days later Halleck finally saw Butler removed from his command; [4] and as soon as Butler left the department Halleck prepared to shift Schofield's corps from Thomas to the North Carolina coast. From there the corps would move inland and join with Sherman as he made his way north. In less than a month Halleck, using the North's material resources and sea power to full advantage, had moved the corps from Tennessee to New Bern, North Carolina. He directed the whole movement and pushed it through without a major hitch.[5] The ease with which it was accomplished only highlighted what Thomas' victory had made obvious—the Confederacy was doomed.

Transferring Schofield's corps was Halleck's last major action of the war. The Union army was well established and perfectly equipped all along the line—now it merely had to wait for good weather before making the final push. By late March Sherman was marching steadily northward, opposed only by a small, mixed force Johnston had managed to gather together. As the roads dried around Petersburg, Grant sent Sheridan, who had just returned from his successful Valley campaign, south of the city to begin the final annihilation of Lee through a series of flanking manoeuvres. By April 9 he had trapped Lee and the pitifully small remnants of the Army of Northern Virginia at Appomattox Court House, where the Virginian finally relinquished the struggle.

Halleck, "amidst the excitement of victory, speeches, &c., on the news of the surrender of Lee's army," remembered to wire Sherman and remark that when Johnston surrendered he should be given the same terms as Grant gave Lee—generous terms that paroled the entire army, allowing the men to keep their horses and the officers their sidearms, but which said nothing about the Southern state governments. "I hope," Halleck concluded, "in a very short time to be able to say and feel that the rebellion is virtually at an end." [6]

But there was one last scene that had to be enacted. On the night

[4] Mallam, "Grant-Butler Relationship," *loc. cit.,* XLI, 265.
[5] *O.R.,* Ser. I, XLV, Part 2, p. 573; XLVII, Part 2, pp. 131, 305, 317.
[6] *O.R.,* Ser. I, XLVII, Part 3, p. 150.

of April 14 a crazed actor assassinated President Lincoln in Ford's theater. The insane act cut like a sharp knife through the victory celebrations. Halleck was one of the few men in the room when Lincoln died.[7] His reaction was immediate: "My God! That even this should befall us!" he cried to Lieber. He blamed the assassination on the entire South and felt that "the murder of poor good Lincoln is no isolated fact . . . it is all, all one fiendish barbarism."[8]

During the excitement following Lincoln's death Stanton virtually took over the government. Among other high-handed acts, he did what the martyred President never desired—the Secretary ordered Halleck out of Washington. The Chief of staff, who now lost that title, would go to Richmond and take over the department there. Halleck stayed in Washington long enough to represent the army at Lincoln's funeral service, then on April 20, left for Virginia.[9] As in St. Louis four years before, he was called upon to bring order out of chaos.

Evidently working on the theory that he had been a success in St. Louis because his first action had been to ingratiate himself with his superiors, Halleck, in Richmond, did everything he could to gain Stanton's approval. The result, however, was the direct opposite to that he had achieved in St. Louis and, because he jumped when Stanton nodded, Halleck suffered a personal tragedy.

When Sherman finally caught up with Johnston and forced him to surrender, the armistice he granted the Confederate included recognition of the existing "rebel" state governments. Ordinarily, this would have caused only a slight stir, but coming less than a week after Lincoln's assassination, it created an uproar. Halleck, meanwhile, had gone to see the bankers in impoverished Richmond almost as soon as he arrived. They had fed him some wild rumors about "Jeff. Davis and his partisans" fleeing with a large amount

[7] Milton H. Shutes, *Lincoln and California* (Stanford, 1943), 104.

[8] Halleck to Lieber, April 15, 1865, Lieber Collection.

[9] *O.R.*, Ser. I, XLVI, Part 3, p. 807; Halleck to Stanton, April 22, 1865, Stanton MSS; Lewis, *Sherman*, 542–50.

of specie, "not only the plunder of the Richmond banks, but previous accumulations." Davis hoped, according to the stories, to get to either Mexico or Europe with the gold after making terms with Sherman "or some other southern commander." Stanton, meanwhile, ordered Sherman to resume hostilities. Halleck, unaware of Stanton's activity, ordered Sheridan to Sherman's headquarters, in Greensboro, North Carolina, telling him to look for Davis and his "wagons" of gold on the way. The next night, April 23, Halleck wired Sheridan: "Pay no attention to the Sherman Johnston truce. It has been disapproved by the President. Try to cut off Jeff. Davis' specie." [10]

Three days later—Sherman was still to be heard from—Halleck was in the same state of excitement. He proudly informed Stanton that he had telegraphed various commanders "to obey no orders of General Sherman, but to push forward as rapidly as possible." He suggested that commanders in Alabama and on the Mississippi River "take measures to intercept the rebel chiefs and their plunder" —which was said to amount to thirteen millions. He was still repeating the orders until April 28, when he received a telegram from Grant telling him that Sherman had made new and satisfactory terms.[11] But Halleck was by now a complete victim, as well as a creator, of propaganda. When Davis was finally captured—without any specie—a rumor went around that he was wearing Mrs. Davis clothes for a disguise at the time; actually it was a cold night and he had wrapped one of her shawls around his shoulders. Halleck, however, wrote to Stanton: "If Jefferson Davis was captured in his wife's clothes, I respectfully suggest that he be sent north in the same habiliments." [12]

By May 8 Sherman was approaching Richmond on his way to Washington and the final grand review of the armies. Old Brains invited him to stay in his headquarters while in the city but Sherman flatly turned him down. "After your dispatch to the Secretary of

---

[10] *O.R.*, Ser. I, XLVI, Part 3, p. 895.
[11] *Ibid.*, 907, 953; Lewis, *Sherman*, 554.
[12] Robert McElroy, *Jefferson Davis* (New York, 1937), II, 701.

War . . . I cannot have any friendly intercourse with you,"
Sherman wrote—"I prefer we should not meet." "Look out for
breakers," the enraged general warned his wife. He was disgusted
with Halleck's complacency with Stanton and with, "worst of all,
his advice that my subordinates . . . should not obey my orders.
Under [them] . . . those Generals have done all they ever did in
their lives, and it sounds funny to us to have H *better* my plans
and orders." [13]

The next day Halleck ordered a corps in Sherman's army to pass
him in review—Sherman forbade it. On the eleventh Sherman
planned to march through Richmond "with colors flying and
drums beating as a matter of right and not by H's favor." He
would take no notice of Old Brains either personally or officially
and dared him to oppose the march. "He will," Sherman told his
wife, "think twice before he again undertakes to stand between me
and my subordinates." [14]

Halleck suddenly realized that Stanton's fleeting approval could
hardly be measured against his friendship with Sherman and tried
desperately to restore the old relationship. Completely humbling
himself, he wrote Sherman: "You have not had during this war
nor have you now a warmer friend and admirer than myself. If in
carrying out what I knew to be the wishes of the War Department
in regard to your armistice I used language which has given you
offense it was unintentional, and I deeply regret it." Sherman,
Halleck claimed, would not attribute to him any "improper motives" if he knew all the facts. At any rate Halleck concluded: "It
is my wish to continue to regard and receive you as a personal
friend." He left the matter in Sherman's hands. [15]

Sherman was too fully incensed to forgive his old chief. After
thinking about it "all night, in connection with that telegraphic
message . . . to Secretary Stanton," he decided he could not "con-

[13] *O.R.,* Ser. I, XLVII, Part 3, p. 435; Howe, *Home Letters of Sherman,*
350.
[14] Howe, *Home Letters of Sherman,* 352.
[15] *O.R.,* Ser. I, XLVII, Part 3, p. 454.

sent to the renewal of a friendship I had prized so highly till I can see deeper into the diabolical plot than I now do." He would march through Richmond "quietly and in good order . . . and I beg you to keep slightly perdu, for if noticed by some of my old command I cannot undertake to maintain a model behavior, for their feelings have become aroused by what the world adjudges an insult to at least an honest commander." [16] The crack had split wide open, and Halleck and Sherman wrote no more to each other.

At the same time that his relationship with Sherman was disintegrating, Halleck was trying to build up Richmond. His first efforts were designed to stimulate the city's trade. The Treasury Department had issued special permits and only those possessing them were entitled to buy or sell in the South. Halleck wanted to "prevent monopolists with special trade permits from swindling those who have anything to sell," and proposed that free access to Richmond from the North be permitted while all permits were revoked. On April 24 Old Brains issued two orders designed to help Richmond back on its feet. Lee's army, he said, had stripped the countryside of all horses and mules, preventing the farmers from putting in their crops. To alleviate the situation Halleck sold the farmers condemned Union animals—they got the money from selling tobacco to Northern troops. "We must," Old Brains commented, "either feed the poor or help them feed themselves." He then sent damaged artillery to the Tredegar Iron Works—one of the South's largest manufacturing establishments—for repair before shipping it to Washington. "This will give employment to mechanics whose families we must otherwise feed to prevent starvation," he noted.[17]

But Halleck's expedients were not working because of the opposition of the Treasury agents, who, for example, allowed no coal or wood to come into the city without a special permit. "It is now perfectly evident that these agents are resolved that no one shall

[16] *Ibid.*
[17] *Ibid.*, XLVI, Part 3, pp. 888, 916, 917.

buy or sell even the necessaries of life except through themselves or their favorites," Halleck fumed. "I know of no better system for robbing the people and driving them to utter desperation." Old Brains' greatest objection was that if the system continued "the military must feed the people or permit them to starve," and he was taking a long range view—he wanted to make the city self-sufficient again so that the army could pull out.[18]

Still Halleck could not resist the temptation to use his power occasionally. On April 28 he issued a series of General Orders, one of which proclaimed: "No marriage license will be issued until the parties desiring to be married take the oath of allegiance to the United States, and no one can marry them unless he has." Proudly he boasted to Stanton: "You will perceive . . . that measures have been taken to prevent so far as possible the propagation of legitimate rebels." To insure that Virginians received proper indoctrination, Halleck closed all churches in which the clergyman refused to read the prescribed prayer for the President—they would be opened by "any other clergyman of the same denomination who will read such service."[19]

While attempting to bring Southern churches under Northern control, Halleck also did his bit in the attempt to prove that secession had been a conspiracy on the part of a few high placed Confederates. He seized former Cabinet member Robert M. T. Hunter's papers and forwarded them to Stanton with the notation that they included "inclosures of most suspicious character."[20]

But Halleck had something more important in mind than proving a fictitious plot. Old Brains, always a suitor for Clio's hand, had as early as 1863 proposed that all official documents and reports of the Union Army "be collected and published in chronological order." Now, in Richmond, he found that the Confederate archives were being burned and stolen and immediately placed a guard over them. He then boxed and shipped the documents to Washington. To keep Stanton interested he remarked that although they might

[18] *Ibid.*, 1072. [19] *Ibid.*, 1001.
[20] *Ibid.*, 1152.

be worthless, still "there may be found among them much evidence in regard to plots of assassination, incendiarism, treason &c." "At any rate," he concluded, "they will prove of great value to those who may hereafter write the history of this great rebellion." Halleck's shipments, 81 boxes weighing ten tons, made up the bulk of the Confederate part of the *War of the Rebellion, the Official Records of the Union and Confederate Armies,* an indispensable tool for Civil War students.[21]

During the remainder of May and the early part of June, Halleck wrestled with many problems—freed Negroes, the court system, city government, and the Tredegar Iron Works. He showed an alarming tendency toward conservatism—advising that the Negroes go to work on the plantations, that Richmond residents quickly elect their own government, that the Tredegar Works remain in the former owners' hands. Stanton, switching over to the Radicals, engineered his transfer to the newly created Division of the Pacific, which embraced the Departments of the Columbia and California. His headquarters were in San Francisco.[22]

So he returned to his home town, not as the conquering hero he had envisioned four years before, but as a misunderstood, maligned, and unappreciated soldier, old far beyond his fifty years. Old Brains returned to the scene of his first triumphs a defeated man, buffetted at every turn, who had already reached his personal height and completed—in the public's eye—the descent back to the bottom. Soon the generals would start publishing their memoirs, and all but one damned Halleck, the convenient scapegoat so different from the rest. He had never won a battle, he had never had a newspaper reporter backing him. He had managed, at one time or another, to irritate almost every general in the army—with one general he paid too little attention, with another too much, he had taken troops from a third and refused reinforcements to a fourth. His name appeared at the bottom of every order removing a general

[21] *Ibid.,* Ser. III, III, 1039; Ser. I, XLVI, Part 3, pp. 889, 1132, 1161.
[22] *Ibid.,* 1173, 1264, 1294, 1297.

from command issued after July, 1862. Halleck was an easy man to hate.

The one exception to the chorus of denunciation came from his oldest and, until 1865, best friend. When, in the 1880's he wrote his *Memoirs,* Sherman forgot a real cause for animosity and gave Old Brains the praise he thought he deserved.

Halleck had little reason to expect that the writers of memoirs would be generous with him since he had seldom been generous with them during his lifetime. As general-in-chief and chief of staff Halleck sent official praise to many generals; only to Sherman did he send private and wholehearted congratulations. Neither was he generous with himself or his feelings, and consequently he was misunderstood as often as he failed to understand others. Only Sherman and Francis Lieber shared Halleck's emotions and knew the man. Old Brains' almost utter inability to communicate with unsympathetic officers and officials added to his suspicious nature to make an open and trusting relationship with others difficult for him. Halleck operated secretively partly out of necessity, partly out of choice. As a result, many of those with whom he came into contact quickly—and falsely—judged him a mere schemer.

Old Brains had a similar opinion of most of his contemporaries. In Washington, Halleck saw himself as perhaps the only high official unselfishly devoted to the cause of the Union. In 1863 he informed Lieber that "the patriotic sentiment of the people is improving," but felt that "unfortunately . . . there is no unity of feeling either in the cabinet or among the generals. *Self,* and that pronoun 'I' are too prominent in the minds of our would be great men." Halleck fancied himself to be above the party politics which were destroying the Union by subverting men's better instincts. "Party politics! Party politics! I sometimes fear they will utterly ruin the country," Halleck cried to Lieber.[23] As 1864 approached he admitted that he would be optimistic about the outcome of the war "if it were not for the interference of political combinations

[23] Halleck to Lieber, April 15, 1863, Lieber Collection.

and political intrigues. They spoil everything." Patriotism, he believed, "seems to be swallowed up in personal ambition and selfish-
ness." [24]

But Old Brains was not as self-effacing as he himself believed;
he had shown that after the Donelson campaign. He detested
politicians not because they were traitors, but because they made
the professionalization and an efficient operation of the army difficult. In the spring of 1864 he returned to a theme he had advanced eighteen years before in his *Elements:* "It requires a *professional* man to conduct a law suit where a few thousand dollars are
involved; but *mere* politicians can conduct armies where thousands
of human lives, millions of money and the safety of the Government
itself are involved." He spoke of "military charlatans," having in
mind especially Banks and Butler, and concluded: "If this cannot
be stopped, and the right man [i.e., professionals] put in the right
places, we need not hope for success." [25] Earlier he had complained
to Lieber: "The great difficulty we have to contend with is *poor,
poorer,* worthless officers. Many of them have neither judgment,
sense nor courage. . . . Recent appointments are worse if anything than before. Politics! Politics! They are utterly ruining the
country." [26]

Halleck opposed the politicians partly because their orientation
towards war was militaristic, not military. They thought of war as
romantic, glorious, and noble; Halleck, like Grant and Sherman,
saw it as a huge, ugly task to be completed as quickly and ef-
ficiently as possible. One reason for Old Brains' unpopularity was
that he tried to remove all comfort and glory from war. Many
commanders objected to Halleck's policy of reducing the amount
of personal baggage an officer could carry. Ben Butler could never
forgive Halleck for his opposition to the Fort Fisher fiasco, a
perfect example of a militaristic action. It was glorious but peripheral, romantic but time wasting and life consuming; it could

[24] Halleck to Lieber, December 27, 1863, *ibid.*
[25] Halleck to Lieber, May 1, 1864, *ibid.*
[26] Halleck to Lieber, April 30, 1863, *ibid.*

hardly hasten the final victory, and was designed primarily to enhance Butler's reputation. Halleck maintained that operations of that type had no place in modern warfare and the easiest way to eliminate them was to eliminate the politicians.[27]

Like his own image of the politicians, Halleck often was petty, vindictive, and unforgiving, as his relations with Hooker, McClernand, Banks, and Butler demonstrated. But he was an always competent, intelligent, well-organized, and sometimes brilliant administrator. His services, in St. Louis, as general-in-chief, and as chief of staff, were essential to victory; he shaped, and shaped well, the tools that others used.

Old Brains seldom suggested uses for the tools which he supplied. Shortly after Halleck arrived in Washington to take up his duties as general-in-chief, Grant complained to Halleck that he had "never suggested to me any plan of operations," nor informed him of the activities "of those Commanders to my right or left." Grant therefore had no plans, but was "ready . . . to do with all my might" whatever Halleck might direct.[28] At one time or another, almost every field commander sent the General-in-chief a somewhat similar letter.

Halleck had few directions for the perplexed generals. Even when he did offer advice—based on Jomini's principles—such as effective pursuit following a victory (with Meade, after Gettysburg), or concentration (with Buell during the Donelson campaign) he could not make himself understood. Unable to give of himself, he was unable to communicate. As a director of the field operations his administrative ability made possible, Halleck was a failure.

Old Brains had few original ideas and he made no outstanding contribution to either tactics or strategy. The tyranny of the past hung heavily upon him. He never recognized fully and therefore did not exploit adequately the communications revolution; he ignored the full possibilities of both the telegraph and the railroad.

[27] I am following Alfred Vaught's definition of militarist.
[28] Grant to Halleck, October 26, 1862, U. S. Grant Papers.

Strategically, especially in the Eastern theater, he did break with
Jomini, but his alternative—advocating the defeat of Lee's army
rather than concentration on Richmond—was hardly a theoretical
innovation. In the West he usually followed the master's lead.
New approaches to tactics and strategy did come during the Civil
War, but the originators were field generals operating in practical
situations, not theorists in Washington. Henry Halleck was a key
figure in the greatest war of Western civilization to occur between
1815 and 1914; he completely failed to use that war as a basis for
making a contribution to the elements of military art and science.

He did make important and lasting contributions as an administrator. He was a major figure in the shift from 18th century,
limited warfare to modern, total war. Halleck had immense pride
in his chosen profession; as a part of that pride he wanted to create
for the United States a powerful, modern, centralized army. He was
anxious to use the Civil War to build up the regular army (as
opposed to an armed mob composed of state militia troops) serving
under nationally trained professionals.

From the day they mustered in until the day they mustered out,
Halleck tried to make the Federal troops feel the hand of the
national army. Conscription, which increased the power of the
nation and its army as opposed to the states and their militia forces,
received active support from Halleck. Like his European counter-
parts, Halleck approved of both the theory behind and the practice
of the nation in arms. He believed it was essential to Union success
and the "only possible means of keeping up the army." [29] He felt
that the conscripts fought well: "They grumble and complain but
this avails them nothing. When conscripts are once in the ranks they
fight about as well as those who voluntarily enlist. Such has been
the case in Europe and our people are no exception to the general
rule." [30] He convinced himself that opposition came not from
idealists but from traitors. During the New York draft riots of
1863 he wrote Lieber: "I perceive that the opposition to the draft

[29] Halleck to Lieber, September 26, 1863, Lieber Collection.
[30] Halleck to Lieber, February 22, 1864, *ibid.*

comes almost exclusively from those of secesh proclivities . . .
If these traitors can delay the draft two or three months, they think
our armies will be driven back. . . . There is abundant evidence
of an understanding between the Peace Men of the North and
the Secesh of the south." He had no qualms about the means used
to enforce national conscription: "Loyal men at home *must* act at
home," he felt. "They must put down the slightest attempt at dis-
order." [31]

Halleck saw to it that conscription was merely the beginning of
the contacts with the federal government and its army that the
American citizen soldier experienced. Once the men were in the
service, Halleck and his staff, rather than the state governments,
supplied their needs. The federal army gave the troops their clothes
and shoes, their arms and ammunition, their horses and fodder;
it trained them, transported them, and supplied the officers who led
them. By 1865 Halleck, aided by his fellow West Pointers, had
eliminated all amateurs from important commands—the heroes
of the war were West Point graduates. Grant, Sherman, Thomas,
and Sheridan led the victorious armies; Banks, Butler, McClernand,
and Fremont watched from the sidelines. The operating procedure
was brutally simple and efficient; and it was part of a general trend
toward centralization in all areas of American life. The total result
was a revolution.

The most obvious symbol of the transformation Halleck had
wrought in the military sphere came at the end of the war. In 1861
state regiments, representing Massachusetts and Rhode Island and
supplied and led by the states, had rushed to Washington to protect
the captial of the Union. In 1865, during the Grand Review of the
Army, regional armies, representing the national state and led by
national officers, marched down Pennsylvania Avenue to receive
their reward for saving the nation.

And it was a nation, not a Union, that the troops had saved.
Politically, economically, socially, and militarily, the Civil War had

[31] Halleck to Lieber, July 26, 1863; August 14, 1863, *ibid.*

created a new nation upon the wreck of the old Union. Halleck, who realized that the powerful army he wanted needed a powerful nation to support it, was an important agent in the revolution. He used troops to quell draft riots, break strikes that threatened the national effort, ensure Republican victories at the polls and suppress traitorous politicians.[32]

Halleck never faced directly the theoretical problems inherent in his position as military head of a citizen army in a democracy; he rejected the democratic ideal that opposition is not only loyal but necessary. He constantly condemned those who opposed, not just Lincoln's administration, but the whole fabric of centralization; he believed that only centralization could lead to victory. During the political campaign of 1864, Halleck supported Lincoln as the lesser of evils. "Although Mr. Lincoln has not the qualities wished at times like the present"—Halleck would have preferred Lincoln to act with Bismarckian ruthlessness—Old Brains could not support the Democrats. "If both parties had been pledged to the prosecution of the war," he explained, "I should have considered the country safe. Moreover, in many respects a change of administration on that basis would have been desirable," as it would have brought Democratic strength to the war effort, and by implication at least, to centralization. "But now, with the possibility, if not a probability of the success of a treasonable faction at the north" (because of the peace clause in the Democratic platform), Halleck "considered [the] country in great peril."

But although Halleck thought Lincoln weak and the Democratic candidate McClellan a traitor, he was not overly concerned because he recognized that "in this contest Lincoln and McClellan are mere bubbles on the surface of the rushing waters the course

---

[32] Halleck easily convinced himself that the Copperheads—States' rights Democrats in the West—were in league with the South and were willing "to plunge the whole north into anarchy and thus secure the complete success of Jeff. Davis' rebellion." Acting on those assumptions, shortly before the election of 1864 he sent troops to Ohio and Indiana, Copperhead strongholds, which were, he believed, "on the brink of a revolution." See Halleck to Lieber, October 16, 1864, *ibid.*

of which neither of them can control." [33] Old Brains realized that America's entrance into the modern world might be slightly hindered, or slightly helped, by individuals, but that by 1864 it could no longer be halted. Politically, socially, economically, and militarily, centralization had become institutionalized; Halleck had done his share in making that result possible.

By all the touchstones used to judge the great captains of the past, Halleck was a failure. He lacked the genius of Alexander and Napoleon; Epaminondas and Fuller made far more significant tactical innovations, as did Jomini and Clausewitz in the fields of strategy and general theory; the audacity of Forrest, Rommel and Patton was not a part of Halleck's character; he missed the tenacity that inspired Frederick and Grant; he could not lead as Lee could. For a *field* general, these touchstones are vital; for a *manager* of modern war, they are peripheral and irrelevant. A democracy waging a modern, total war requires a businessman-soldier to manage the war machine. This Halleck did.

Halleck lived only until 1872. Instead of writing memoirs he dragged out his existence fighting Indians, dedicating statues in California, speaking at state dinners, advocating the acquisition of British Columbia before a disinterested audience. Indicative of his loss of spirit was his failure to leave the army and return to his law-business career. In 1869 he left California to assume his new duties as commander of the Division of the South, with headquarters in Louisville, Kentucky. In early January of 1872 he suddenly became ill. His cousin, Bishop Whipple of Minnesota, visited Louisville in time to administer the sacrament of baptism and give Halleck the Holy Communion. He died on January 9, 1872, six days short of his fifty-seventh birthday. A few personal friends accompanied his funeral train to the family burial grounds in Greenwood Cemetery, Brooklyn, where he was interred on January 25.

The newspapers hardly noticed his passing, but the *Army and*

[33] Halleck to Lieber, September 2, 1864, *ibid.*

Navy Journal allowed Halleck's chief of staff, George W. Cullum, a column for a eulogy. Cullum ignored his war services but made much of Halleck's death-bed baptism, his "open acknowledgement of the source of all his strength." [34] Yet Henry Halleck had been more than a tired general who died with belated atonement—he had been the "Old Brains" of the Union Army in the time of the testing of the nation.

[34] Shutes, *Lincoln and California,* 195; Friedel, *Lieber,* 388; *American Annual Cyclopaedia* (New York, 1873), 375; Henry Benjamin Whipple, *Lights and Shadows of a Long Episcopate* (New York, 1912), 103; *Army and Navy Journal,* January 27, 1872, and February 3, 1872.

BIBLIOGRAPHY

Manuscripts

C. P. Buckingham Papers, Illinois State Historical Library, Springfield, Illinois.

Zachariah Chandler Manuscripts, Library of Congress, Washington, D. C.

Ulysses S. Grant Papers, Illinois State Historical Library.

Adam Gurowski Papers, Library of Congress.

Henry Wager Halleck Letter Book, Library of Congress.

Francis Lieber Correspondence, Library of Congress.

Francis Lieber Correspondence, Henry Huntington Library, San Marino, California.

Robert Todd Lincoln Papers, Library of Congress.

George B. McClellan Papers, Library of Congress.

John A. McClernand Manuscripts, Illinois State Historical Library.

Unpublished manuscript biography of General John A. McClernand, possibly written by Adolph Schwartz, McClernand's chief of staff, annotated by General Edward J. McClernand, Illinois State Historical Library.

John M. Schofield Manuscripts, Library of Congress.

John Sherman Manuscripts, Library of Congress.

Edwin M. Stanton Papers, Library of Congress.

State of Wisconsin Executive Department Administration files (Organization and Administration of the Army), Series 1/1/5–11, Archives Division, State Historical Society of Wisconsin, Madison, Wisconsin.

Newspapers

Army and Navy Journal, 1872.
Chicago *Tribune,* 1862–1865.
The New York *Herald,* 1862–1865.
New York *Tribune,* 1861–1865.
New York *World,* 1861–1865.
Wilkes' Spirit of the Times, 1865.

Secondary Sources

Agassiz, George (ed.). *Meade's Headquarters 1863–1865: Letters of Colonel Theodore Lyman from the Wilderness to Appomattox.* Boston, 1922.
American Annual Cyclopaedia. New York, 1873.
Athearn, Robert G. (ed.). *Soldier in the West: The Civil War Letters of Alfred Lacey Hough.* Philadelphia, 1957.
Basler, Roy (ed.). *The Collected Works of Abraham Lincoln,* 8 vols. Rutgers, 1953.
Bates, David Homer. *Lincoln in the Telegraph Office.* New York, 1907.
Blaine, James G. *Twenty Years of Congress.* 2 vols. New York, 1884.
Bradford, Gamaliel. *Union Portraits.* Boston, 1914.
Browne, J. Ross. *Report on the Debates in the Convention of California.* Washington, 1850.
Catton, Bruce. *This Hallowed Ground.* Garden City, 1956.
Catton, Bruce. *Grant Moves South.* Boston, 1960.
Chittenden, L. E. *Recollections of President Lincoln and His Administration.* New York, 1891.
Church, William Conant. *Ulysses S. Grant.* New York, 1897.
Clausewitz, Carl von. *On War.* 3 vols. London, 1956.
Donald, David (ed.). *Inside Lincoln's Cabinet: The Civil War Diaries of Salmon P. Chase.* New York, 1954.
Doster, William E. *Lincoln and Episodes of the Civil War.* New York, 1915.
Dupuy, R. Ernest. *Where They Have Trod; The West Point Tradition in American Life.* New York, 1940.
Durant, Samuel W. *History of Oneida County, New York.* Philadelphia, 1878.
Ellison, Joseph. "The Struggle for Civil Government in California."

California Historical Society Quarterly. Vol. 10. San Francisco, 1929.

Fessenden, Francis. *Life and Public Services of William Pitt Fessenden.* 2 vols. Boston and New York, 1907.

Freidel, Frank. *Francis Lieber: Nineteenth-Century Liberal.* Baton Rouge, 1947.

Fuller, J. F. C. *The Generalship of Ulysses S. Grant.* London, 1929.

General Orders, Department of the Missouri and Mississippi, 1861–1862. n.p., n.d.

Gurowski, Adam. *Diary 1863–1865.* Washington, 1866.

Halleck, Henry Wager. *Elements of Military Art and Science.* 2nd edition. New York, 1861.

Halleck, Henry Wager. "Report on the Means of National Defense." 28th Congress, 2nd session, Senate Document 85, series no. 451.

Hallock, Charles. *The Hallock-Holyoke Pedigree.* Amherst, 1906.

Harrington, Fred Harvey. *Fighting Politician: Major General N. P. Banks.* Philadelphia, 1948.

Hassler, Warren W. *General George B. McClellan: Shield of the Union.* Baton Rouge, 1957.

Haupt, Herman. *Reminiscences.* Milwaukee, 1901.

Howard, Oliver Otis. *Autobiography.* 2 vols. New York, 1908.

Hesseltine, William B. *Civil War Prisons, A Study in War Psychology.* Columbus, Ohio, 1930.

Hesseltine, William B. *Ulysses S. Grant, Politician.* New York, 1935.

Hittell, Theodore H. *History of California.* 3 vols. San Francisco, 1885.

Hittle, Lt. Col. J. D. *Jomini and His Summary of the Art of War.* Harrisburg, 1947.

Howe, M. A. DeWolfe (ed.). *Home Letters of General Sherman.* New York, 1909.

Johnson, Ludwell H. *Red River Campaign; Politics and Cotton in the Civil War.* Baltimore, 1958.

Johnson, Robert Underwood, and Buel, Clarence Clough (eds.). *Battles and Leaders of the Civil War.* New edition, 4 vols. New York, 1956.

Joint Committee on the Conduct of the War, Report. 3 parts. 37th Congress, 3rd session, Senate Report no. 108, serial no. 1152.

Kamm, Richey. *The Civil War Career of Thomas A. Scott.* Philadelphia, 1940.

Lewis, Lloyd. *Sherman, Fighting Prophet.* New York, 1932.

Long, E. B. (ed.). *Ulysses S. Grant Memoirs*. New edition. Cleveland and New York, 1952.

Lord, Francis A. "Army and Navy Textbooks and Manuals Used by the North During the Civil War," *Military Collector and Historian*. Washington, D. C., 1957.

Macartney, Clarence. *Grant and His Generals*. New York, 1953.

Mahan, D. H. *An Elementary Treatise on Advanced Guard, Out Post, and Detachment Service of Troops*. New York, 1847.

Mallam, William D. "The Grant-Butler Relationship," *Mississippi Valley Historical Review*. September, 1954.

McClellan, George B. *Own Story*. New York, 1887.

McElroy, Robert. *Jefferson Davis*. 2 vols. New York, 1937.

Nicolay, John G., and Hay, John. *Abraham Lincoln, a History*. 8 vols. New York, 1886.

O'Reilly, Miles (pseudo. for Charles G. Halpine). *Baked Meats of the Funeral*. New York, 1866.

Papers of the Military Historical Society of Massachusetts. 10 vols. Boston, 1908.

Pratt, Harry S. (comp.). *Concerning Mr. Lincoln*. Springfield, 1944.

Richards, G. W. *Lives of Generals Halleck and Pope*. Philadelphia, 1862.

Sheridan, P. H. *Personal Memoirs*. 2 vols. New York, 1888.

Sherman, W. T. *Memoirs*. 2 vols. New York, 1875.

Shugg, Roger W. *Origins of Class Struggle in Louisiana*. Baton Rouge, 1939.

Shutes, Milton H. "Henry Wager Halleck, Lincoln's Chief-of-Staff," *California Historical Society Quarterly*. September, 1935.

Shutes, Milton H. *Lincoln and California*. Stanford, 1943.

Smith, T. C. *The Life and Letters of James Abram Garfield*. 2 vols. New Haven, 1925.

Sorrel, G. Moxey, *Recollections of a Confederate Staff Officer*. New edition. New York, 1958.

Stackpole, Edward J. *Drama on the Rappahannock: The Fredericksburg Campaign*. Harrisburg, 1957.

Summers, Festus P. *The Baltimore and Ohio in the Civil War*. New York, 1939.

Thorndike, Rachel Sherman (ed.). *The Sherman Letters*. New York, 1894.

The Union Army. 8 vols. Madison, Wisconsin, 1902.

Vandiver, Frank. *Mighty Stonewall.* New York, 1956.

Vaughts, Alfred. *A History of Militarism.* Revised edition. New York, 1959.

Wager, Daniel E. *Our County and its People.* Boston, 1896.

Wallace, Lew. *Autobiography.* 2 vols. New York, 1900.

War of the Rebellion, Official Records of the Union and Confederate Armies. 128 vols. Washington, 1880–1901.

Weber, Thomas. *The Northern Railroads in the Civil War, 1861–1865.* New York, 1952.

Weisberger, B. S. *Reporters for the Union.* New York, 1954.

Welles, Gideon. *Diary of Gideon Welles, Secretary of the Navy Under Lincoln and Johnson.* 2 vols. Boston and New York, 1909.

Whipple, Henry Benjamin. *Lights and Shadows of a Long Episcopate.* New York, 1912.

Wiley, Bell Irvin (ed.). *"This Infernal War," The Confederate Letters of Sgt. Edwin H. Fay.* Austin, 1958.

Willey, Rev. S. H. "Recollections of General Halleck as Secretary of State in Monterey, 1847–1849," *The Overland Monthly.* I, 1872.

Williams, K. P. *Lincoln Finds a General.* 5 vols. New York, 1948–1959.

Williams, T. Harry. *Lincoln and His Generals.* New York, 1952.

Williams, T. Harry. "The Military Leadership of the North and the South," *The Harmon Memorial Lectures in Military History, Number Two.* United States Air Force Academy, Colorado, 1960.

Wilson, James Grant. "General Halleck, a Memoir," *Journal of the Military Service Institution of the United States.* Vols. 35 and 36, 1905.

Wilson, James Harrison. *Under the Old Flag.* 2 vols. New York, 1912.

INDEX

plans Corinth campaign, 47–
49; and Sheridan, 49; marches
for Corinth, 49, 50; criticized
for Corinth operation, 50–54;
takes Corinth, 52; pleased with
Corinth campaign, 53, 54;
abandons pursuit of Beauregard, 55; plans for summer of
1862, p. 56; sends Buell towards Chattanooga, 57; refuses
to send reinforcements east, 58,
59; made general-in-chief, 59–
61; regrets to leave West, 61;
praises Sherman, 62; contributions of in West, 63; relations
with Lincoln, 65, 66; meets
with McClellan, 66, 67; criticizes McClellan, 68; withdraws
McClellan from Peninsula, 69;
complains about position as
general-in-chief, 70, 143, 158;
during Second Bull Run campaign, 70–76; on McClellan,
79, 80; used by Lincoln, 80,
81; and Antietam campaign,
81–87; protects Buell, 88–92;
relieves McClellan, 92; and
Fredericksburg campaign, 94–
99; after Fredericksburg, 99–
102; and army reforms of,
102–105; argues with Rosecrans, 105–108; and Vicksburg
campaign, 108–122, 140; argues with Rosecrans, 123–26,
189–91; reinforces Grant at
Vicksburg, 127, 128; and
Lieber, 128–31; and General
Orders, No. 100, pp. 129–31;
and army reforms of, 131; relations with Hooker, 131–135;
and Meade, 137, 138; during
Battle of Gettysburg, 137–39;
urges Meade to fight Lee, 140–
44, 147–49; reforms Army of
the Potomac, 144, 145; and

Red River campaign, 145;
urges Rosecrans to advance,
150–52; and Chattanooga campaign, 152–56; views of on
Reconstruction, 156, 157; contributions of as general-in-
chief, 158–61; analyzed by
Sherman, 160, 161; made chief
of staff, 161; activities of as
chief of staff, 162–64; and
Wilderness campaign, 165–67;
complains of position as chief
of staff, 167, 168; works to
eliminate Banks, 168–70; to
eliminate Butler, 170–73; during Early's Valley campaign,
173–78; and Atlanta campaign,
178–80; advocates total war,
181, 187; and Sherman's
March to the Sea, 182–87; and
administrative reforms of, 187–
89; and Nashville campaign,
189–95; urges Sherman to
march through Carolinas, 197;
opposes Fort Fisher operation,
197, 198; transferred Schofield,
198; ordered to Richmond,
199; fights with Sherman, 199–
202; in Richmond, 202–204;
inability of to communicate,
205; criticizes politicians, 205–
207; failures of, 207, 208, 211;
contributions of, 208–11; fa-
vors centralization, 209–11;
death of, 211–12
Halleck, Joseph, 4
Hamilton, Alexander, 8
Hamilton, Elizabeth, 8
Hamilton, Schuyler, 211
Hamilton, Mrs. Schuyler, 40
Harper's Ferry, Virginia, 82–85,
134, 135, 138, 141, 174
Harrisburg, Pennsylvania, 139
Harrison's Landing, Virginia, 66,
69